TERRA MORTIS

TERRA MORTIS

IS THE EARTH DYING? A JUNGIAN AND INDIGENOUS VIEW

PART I: A FEW ROUGH BEASTS

MICHAEL OWEN

KAHURANGI

PRESS

Published in 2024 by Kahurangi Press, Tauranga, New Zealand

www.kahurangi-press.com

National Library of New Zealand Cataloguing-in-Publication Data

Terra Mortis: Is the Earth Dying? A Jungian and Indigenous View / Michael Owen. Includes bibliography and index. Part I: A Few Rough Beasts.

ISBN 978-0-473-72275-3

Book design and typography by Michael Owen.

The cover is a poster I bought in Vancouver BC in the 1980s. Above the logging slash is a quote from Shakespeare's *Julius Caesar* (Act III, Scene I). Mark Antony stands over Caesar's body, slain by Brutus: "O, pardon me, thou bleeding piece of earth / That I am meek and gentle with these butchers!" (The rest of Scene I is worth a read and relevant to our theme).

It has travelled with me all these years and it seemed right for it to come out of its tube and show its face. And it seemed right as an expression of the destruction already caused and the burden of rage our children's children will carry. It's a photo of clear-cut logging in BC, late winter or early spring I would guess. I have tried to track down the provenance to no avail and would be glad to be advised.

To the lasting memory of David.

With love and gratitude to Walks Slow Woman for your many gifts.

Thirteen thankyous to the 17s who continue to teach and to the bird who continues to delight.

Western science, following Roger Bacon, believed man could force
nature to reveal its secrets; the Sioux simply petitioned nature for
friendship.
—Vine Deloria Jr.

If it keeps on raining, the levee's going to break
When the levee breaks, have no place to stay
Crying won't help you, praying won't do you no good
When the levee breaks, mama, you got to move, ooh
—Kansas Joe McCoy and Memphis Minnie, "When the Levee Breaks."

CONTENTS

WHAT'S THIS ALL ABOUT?
A PREFACE

This book is a collection of essays written over the last thirty years and only recently have they wanted to come out of the writer's closet. Some are pretty much in their raw state, still stunned by the daylight, others have been scrubbed up a bit for polite company. They are neither a work of scholarship nor are they twittery and tabloid. Hopefully I have found a middle way that reflects my own voice.

Over the years the emergent theme has not been the collective narcissism of "the end of the human race" (which would solve the problem in one swell foop) but something more difficult to think about —the death of the Earth itself.

In Part I: A Few Rough Beasts I talk, amongst other things, about indigenous consciousness; ancient and modern oracles that foresaw the coming troubles; the metastatic growth of growth; and the psychotic break with planetary reality of the USA and global culture.

In Part II: All the Rough Beasts (due in 2025) I discuss indigenous knowledge about the death of the Earth; ailments related to Earth changes; the revenge of matter; the subjectivity of science; the Earth as the ancestor of the Self; Jung's Answer to Job; monotheism as a holocaust for the Earth; and finally some suggestions and remedies, perhaps.

The planned Preface ended up being way too long and it pushed and bullied its way to the head of the queue and wanted to be promoted to First Chapter. But no, that would have completely messed up the pagination and the index had already been done. Heroically, I stood my ground and told it to stay in its lane. But I did offer the consolation of a fancy title, *What's This All About?* It seemed to settle down after that.

Thinking the Unthinkable

To think the unthinkable allows what does not have a home to find a home. Then it will not appear in matter the same way as it might have done. Perhaps.

It may be that this planet will die, is dying or has died—but we don't know it yet. She may right herself without help or interference from us. I hope so. Or if her life is in danger she will let her children die without sentiment so that she may live. However, all possible futures may not be open, we may have gone past a tipping point, and there may not be enough time. God, Goodall and Attenborough won't save us. So I ask the reader to welcome, as an unknown guest, the immigrant possibility that the Earth will die. (But that's NEGATIVE THINKING you might say! I say, OK, no need to shout, if your positive thinking works so well, how come we're in this mess? Go on, give it a try). Maybe we can prevent it, forestall it, or make suitable funeral arrangements.

We've run out of planet. Humans have exhausted the gifts that the Earth provides. A whole 1.7 planet's worth. The Great Barrier Reef is dying. The great dying will gather pace until we hit rock bottom. Our grandchildren's children will be bereft, left only with dust and diesel.

The trees have nearly given up. The animals have done what they can. 9/11, the GFC and Covid have tried their best to warn us. Monotheism has abandoned the earth for heavenly rewards. Indigenous peoples are now only 5% of the world's population. 55% of the world's population lives in cities. And our relationship with beauty has been lost.

There are mountains and oceans of evidence about the perilous state of the planet. There's no need for more and we must ask, "What forces compel us to continue to deny the obvious?"—other than the obvious political and financial ones. We think we have time. Maybe we don't. So let's begin to make space within ourselves to entertain the thought that this planet of infinite beauty may die. Now stand back and watch the reactions, your own and others, to such a notion. Then read on.

If all this sounds too weighty and depressing, please read the chapters on hope and despair, or you could just think about the whole thing as a "thought-experiment". Failing that, let your grandchildren handle it.

Upbeat title, eh?

It's Latin for the death of the Earth. Is the Earth dying? Maybe. Is it already dead? Don't know. Ecological activism, reducing waste, and reports on climate change are all fiddling around the edges, slant ways of talking about what cannot be said. We are killing the being that gives us life and in twenty, fifty, a hundred or two hundred years this planet may no longer be able to support life. But there is little space in the collective to think the unthinkable. The forces against—religious, financial, political, and psychological—are legion.

So these scribblings are about the spiritual and historical ancestors of this profound contempt for matter, the fallacy of optimism, and the psychological children (grief, nostalgia, melancholy, depression, suicide, and loss of memory) that have been born from this chronic, monotheistic, and possibly terminal, illness.

Possums

The only tragedy would be to not see it coming and get run over like a possum in the headlights. For those who live in remote places like the northern hemisphere, a possum is a nocturnal marsupial, about the size of a raccoon, that somehow crossed the Tasman from Australia and has taken up residence in the New Zealand bush. About 30 million of them. They breed like, er, possums, kill the indigenous forests, and enjoy standing, hypnotised, on the white line at night. Marsupial road kill.

Robust and thoughtful pessimism

A dose of robust and thoughtful pessimism is needed, not because it is the "truth" or more "right" but to compensate the mindless optimism that infects the collective. With optimism being so widespread (even Jane Goodall says there's still time) it begs a swing to the opposite. I have no skin in this game—I would be glad if the Earth survived. But no-one seems to be thoughtful about the possibility that she will not. In the great democracy of ideas this one is an unwanted immigrant, with the exception of some science fiction writing and apocalyptic movies. (It seems that Hollywood, perversely, dreams for the collective). In other words, the possibility of her death has gone all denied, dissociated and unconscious.

Oh, they cry, he's a pessimist! An acquaintance once said to me, "You're a pessimist, you're spewing doom and dread". I thanked them for the compliment. It's rubbish, they say! All this religiose talk about the end of the world. The apocalypse. The end is nigh. Been shouted about for 2000 years and hasn't happened yet! But these opinions betray the psychology of those who hold them. The outward-looking conquistadors, eyes on the horizon of possibility, manifest destiny, hey guys let's go to Mars, anything-is-possible folks—all these have reached their limit but don't know it yet. They will collapse into smallness—a land they never knew existed. We live on a finite planet.

Evidence

I have no scientific evidence, if that's what you might be looking for, for the notion that the Earth will die. On the other hand, there is no evidence that she will survive our new-kid-on-the-block occupation. And by the time any such scientific evidence arrives it will be stating the obvious and past its useful date. But I do know where the arrow is pointing. I also know that our collective short-sightedess, from denial or ignorance, only sees as far as climate change. The eye-opener might be when Phoenix and Las Vegas become unliveable.

Notwithstanding the forces and interests against such, I suppose if billions worked together then the ship could be turned around. But that degree of collective cooperation flies in the face of history or, if it does occur by force of circumstance, it may too little, too late. In the meantime there is a blank space, open country, a vacuum, that is all the more influential by its absence, that has been uninhabited by thought or imagination. This book might fill that *terra nullius* that was so eagerly explored 300 years ago. Now, not so eager but reluctant, unwilling, or "We can't afford it".

At some point the decline, long past reversible, will become obvious to collective consciousness. It will rise to the surface and become fast food at your favourite media restaurant. The deniers and sceptics and diggers and drillers will have passed away and we will think: "How did it to come to this?" Heroic optimism will not save the day and the keening and wailing will begin. This planet may no longer give life or hold life.

Gnawing at the roots of monotheism

So there you have it. I have set the tone, stated my thesis, summarised the book, and got the possum off the road. Along the way I shall try my best to sneer at the starry-eyed demon of optimism, evade the monster of denial, drown unsuspecting readers in melancholy, gnaw at the roots of monotheism, and generally try to paint a picture of the mess we're in. What follows is a long and winding, perhaps long-winded, riff on that sentence. None of this will kill you.

The tendrils of possibility, revolution, and disruption creep in from the outside the zeitgeist, never from the inside. New possibilities show up as an outlier, a group or party or movement that appears to drive social change. It's often overly chuffed with itself and devoted to X or Y but really it's an emerging archetype whose time has come and having its way with us (more on those later). The friction of the revolution always goes for the most vulnerable and flammable first—those with strong opinions and passionate views about everything; those who are as-yet unformed (adolescents and young adults); and those who are beholden to the collective (most of us).

Nothing worth defending

This book will have little to say about climate change, environmental action, or sustainability. These matters are more suited for a final chapter and we haven't reached the first chapter yet. So please do not assume I have a solution. The irritable reaching after fact and reason would interrupt a necessary suffering, a realisation of the full weight of our destructiveness. Then and only then might the collective turn to what it knows little of. The repair of the damage, if there will be such a thing, will have its own will and intention and needs to come in its own time.

If you are looking for solutions to the mess we are in—drop the book right now, step away and put your hands in the air! You are the kind of reader who will end up frustrated, full of opinions, and feel you have wasted your time and money. Yes, but what are we going to DO!, you say. If you are willing to suspend the urge to heroic action for just a while then read on at your own risk. Satisfaction is not guaranteed.

I don't care if what I am saying is true or not. The possible future I'm describing may come to pass or not. But read on anyway. I don't have much to lose. I am not an academic—I have no reputation to uphold, no papers to publish. I am at a late stage of my professional career so I have no credibility to protect. And I like to think that I don't have any personal, political or religious beliefs that are really worth defending.

Saviours, meh!

An Earth that is alive and fertile and healthy is not the subject of this book. She has been doing that for five billion years without our help, thank you. Saviours, meh! She doesn't need them. A living future cannot be materialised until we feel the full weight of the condition we are in. Until that happens any assertion of hope and optimism remains false and insubstantial. We want a quick solution, cognitive-lite without the weight of experience, we want to sneak around the grief, the pain, the terrible choices, the humiliation, and the downsizing. But we may have overshot the tipping point and gone already past the point of no return. Even the best of ancient knowledge may not be able to save us.

Jung and the five faces of the aeon

Back in the early 1980s, I became acquainted with the *Xultun Tarot*, the first of the modern indigenous tarot decks, created by a New Zealand artist, Peter Balin. Some years after writing *Jung and the Moon Cycles* I turned my attention to writing *The Maya Book of Life: Understanding the Xultun Tarot*, a companion text for the deck. The ideas in both these books also form some of the strands of this book.

The Greek word *aion* translates to aeon in English meaning age, epoch or era. Jung published *Aion: Researches into the Phenomenology of the Self* when he was seventy-six and it was his last major work but one. In it, he wrote about the lifespan of the Christian epoch over the last two thousand years.

We can think of an aeon as having four different faces or aspects. The south face is the lifespan of the individual. This was the subject of *Jung and the Moon Cycles* where I put Jung's life on the Moon Cycles, an indigenous teaching about the lifespan development of an invidiual. The north face is about the lifespan of the group or the collective—this was the subject of *The Maya Book of Life*. The west face is about the lifespan of human culture—which is the subject of this book. In the east is the history and lifespan of all cultures that have lived, are living, and will live, on this planet. I speak here not only of human cultures but also of the great societies, traditions, domains and nations of the winged ones, the crawlers, the four-leggeds, the spores, the bacteria, the minerals and the elements themselves. Modern science might call this evolution. The centre and fifth face is the lifespan of what reflects and gives life, blood and breath to all four faces—the Great Smoking Mirror, the Earth itself.

Spiritual dementia

Jung's work has been invaluable in helping me sketch the arc of this book. But his scope was Gnostic and alchemical, limited mostly to the last 2000 years, and he held (in part) a primitive view of "primitive" peoples. In the tradition of the Enlightenment and scientific progress —and he was frequently at pains to be scientific—he said that culture evolved from less differentiated to more differentiated, from less consciously human to more consciously human. As we shall see, alongside our apparent ascension to bigger and better things over the last, oh let's say, ten thousand years, there has been a complementary descension, a loss of consciousness, a gradual onset of spiritual dementia—a great forgetting about our place in the Great Circle of Life.

Jakkals pad

This is a wandering story and I beg of the reader's patience that I might take a jakkals pad (a jackal's path) to pass by what I have written in the past thirty or so years. This has been mostly for my own introverted amusement. I am encouraged by the story of the extroverted advertising executive who said, "Running a company without advertising is like winking at someone in the dark, you know what you are doing but no one else does." The introvert, on the other hand, might think (but wouldn't say), "He just doesn't get it... that's the whole point!"

In writing I find that the thought-birds land somewhere, often unexpectedly. They have an independent existence but I have the laptop. So it works for both of us and I begin to understand more of what I think and what I feel. I will jump around so do not expect any logical progression and well-reasoned arguments. I hope to be descriptive rather than inspirational. I'll venture to raise questions but not spoil them with answers. And I will try not to encourage you to take action.

Room at the Inn of Exaggeration

I have no idea if what I write is prediction, prophecy, fantasy, phantasy, or projection. I'd be happy with any of those. But there's enough hard evidence for me to flatten my understanding into words, pull out the bath plug, and release it into the wild. I'll talk about big things so please allow me lots of slack for hyperbole, exaggeration, drama and the like.

The problem is big enough such that it cannot be overstated. So there is lots of room for inflation.

Jeremiads and prophecy

I will use informal language and speak plainly. If I appear sarcastic, judgemental and critical, it's because I am so. The sentimental correctness of being "non-judgemental" may hide its dishonest shadow—a lack of courage, a failure of nerve, an avoidance of conflict and guilt, the preening maintenance of neutrality, or the inability to speak clearly and directly about one's own shortcomings or those of another.

So I would like to speak of a massively denied emotional and physical reality. Let me be clear that this is not doomerism although some might think it to be so. This accusation is usually emitted by those who have not seen the magnitude of the problem, and who are overly friendly with optimism and denial.

Neither is this a jeremiad of which Wikipedia says: "A long literary work, in which the author bitterly laments the state of society and its morals in a serious tone of sustained invective, and always contains a prophecy of society's imminent downfall.... The jeremiad was a favourite literary device of the Puritans especially in sermons.... In contemporary usage, it is frequently pejorative, meant to suggest that the tone of the text is excessively pessimistic and overwrought". Whew, I hope it's not like that—overwrought anyway.

The problem with writing about all this is that it's hard not to sound like prophecy. It's not. It's a best-guess extrapolation, informed by multiple sources—from indigenous knowledges, from observation, from what's obvious now, and what has been obvious for the last 50, 500 or 5,000 years—take your pick. I will wobble between the certainty of "will" and the uncertainty of "maybe". I would ask the reader to adapt accordingly. It's good practice for the future.

Global humiliation:

In some way, at some time, our global civilisation will experience a violent upheaval and be brought down to earth. There will be a reality check, a rude awakening, and things will be turned upside-down. This means the collapse of old values and beliefs, the destruction of long-established situations, the puncturing of inflation, the discarding of what has petrified, or the dismantling of towering ambition, pride and arrogance. What has been built brick by brick is destroyed in a flash and cultural norms and hopes are shattered. But perhaps, you say, this has been said before by Jeremiahs of all times and all cultures. But, I say, this is different. What is at risk is not just a culture, society, or religion, or even humankind, but the Earth itself.

Growth and coercion

The excesses of humankind are the cause of this great dying. We are a life form that has removed itself more than four paces from the community of life around us. We have fallen out of the Garden of Eden. There are two possible reactions to this state of affairs: The first is to ignore it, dismiss it, argue against it, or refuse to be aware of it. The second is to over-identify with it, to take it all-of-a-serious on one's shoulders and start a protest movement. This position is as arrogant as the first. It breeds all kinds of -isms, paint-throwing, lab-bombing, tree-hugging, cow-cuddling, marching, de-platforming, cancellation, direct action, and coercion-by-principles. Both reactions are unhelpful.

These two themes—bigness, giantism, expansion, inflation, growth and denial on the one hand, and guilt, over-responsibility, humiliation, and down-sizing on the other—are not obviously related but they do graze in the same paddock. They form the central theme of this book around which the rest twists and spirals.

Up until now, those who know better than I have softly and consistently discouraged the release of this book, repeatedly saying it's not time yet. But the pace has quickened and now it's time.

So I write, tentatively but with sufficient desire to feel that it is worth the effort, about the coming catastrophe that is already here. The apocalypse, demise, disaster, collapse, crisis—call it as you wish—which means that this planet we live on, that has sheltered us, that has given us life and death and beauty, may die.

Herding cats

If it has legs and heart this book will find its own way. I will follow. I
have resisted the temptation to give more order to its contents than you
see before you. More accurately, the book has resisted any order I have
tried to impose on it. The chapters are a nuisance of cats, loosely herded,
that I have written over the years—some recent, some over thirty
years ago.

Lineage

I want to speak of some of the ancestors of this book to give it some
lineage and continuity. It has sprung out of a wandering story that has
been telling itself over the years, though not from a political standpoint
or an "outrage" at "society." Although there is plenty to be outraged at,
that hopeful pursuit is best left to adolescents or young adults whatever
their age. Rather, it comes from knowing that this Earth and all its children are living, breathing, intentional beings. Yes, the planet breathes
and has intent.

In New Zealand, Maori who speak on the marae introduce themselves by naming their waka (one of the seven canoes in which Maori
came to Aotearoa, Land of the Long White Cloud), their maunga
(mountain), their awa (river), their iwi (tribe), their hapu (extended
family), and their name. In a similar way I want to voice a genealogy for
this book, just enough so you may know its whakapapa, hear its ancestors, see its face, and share its breath.

Way back, as a third-year zoology student, I had to specialise. Was it
going to be animal behaviour and the dances of honey bees? Karl von
Frisch had recently published his work on their language and I was also
fascinated by Niko Tinbergen's work on animal instinct. Or was it to be
palaeontology like my best mate Roger, later of the British Museum?
Dissecting a primate forearm together for the comparative mammalian
anatomy course was a hoot. But no, what got me was two things:
ecology and evolution. My psyche chose history and nature.

Evolutionary studies, then. From 1931 to 1963, H G Cannon FRS
(1897–1963) was head of department and Beyer Professor of Zoology at

the University of Manchester. When I arrived the year after he passed, an air of embarrassment hung over Cannon's legacy, as he had believed in Lamarckism in contrast to the Darwinian zeitgeist of the time. Strangely, I still have Cannon's small book *Lamarck and Modern Genetics* which has survived in my library over many years and much travelling. Epigenetics and the intergenerational transmission of trauma have finally caught up with Lamarck.

The Darwinian banner is still carried by Richard Dawkins. At Oxford, Dawkins studied under A J Cain, an evolutionary biologist, who replaced Cannon as Professor shortly after I arrived at Manchester. Dawkins is the Donald Trump of evolutionary biology. Sometime after the majority of this book was written Trump became President. He is the hapless embodiment of the problem I write about and I shall refer to him for clarity, hilarity and immediacy of example.

As for ecology, no-one in the department was interested. It was all pseudoscorpions, mammalian anatomy, *Drosophila melanogaster* fruit flies, and *Cepaea nemoralis* snails. Ecology was a new and fluffy field far from the Victorian gravitas of taxonomy, embryology, and comparative anatomy. As a discipline, ecology only began to gather traction in the 1960s. In his 1963 book, *Ecology*, Eugene Odum said he had been inspired to "seek more harmonious relationships between man and nature."

As fortune would have it, on graduating I was offered a place in a Master's program studying the ecology and physiology of freshwater fish in the Duck Mountains northwest of Winnipeg—probably because I had done two years of physiology with the medical students unlike all my other fellow students who stuck with botany. But life had other plans for me. I was inevitably captured by my own ecology—the workings of my inner world with its anatomy, palaeontology, plants and predators, its ecology and evolution.

By turn of fate, I then worked for six years in an innovative residential treatment centre in Canada for "emotionally disturbed" children and adolescents. After that I went on to post-graduate studies at the University of Toronto. Guess where I learned the most about kids, others and myself!

My life has led me to walk two different but parallel paths over the years—psychotherapy and its overly scientific cousin, clinical psychology; and work with indigenous elders, medicine people, and sangomas. I continue to be deeply grateful for the presence of those ones who do not wish to be named.

Michael Owen
Tauranga and Maenam

1

INDIGENOUS
THE ELDER BROTHERS

Five hundred years ago, you came to our pristine lands of great forests, rolling plains, crystal clear lakes and streams and rivers. And we have suffered in your quest for God, for Glory, for Gold. But, we have survived. Can we survive another 500 years of "sustainable development?" I don't think so.

THESE WORDS WERE SPOKEN by Chief Oren Lyons at the Opening Address to the United Nations "The Year of the Indigenous Peoples" in New York City, December 10, 1992.[1] Lyons is Faithkeeper of the Turtle Clan of the Onondaga Nation, one of the Six Nations of the Haudenosaunee (People of the Long House) whose territory once encompassed most of New York, Pennsylvania, and parts of Ohio in the USA, and Ontario and Quebec in Canada. They are also known as the Iroquois Confederacy. The Six Nations includes the Onondaga, Mohawk, Seneca, Cayuga, Oneida, and Tuscorara nations. The Haudenosaunee form of government is based on a more than 1,000-

---

1. https://ratical.org/many_worlds/6Nations/OLatUNin92.html. See also Oren Lyons and John Mohawk, eds. *Exiled in the Land of the Free: Democracy, Indian Nations, and the U.S. Constitution*, 1992.

year-old oral constitution called the Great Law of Peace whose democratic ideals served as inspiration for the framers of the US Constitution.

The English word indigenous comes from the Latin, *indigenus*, meaning born of a land or to a group of people who have ancestral connections to a geographical place. Worldwide, there are over 5,000 distinct indigenous cultures in over seventy countries. Generically, indigenous peoples are referred to as Aboriginal, Native, or First Nations. Maori are the indigenous people of New Zealand who came here in seven great wakas (ocean canoes) from Hawai'iki. All Maori can trace their ancestry (whakapapa) back to one of these wakas. In te reo Maori (the Maori language) the uncapitalised word maori means normal, natural or ordinary. Maori refer to themselves as tangata whenua, meaning People of the Land. In te reo the English plural Maoris is not used as Maori is already a collective noun. Often, if a name is used in the press, it is usually followed by the person's iwi affiliations. In Maoridom whanau (extended family), hapu (sub-tribe) and iwi (tribe) are everything and you would not be wrong to say that in Maoridom there is no such thing as an individual.

In New Zealand Maori speak of their whakapapa, their heritage and genealogy. The following is taken at random from a website of a regional council in New Zealand.

> Genealogy recites for us our divine inheritance,
> Through the union of Earth Mother and Sky Father
> Who gave birth to our resources
> And entrusted their care into our hands,
> The land and the sea
> The forests and the birds,
> The animals and plants,
> All these treasures, bestowed upon us as nurturers
> To sustain the people.
> —Tangata whenua/Northland Regional Council

At the other end of Aotearoa (The Land of the Long White Cloud), Ngāi Tahu are the iwi of the south island of New Zealand. In te reo Maori the south island is called Te Waipounamu—the Greenstone

Island. They say that "whakapapa speaks to more than our relationships with each other; it links us with the land, the sea, the environment, our world and our universe. It permeates all things Ngāi Tahu, helping us understand who we are and where we come from. It lies at the core of Ngāi Tahu knowledge and understanding—it provides an unbroken link and chain of descent between the spiritual and the material, the inanimate and the animate".[2]

The Earth is our first mother. The majority of humans in the history of the planet have viewed the Earth this way. The ground beneath our feet is sacred. For this to be considered by the collective as tree-hugger, get-a-life, space cadet nonsense, or a quaint notion of so-called primitive cultures, or as some unanalysed mother complex, is in itself strange. Monotheistic contempt for her is a recent aberration. So let me give voice to a few of her many names: Papatuanuku (Maori), Pachamama (South America), Gaia (Greek), Nokomis (Algonquin), Ala (Ibo), Bahuba (Zaire), Mari (Basque), Ishtar (Babylonian), or Umhlaba (Zulu). We are all descended from her.

Up to about 1,000 years ago most of the world had an indigenous consciousness and lived an indigenous way of life. These were farming or hunting and gathering cultures which were self-supporting. They were non-urban, either settled in a region or nomadic, and community-oriented rather than individualistic. Now, indigenous peoples living a mostly traditional lifestyle comprise only about five percent of the Earth's population. The European "discovery" of the Americas was the beginning of the colonisation and decimation of indigenous cultures world-wide. In colonial times, indigenous peoples were referred to as "savages," "primitive," "backward" or "uncivilised."

I will use the term indigenous to indicate not a race, people or culture but a particular consciousness or world-view. The characteristics of this world-view include the interrelatedness and livingness of all creation, a close relationship to the natural and the spirit world, and the attachment to a particular place, land or territory. I shall use the term "Western" to refer to the Judeo-Christian-Islamic—yes, they all graze in

---

2. https://ngaitahu.iwi.nz/ngai-tahu/whakapapa

the same paddock—economic, scientific and religious tradition that has lost its indigenosity and has now become globalised.

Although the indigenous way of life and indigenous culture has been lost to most humans, the question remains: Is it possible to retain an indigenous consciousness without a culture?

The opposite of Western is not Eastern but indigenous. West and East are similar in their different ways. As witness, Western culture has long had a fascination with Eastern cultures on account of their different "civilisations." Japan, China or India, for example. Japan and China were long closed to the West but India became the "jewel in the crown" of the British Empire because of its "advanced" culture. Yes, they were one of the "dusky races" but at least they were not black or yellow and looked more like the English than Africans or Chinese did.

One could not imagine, say, Bushman or Aboriginal culture being held in the same regard by Queen Victoria as were Chinese or Indian cultures. Both East and West are estranged from their indigenous roots. However, the East has retained more of a connection although it has arrived at the same place in its broken relationship to the Earth, as witness the trillion dollar Silk and Belt Road that will connect China and Europe.

Indigenous people are as much a part of a culture, with its attendant benefits and restrictions, as those who live within Western culture. But the distinguishing difference is that they have not lost their connection with the Earth and what Don Juan called "silent knowledge".

A recent BBC story illustrates this indigenous consciousness that must be lived in relationship to the land underneath our feet. I summarise and quote at length from Christopher Baker's 2019 article "The Ancient Guardians of the Earth".[3]

Weaving the world

Luis Guillermo Izquierdo, a *mamo*, or spiritual leader, of Colombia's Arhuaco indigenous people says, "The Younger Brother is damaging the world. He is on the path to destruction. He must understand and

---

3. www.bbc.com/travel/story/20190329-the-ancient-guardians-of-the-earth

change his ways, or the world will die" handing Baker a piece of thread representing the umbilical cord tethering him to Mother Earth. He wears a woven white conical hat in reverence to the snow-capped peaks of the sacred Sierra Nevada de Santa Marta mountains.

The Arhuaco are descended from the Tairona culture. When the Spanish conquistadors invaded in the 16th century, the Tairona retreated into the Sierra Nevada de Santa Marta—the world's highest coastal mountain range—which encompasses distinct ecosystems from coastal wetlands and equatorial rainforest to alpine tundra and glacial peaks. The mountain range was named as the most irreplaceable ecosystem on Earth by Science journal in 2013.

The Arhuaco-Kogi-Wiwa community of about 90,000 is one of the world's last indigenous civilisations to have survived culturally intact since the time of the Aztecs and Incas. They call themselves the 'Elder Brothers' with a *mamo* priesthood based on the custodianship of Mother Nature. Izquierdo, like fellow mamos, spent his entire youth in intense spiritual training. Chosen by divination and sequestered for 18 years from birth to adulthood near the summit of the Sierra Nevada de Santa Marta, they possess a consciousness that enables them to commune with the planet directly. "They learn to work as hidden spirit-midwives to all life, keeping it in balance," explained Alan Ereira, a documentary filmmaker and founder of the Tairona Heritage Trust.

"The thoughts of our ancestors are embedded in every rock and other element in which humans have contact," said Izquierdo, who holds to Arhuaco belief that we exist in a conscious universe where all material things have life and awareness. This "lost" indigenous people lived for five centuries in almost complete isolation, steadfastly guarding their territory against outside intrusion. Despite, and because of, this isolation their consciousness charges them with the responsibility of maintaining the balance of nature on behalf of all mankind.

Three decades ago, the Arhuaco realised that the sacred Sierra Nevada de Santa Marta snow caps—for them, the heart of the world—were melting. The páramos (the high-altitude savanna) were drying up. Amphibians and butterflies were disappearing. In 1987, concerned that climate change was impacting the cosmos, the Arhuaco came out of centuries of isolation to send us, their "Younger Brothers", a message.

Two decades later their pleas of ecological disaster have fallen on deaf ears.

"The entrance of non-indigenous is prohibited" reads a sign above the entrance gate to the sacred inner sanctum of the capital, Nabusimake. Photography is forbidden.

Every knot in their intricately crafted *zijews* and clothing represents a thought or memory. Men perched on low wooden stools wove cloth on ancient looms, deep in concentration as their deft fingers wove together the material world with that of spirit. Every aspect of Arhuaco life is permeated with the symbolism of weaving. "Their central metaphor is a loom," Wade Davis said.

The Sierra Nevada de Santa Marta is the very spindle from which the all-knowing Mother's thread unwinds, turning possibility into reality, dreams and memory. Their embedded thought is the very weft to the warp of the cosmos.

West is not the opposite of east

> Words are eggs. Brood over them, warm them, and they will hatch. — Russell Lockhart

> I am not so lost in lexicography as to forget that words are the daughters of earth, and that things are the sons of heaven. —Samuel Johnson

> There is nothing wrong with language except its tyranny. —Anon.

The west is the place where the sun goes down. That sentence betrays our anthropocentrism. The sun never sets, Grandfather Sun is always at work. He rises each day for work, leaving the House of the East, and climbs up the steep stairway of the sky sweating, showing us his face, and biting us with his teeth. He rests briefly, not moving, at the Top of the Sky. He then falls longingly into the arms of Grandmother Earth and they embrace, hidden in the House of the West. With the prayers of the People that our Heavenly Father may not tire in his journey, the world is renewed each day so that life may jump up and live.

Instead of west we could say "There is the sun-going-down-place," pointing, like my Zulu friend, with the elbow not the finger as a mark of respect for the mountain or the river. Or we could glimpse the small rodent that lives in burrows, calling it "disappearing-over-the-hill-with-teeth", but known mundanely in English by the noun "groundhog". The Cape Dutch and their Boer descendants have always been farmers and close to the land. The word *boer* is Afrikaans for farmer. In Afrikaans when something is hard to understand it is *bo my vuurmaak-plek* or "above my fire-lighting place". What a wonderful image! The closer the people, language or culture is to the land the less abstract are descriptions of everyday happenings—and here I resist the temptation to write "everyday things" and fix the process in the nominative formaldehyde of time and space.

What's the difference? An object here, a subject there. Meh! The particular kind of consciousness that gave rise to English and other similar languages turned the "sun-going-down-place" into the "west". Just as with the rise of monotheism and the People of the Book (the Torah, the Bible and the Koran) the word obliterated the process, matter was relegated to second place, words became things-in-themselves divorced from the essence of what they described, and we took a step away from the world underneath our feet and a step up into our minds. And hairs became much easier to split.

In all the monotheistic religions, the Book, and its exegesis and commentary, is the root of tradition and has been made holy—the Torah, the Bible, the Q'uran. Now human interest turns to the abstract, something that does not exist in the natural world. Faith, belief, creed and doctrine do not have blood and breath—they only exist in ink on paper.

The quoting of the Bible, chapter and verse; the endless spats over its literal interpretation; the close adherence to what is written in the Torah or the Koran; all worship the Word, literally. This biblical literalism is identical with the constitutional literalism of the US originalists and textualists, and by the scientific literalism that is bound to the wheel of evidence, fact and reason, although the latter prides itself on its neutrality and atheism. But close cousins they are, joined at the head. One adores the Book, another the Constitution, yet another the Evidence.

I use the word "adore" intentionally as it points to the intimate, arouse, haloed and hallowed relationship each has with the object of its awe and affections. Theologically, this relationship is called belief or faith. Constitutionally, it is called patriotism. More on that later. Poke the bear and all groups get surprisingly heated, emotional and shouty—scepticism with science, patriotism with constitutionalism, evangelism with religion. Or they pull up the drawbridge of faith and retire behind the castle walls.

Historically, the ground was well prepared for a swing to the opposites of faith and belief with the emergence of the nihilistic writings of post-modernism. Unfortunately, post-modernism thought it was different but really it was an identical sibling that was just cock-sure of its difference. Post-modernism is largely a reaction to the certainty of scientific efforts to explain reality, or the certainty of faith and belief. Post-modernism is sceptical of explanations which claim to be valid for all groups, cultures, traditions, or races, and instead focuses on the relative truths of each person. Interpretation is everything and reality only comes into being through our individual interpretation of the world. There is no objectivity only subjectivity. Our feet lift off the ground and we float through word-clouds of deconstruction, narrative, discourse, conversation, lenses, lived experience, and many -ists and -isms.

Jacques Derrida (1930–2004) the Algerian-French philosopher and father of deconstruction said, "There is nothing outside of the text". Post-modernism hides in complex sentences, lives in cities, doesn't venture below the neck, and wouldn't survive a week in the bush.

Between obedience to the Word or the Evidence and obedience to one's own interpretation, there is no mediating third, or what Jung called the transcendent function, just a polarised, oscillating debate between two archly human opposites that, over time, change into the other. One says, "One size fits all." The other says, "No size fits all."

Our Western distance from nature and experience allows us to slide unwittingly into the place where we substitute a word, a vocalisation, a belief, some ink on a page, some pixels on a screen, or a philosophical proposition, for the reality of what happens in the world. It is easier to say, "The west is the place where the sun goes down," than "The place where the sun goes down is called the west." But notice the subtle shift, we have lost the medicine, the mana, the essence of the "the all-spirits-go-there place, the sun-going-down place, the love-making, Grandfather Sun-dying-in-the-arms-of-Grandmother Earth place." Instead, we say west.

The 2000-year, chronic, degenerative, and now terminal, disease that is Western culture has made us cross-eyed, unable to see reality right-side up, and incapable of looking at human experience from the outside, that is, objectively in the truest sense.

Samuel Johnson (1709–1784) was an English writer and lexicographer and a major figure in 18th century literature.[4] His writing was largely in defence of reason against the charms of fancy and emotion, and he championed the values of the aesthetic, humanistic, and moral order. His statement that I quote above is an example from the 1700s when the underlying disease process worsened and Western culture took another step toward the west. The zeitgeist of the time thought it was taking a great leap forward in science and exploration and rather than a step toward death. So I would reverse the Johnson quote to read, "Words are the sons of heaven, and things are the daughters of earth."

Please do not misunderstand me. There is nothing wrong with language except its limitations. Without the gifts of language I would not be writing this book, we would not have the beauty of Shakespeare, the art of Maori oratory or whaikorero, there would be no poetry from Blake and Keats, no Bhagavad Gita, no Norse legends, no myth, no story. However, there are human experiences that cannot be quantified or captured in the net of words. Words literalise and flatten our deepest experiences. Why has so much been written on love? Because its hard to describe. The best writing touches a face of the many-faces of our experience. It comes close but is never the experience itself. Music and dance are usually better than words. They all slip away too soon but art remembers these gifts—a Bach fugue rises up through my cells, a Turner painting draws me into its light, Riverdance moves my feet, and Robert Johnson sends me down to the crossroads.[5]

---

4. Samuel Johnson, (1755) *The Dictionary of the English Language.*
5. "Matter delights in music, and became Bach." —Ronald Johnson (1935-1998), American poet.

These experiences of love, of epiphany, of being carried away, are beyond the realm of description and can only be experienced or pointed to. They are ineffable, indescribable, or too sacred for words. But here is the problem. These experiences can happen to anyone (pretty much). Spirit, the Holy Ghost, the Universe, is sometimes not too choosy with its bolt-out-of-the-blue. Like the lightning bolt, in its exercise of free will it just wants to connect with matter, fertilise, and stir things up. But the "who" the experience is happening to makes all the difference. The more unconscious, complexed, or mass-minded the person is the more they will be swept away by the ineffable and will go found a religion or find one to follow. Their obedience to the archetypal forces—I've found Jesus, I've seen the light, I am a patriot, I am now guided by X, My life is in the hands of Z, I'm passionate about A, I can manifest B, as well as their willingness to tell everyone who will listen about their profound experiences—lights them up on the rationalist radar. But their experience cannot be replicated, it is unique, and meant for that person only, so it always fails the rationalist test. Reason vs religion—smugness ensues, on both sides.

Nevertheless, words are good. They are psychic eggs. If we brood over them long enough, give them warmth and attention, their unremarkable shells crack, and they hatch and reveal their origins and meaning. The Maya represented speech by a glyph coming from the mouth that meant flower or water. Whether the masculinities of the mind like it or not all things that are physical are born from the earth, à la Samuel Johnson upside-down. All things are born, live and die. They are not immortal, that is not their nature and their gift. We are a recyclable life form. Death is the transference of life. It is the mortal gift of the physical world that spirit, in its permanence and immortality, can only wonder at.

In the West death is sown deep. Our culture is full to bursting with innovation, progress, expansion, growth, development, and advance such that there is no room available for death, contraction, retraction, pause, backwardness, regression, failure and retreat. So, much denied, these things must make room for themselves. Most expansions or colonial movements went from east to west—the Roman Empire, the Vikings, and European colonisation—and took with them the seeds of their own death and transformation which we are now beginning to reap.

Cleanliness is next to godliness said John Wesley in a 1778 sermon. Being clean, physically and morally, not like those dirty savages, is seen as a sign of civilisation. The Western obsession with sprays, deodorants, disinfectants, and its sanitisation of waste is putting lipstick on the pig of its pollution of the body-of-the-world. And my apologies to all swine. Robert Wolff writes about the Senoi of Malaysia who clean out the village, spiritually and physically, every two weeks at the new moon and the full moon by reenacting the battle between Ragda (the chief leyak or witch) and the Barong (a protective monster).[6]

When a culture loosens its attachment to the earth, it begins to die like a great tree that has been uprooted. And when it begins to die it will go west. So all the great migrations, diasporas, resettlements, emigrations, relocations, exodi, journeys, voyages, and treks almost always went west. Or to put it another way when a people are severed from the land there is death and loss: both physical and spiritual. Then we go west.

East (Greek *eos*, dawn) is the place where the Sun is born each day from the body of the Earth. West (Latin *vesper*, evening and, further back, the Sanskrit word *avah* meaning "to go downward") is the place where he dies into her arms and travels into the Underworld to be born again.

The west has always been associated with ending, death, change, twilight and the transition from light to darkness. To the British Tommy in World War I to "go west" meant to be killed and in Ojibway it is "the place where all spirits go." When we come to the remains of the day we are reminded of endings. Dusk is the time for reflection and melancholy. All things are born in the east and when they die they go west. Out global culture lives in the West.

Some indigenous cultures spent half their time in "religious" ceremony honouring the worlds of both matter and spirit. The beauty of prayer and dance and speech feed the other world. This is not just a Sunday morning church service or evening bible readings. In fact, the majority of indigenous life could be considered as ceremonial—the spir-

---

6. Robert Wolff, *Original Wisdom: Stories of an Ancient Way of Knowing*.

and the temporal always walk side-by-side. The corn is never planted without talking to the corn goddesses. The pollen is never gathered without thanks to the spirit of the plants and the Earth. In Bali the women place beauty-offerings, or *canang sari*, of fruit and flowers at temples, altars, gateways and on the street. Every morning. The soul dies without beauty. In Kawi *sari* means essence, and *canang* (*ca*, beautiful; *nang*, purpose) is the small palm leaf tray that holds the offering. The different colour of the flowers point to the gods and goddesses of each of the four directions. The powers of the directions are acknowledged, not just as geographical conveniences or political divisions, but the places where the great Givers-of-life-to-the-People, the Sun and the Earth, are born, marry, make love, and die in each others arms every day.

But Copernicus and Galileo gave us a different view of the sun and the earth. Capitals were dropped, all was explained, their lovemaking was stilled, and their faces no longer smiled. In fact (there's that phrase again which we think makes things real and actual) they have no face—the sun is just a ball of hydrogen and helium that is 4.5 billion years old and 15 million °C in the middle.

Hemisphericentrism was a word I made up to seduce myself into thinking that a noun meant something real, and that maybe I could found an activist movement to root out and de-platform discriminatory hemispheric practices. As well as east and west there's north and south, in English anyway, who (not which 'cos they are alive) tell of our biases. South means "sun-side" because the sun travels to the south in the northern hemisphere. Not so in the southern hemisphere where it travels to the north. World maps always have north at the top. But just to straighten things out have a look here.[7] And New Zealand is often left out.[8]

The first ever photo of the earth from space (called the "Blue Marble") was taken in 1972 by Apollo 17 and is one of the most reproduced images in human history.[9] Originally the photo was taken with

---

7. http://mapco.co.nz/product/upside-down-world

8. www.atlasobscura.com/articles/new-zealand-left-off-world-map

9. The "Blue Marble" is the Substack icon of Terra Mortis. https://terramortis.substack.com

Antarctica at the top.[10] But someone decided to turn it upside-down for the benefit of those in the northern hemisphere who are hemispherically challenged.

But hemispheric biases aside, our body knows her body intimately. She is the lover who does not betray us—but in the human world that is the lover's job. She has no concern for us yet we are one of her children. She births us, holds us, feeds us, and receives us when we die. All experiences of nurturing, feeding, holding, betrayal and desertion belong to the Great Mother, Earth Mother, Grandmother Earth, who is known by her many names.

But we walk among the energetically illiterate, the emotionally deaf, and the science-infested. Our world gifts the other world with opposable thumbs, art, movement, sex and pleasure. The other world gifts this world with meaning and magic. When the Earth stumbles and becomes frail, what will happen to all this psychic energy, this commerce between spirit and matter, that keeps these worlds in good relation?

Silent Knowledge

The first nine months of life—inside the womb—are a time of intimacy and attachment through physical touching (sensation) and non-physical touching (intuition). Similarly, the second nine months of life—outside the womb—are also a time of intimacy and attachment through physical touching (sensation) and non-physical touching (intuition). These two psychological functions, sensation and intuition as Jung called them, are our primary ways of knowing and experiencing. Feeling and thinking come later.

Sensation is immediate, raw perception through the five senses, intuition is immediate, raw perception through the unconscious or the sixth sense.[11] The natural world physically touches us with wind, rain, birds and the sea. Our kinship with nature's gentleness and healing, as well as our fear and respect for nature's disregard, awakens our intuition,

---

10. https://en.wikipedia.org/wiki/The_Blue_Marble#/media/File:Apollo_17_Blue_Mar
ble_original_orientation_(AS17-148-22727).jpg
11. CW 9i, par. 504.

our indigenous soul. The other two functions—thinking and feeling—judge, evaluate, and sort our perceptions. Thinking is objective judgment and feeling is subjective judgment. Our thoughts and feeling judgements may catch up weeks, months or years later after the experience. And beware of those who profess to be "non-judgemental".

Our indigenous soul is our evolutionary heritage. This quiet animal keeps itself dappled, glimpsed but not seen, until the holiday-maker, the wage earner, the mother, the student, the seeker or the anthropologist within us is ready to ask the right question, to be still, to find the right attitude, to kneel. Then our indigenous soul smells us, and only after long years of sniffing, does it reveal its wildness to us. Its "silent knowledge", or intuition, is our original knowing and being known by the world around us. Don Juan explained:

> Inside every human being was a gigantic, dark lake of silent knowledge which each of us could intuit... "Silent knowledge is something that all of us have," he went on. "Something that has complete mastery, complete knowledge of everything. But it cannot think, therefore, it cannot speak of what it knows. Sorcerers believe that when man became aware that he knew, and wanted to be conscious of what he knew, he lost sight of what he knew. This silent knowledge, which you cannot describe, is, of course, intent—the spirit, the abstract. Man's error was to want to know it directly, the way he knew everyday life. The more he wanted, the more ephemeral it became." "But what does that mean in plain words, don Juan?" I asked. "It means that man gave up silent knowledge for the world of reason," he replied. "The more he clings to the world of reason, the more ephemeral intent becomes."[12]

Up until about 50 years ago humanity could go it's own way and was not a threat to the planet. To itself, yes, but not to the Earth. Beginning in the 1970s, indigenous elders around the world began to respond to the increasingly dangerous state of imbalance on the planet by sharing knowledge that had been previously kept hidden. In Aotearoa/New Zealand the Waitaha elders say:

---

12. Carlos Castaneda, *The Power of Silence*, 164, 167.

We are Waitaha. Until now we have hidden our beginnings, and all that followed, in the shadows. In this way we protected our knowledge in the silence of the Whare Wananga, the School of Learning of Waitaha. Tuatara, the Keeper of the Knowledge, guards the trails of the mind and spirit that gave us life. We lead you past Tuatara, The tuatara is a lizard-like reptile that is a "living fossil" found only on a few islands off the coast of New Zealand. The species is the sole survivor of an order that became extinct about 200 million years ago even before the dinosaurs disappeared. It has a highly developed third or pineal eye on top of the head. our ever vigilant kaitiaki [guardian], and invite you to share the words and the wisdom of our ancestors. For it has been decided it is time for our treasures to be brought in to the light.... We kept safe this knowledge of the Tides of Life that flow from Marama, the Moon. Our Star Walkers joined the stars to the land. These kete [baskets] are the treasures of the peoples of the Nation of Waitaha. We have kept them safe through sixty-seven generations, for they are the sacred songs of our ancestors. Now we share them with all born of these mountains, and all who call this land home, for you are of this land as we are of this land.[13]

Vusamazulu Credo Mutwa, a Zulu sangoma, wrote:

"Ultimately I saw that the lore of my people was destined to die with those of us who knew it, and that it would then die forever. I felt I gradually recognised that by breaking my oath—something originally made to protect the sacred lore in times that were very different from these times—I was doing something for my own people, preserving the eternal wisdom that has been carried on for centuries; and also doing something for mankind as a whole. For there are people of many lands and many races who share in this wisdom and learn the wonder of these stories—they existed for the good of our people, but also now for all people".[14]

---

13. Ngati Kowhai o Waitaha, *Song of Waitaha: The Histories of a Nation*, 10.
14. Credo Mutwa, *Song of the Stars*, xiii.

Lorraine Mafi Williams, an Aboriginal elder said, "In 1975 our elders prophesied a shift, and have been preparing our people for it... the ancient teachings are being revived by the elders around the Earth".

This indigenous capacity to see, backwards and forwards, for seven generations and seven times seven generations has been leached from the soil by the solvents of progress, development, and the narcissism of human democracy. But this wisdom is in need of restoration. It is the only way to survive.

I have had the good fortune to have been associated with indigenous elders over the last forty years. Some say that there are ten ways in which the Earth keeps herself in balance and beauty, that is, how she keeps her body in good health. We might call these ecological laws. If too many of these laws are broken then she can no longer be a fertile planet and give birth to her children—the rock peoples, the plant nations, the animal brothers and sisters, the humans, and the ancestors—and she will eventually die.

They also say that there are four universes—the heart, mind, body, and spirit—that make up the wholeness of the Creator just as we are made in its image. We are in the south, child or heart universe. In this universe there are 12 stars that have planets with human life. We are the only planet with humans in physical form. We are the south planet in the south universe. In other words, we are the youngest planet in the youngest universe of the Creator. Our closest elder brother is Sirius and our closest elder sisters, the aunties, are the Pleiades, or Matariki in te reo Maori.

As the south planet in the south universe the Earth carries the heart, the emotions, the joy and the woundedness, of the child aspect of the Creator. This is why emotions, personal and archetypal, and their transformation into unique, personal feeling values—the great enterprise of individuation—is so important on this planet. It is our part in the Creator's creation of itself. But if this small green planet dies something will happen that is beyond human vision and comprehension. The feeling heart of the child of the Creator will die.

Will the Earth disappear? Yes. No. Perhaps. But she may no longer give birth to life that jumps up and lives. Grandfather Sun will have no one to make love to each day. His tears of fire will fall on the greyness of her face. Creation will become a colder place.

Idealisation?

Lest the reader may think I idealise indigenous peoples I will say that at various times they were as rapacious, stupid, cruel, grandiose, and sexist as modern peoples. Jared Diamond puts it tolerably well:

> Not surprisingly, Native Hawaiians and Maoris [sic] don't like paleontologists telling them that their ancestors exterminated half of the bird species that had evolved on Hawaii and New Zealand, nor do Native Americans like archaeologists telling them that the Anasazi deforested parts of the southwestern U.S. The supposed discoveries by paleontologists and archaeologists sound to some listeners like just one more racist pretext advanced by whites for dispossessing indigenous peoples.
>
> Some of the indigenous peoples and the anthropologists identifying with them go to the opposite extreme. They insist that past indigenous peoples were (and modern ones still are) gentle and ecologically wise stewards of their environments, intimately knew and respected Nature, innocently lived in a virtual Garden of Eden, and could never have done all those bad things.... Only those evil modern First World inhabitants are ignorant of Nature, don't respect the environment, and destroy it. In fact, both extreme sides in this controversy —the racists and the believers in a past Eden—are committing the error of viewing past indigenous peoples as fundamentally different from (whether inferior to or superior to) modern First World peoples. Managing environmental resources sustainably has always been difficult, ever since Homo sapiens developed modern inventiveness, efficiency, and hunting skills by around 50,000 years ago.[15]

What about cultures and civilisations that did not collapse—where life was supposedly nasty, brutal and short as Thomas Hobbes would have us believe? As Diamond points out, it's complicated. He gives the exam-

---

15. Diamond, *Collapse: How Societies Choose to Fail or Succeed,* 8-9.

of Iceland and Tikopia, two island cultures that were able to manage their environment. He also lists also eight reasons why ancient societies collapsed: deforestation and habitat destruction, soil erosion, water management, over hunting and fishing, and human population growth. All signs of human excess.

He says that indigenous peoples are not fundamentally different from modern first world peoples. I say that they were and are but not measured by whether their societies collapsed or not—that's the modern, extroverted view. In other ways they were fundamentally different—but in ways that you can't see or measure. Diamond also fails to point out that in the last 50,000 years the life of the planet was not at risk and the foibles and failings of indigenous peoples had not yet run up against absolute limitation. Nature took care of them, or not. She can't any more.

In traditional cultures the relationship with the surrounding environment was different and they retained a connection with the human heritage of silent knowledge. Not that this prevented them from exhausting their resources and cultural collapse but that's a judgement based on the outer appearance of things and it misses the point. All cultures have had difficulty managing the environment they existed in. Most importantly, previous collapses were a local affair. Now it's global and we may have reached the limit of the island we live on.

Participation mystique

For the most part, Jung and Jungians have had an ambivalent—and primitive—relationship with the "primitive". One has only to sample Meredith Sabini's *The Nature Writings of C G Jung,* or the photo of Jung with bare feet in the mud cooking at the camp fire, to appreciate Jung's deep connection with the natural world. On the other hand, he was also a European of his time. His experience of indigenous cultures was sparse, with personal contact limited to a visit to Taos Pueblo, New Mexico on January 5-6, 1925, and three weeks at Mount Elgon, Kenya in 1926. The rest of his information was derived from European anthropological texts. For example, his references in the Collected Works to

Australian aboriginal peoples. Some of Jung's writings show a decidedly "primitive" view of the "primitive mentality".

> Primitive people and animals have nothing like that capacity for reviving memories of unique impressions which we find among civilized people.[16]

> Not only primitive man but animals too have a mighty dislike of all intentional effort, and are addicted to absolute laziness until circumstances prod them into action.[17]

> The primitive mentality can be directly experienced by us only in the form of the infantile psyche that still lives in our memories.[18]

> If you can put yourself in the mind of the primitive, you will at once understand why this is so. He lives in such "participation mystique" with his world, as Lévy-Bruhl calls it, that there is nothing like that absolute distinction between subject and object which exists in our minds. What happens outside also happens in him, and what happens in him also happens outside.[19]

> It is true that primitives are simpler and more childlike than we, in good and evil alike.[20]

From an ethnocentric viewpoint Jung suggests that "primitive" cultures were less differentiated, less conscious, and more subject to a *participation mystique* with the surrounding world, than "civilised" cultures.[21] In many places he equates the primitive with the infantile in the sense that the primitive is undeveloped, uncivilised and undifferentiated. Edward Edinger expands similarly:

---

16. CW 4, par. 404.
17. CW 4, par. 470.
18. CW 8, par. 97.
19. CW 8, par. 329.
20. CW 10, par. 112.
21. CW 10, Archaic Man.

Children share with primitive man the identification of ego with the archetypal psyche and ego with outer world. With primitives, inner and outer are not at all distinguished. For the civilised mind, primitives are most attractively related to nature and in tune with the life process; but they are also savages and fall into the same mistakes of inflation as do children. Modern man, alienated from the source of life meaning, finds the image of the primitive an object of yearning. This accounts for the appeal of Rousseau's concept of the "noble savage" and other more recent works which express the civilised mind's nostalgia for its lost mystical communion with nature.

This is one side, but there is also the negative side. *The real life of the primitive is dirty, degrading and obsessed with terror.* [italics added] We would not want that reality for a moment. It is the symbolical primitive for which we yearn. When one looks back on his psychological origin, it has a twofold connotation: first. it is seen as a condition of paradise, wholeness, a state of being at one with nature and the gods, and infinitely desirable; but secondly, by our conscious human standards, which are related to time and space reality, it is an inflated state, a condition of irresponsibility, unregenerate lust, arrogance and crude desirousness. The basic problem for the adult is how to achieve the union with nature and the gods, with which the child starts, without bringing about the inflation of identification.[22]

But Edinger arrives at the right place. Western civilisation has brought upon itself the inflation of separation and the dis-identification with nature. So the question is, "How can we relate to the natural world around us without the inflation of 'civilisation'?". As I have suggested a "primitive" way of relating to the world around us is basic to our human nature, has been refined as a psychotherapeutic skill in establishing a relationship with the unconscious, and is the just about the only thing that will save us and the planet. It will bring about a needed humiliation.

In reading Jung's writings on indigenous consciousness we should keep in mind that what he wrote is not necessarily what he thought,

---

22. Edinger, *Ego and Archetype*, 11.

although others have described him as a "pagan".[23] Perhaps Jung did not want to commit himself publicly to a view that would have been at odds with the prevailing colonial and Eurocentric sentiment with regard to "primitive" peoples.

The phrase "participation mystique" was coined by the French anthropologist Lucien Levy-Bruhl (1857–1939) in his book *How Natives Think* (1910) to denote a particular kind of psychological connection with objects, where the subject cannot clearly distinguish him- or herself from the object. He proposed that there were two human mindsets, primitive and Western. The primitive mind does not differentiate the supernatural from reality, but rather uses "mystical participation" to engage with the world. The Western mind, by contrast, uses speculation and logic. He believed in a historical and evolutionary process leading from the primitive mind to the Western mind. Jung wrote:

> [Participation mystique] is a phenomenon that is best observed in primitives.... Among civilized peoples it usually occurs between persons, seldom between a person and a thing".[24]

> The primitive cannot assert that he thinks; it is rather 'something that thinks in him'.... His consciousness is menaced by an almighty unconscious: hence his fear of magical influences which may cross his path at any moment.... Owing to the chronic twilight state of his consciousness, it is often impossible to find out whether he merely dreamed something or whether he really experienced it.[25]

> I use the term identity to denote a psychological conformity. It is always an unconscious phenomenon.... It is a characteristic of the prim-itive mentality and the real foundation of participation mystique, which is nothing but a relic of the original non-differentiation of subject and object, and hence of the primordial unconscious state. It is

---

23. Noll, *The Jung Cult: Origins of a Charismatic Movement*. Presumably Noll thought the word pagan was pejorative.
24. CW 6, par. 781.
25. CW 9i, par. 260.

also a characteristic of the mental state of early infancy, and, finally of
the unconscious of the civilized adult.[26]

We might liken these generalisations, which were Jung based on Jung's
brief contacts with a few indigenous people, to Ochwiay Biano—the
Taos Pueblo Jung met in 1925 on his visit to the USA—thinking that all
Europeans were like Jung.

Jung suggests a hierarchy: discrimination between subject and
object is more "civilised," and identity between subject and object is less
"civilized." Differentiation is the more conscious, and identity the less
conscious, mode of being. Many individuals in indigenous cultures are
differentiated and conscious, but in ways contrary to how differentiation is understood—psychologically, anyway—in Western culture. A
state of identity, temporary or permanent, is not always unconscious,
and we need look no further than Jung to find examples. It was he who
said that the meeting of two personalities is like a chemical reaction; if
anything happens, both are changed. It is a conscious identification that
allows psychotherapy to take place. Empathy identifies with the other's
distress, and it is the consciousness with which this meeting happens
that differentiates therapy from most other human encounters. Most
importantly, it is conscious identity, a conscious participation mystique,
that is the basis for the eros, the aroha, that the People have for the Land.

In *The Spirit Mercurius*, written in 1942, Jung clearly understands
the indigenous consciousness. He relates a story of a soldier in Nigeria
who, when he heard his tree spirit calling him, desperately tried to break
out of his barracks and go to the tree. When the soldier was questioned
about it, he said that all those who bore the name of the tree would
occasionally hear its voice and be obliged to respond. Jung did not
dismiss this as animism or superstition. He elaborates:

These psychic phenomena suggest that originally the tree and the
daemon were one and the same, and that their separation is a secondary
phenomenon corresponding to a higher level of culture and consciousness.... Since at the present level of consciousness we cannot suppose

---

26. CW 6, par. 741.

that tree daemons exist, we are forced to assert that the primitive suffers from hallucinations, that he hears his own unconscious which he had projected into the tree. If this theory is correct—and I do not know how we could formulate it otherwise today—then the second level of consciousness has effected a differentiation between the object "tree" and the unconscious content projected into it, thereby achieving an act of enlightenment. The third level rises higher still and attributes "evil" to the psychic content which has been separated from the object.

Finally a fourth level, the level reached by our consciousness today, carries the enlightenment a stage further by denying the objective existence of the "spirit" and declaring that the primitive has heard nothing at all, but merely had an auditory hallucination. Consequently the whole phenomenon vanishes into thin air—with the great advantage that the evil spirit becomes obviously non-existent and sinks into ridiculous significance. The fifth level is of the opinion that something did happen after all.... [it] assumes that the unconscious exists and has a reality just like any other existent. However odious it may be, this means that the "spirit" is also a reality.[27]

Jung chooses his words carefully here, suggesting that it could not be imagined otherwise in his day. But he ends up taking the position that what was heard was real. If we are not burdened by too much civilised behaviour and can walk without shoes then we can hear the voices of the trees that are drowned out by the concrete, the real estate deals, and all manner of trumpery.

The movements of modern psychology including behaviourism and psychoanalysis both succumb to the same scientific fallacy that overly separates inside and outside. Each denies that there is another end to the stick. With behaviourism what you see is all you get. With psychoanalysis what you see is never what you get. One privileges outside, the other privileges inside. To be fair (but not to overdo the generosity) in comparison to the 1950s, 60s, and 70s, both of them are slowly unclenching and coming to an acknowledgement of each other.

Jung was the first of modern clinicians to consider that inside and

---

27. CW 13, pars. 247-248.

outside were connected and that matter and spirit were but two forms of the same thing.[28] Although I imagine that even he would be pushed to entertain the notion that the Maya spirit house *is* the universe, or the Navajo sand painting *is* the world, or the Maori whenua (the land) *is* the body of Papatuanuku.

He proposed that a symbol is a transformer of archetypal energy, "The psychological mechanism that transforms energy is the symbol."[29] Symbols are the many ways an archetype speaks to us in human images. But, the fact that we have had to invent an intermediary we call a "symbol" tells us that we have drained spirit of life and blood and body and it cannot be experienced directly. It then only inhabits cool and lofty places with angelic wings where there is no place for death and grief, betrayal and war, birth and love-making. Matter and nature are rendered coarse, dumb, mute and insensible. They become dirt that has no life or spirit, cannot talk or think, is under the dominion of man, and can only be understood by observation or dissection.

Dissociation mystique

Western culture has had over two thousand years, perhaps five to ten thousand, to adjust to the process that Jung described in his penultimate work, *Aion*, of being severed from the land. Indigenous cultures, however, have been dispossessed over the course of a few centuries. Similar to their vulnerability to alien physical diseases—like smallpox during the colonisation in the Americas—indigenous cultures have little immunity against the psychic infections of Western culture, the worst of which (alcoholism or suicide, for example) become amplified. With colonisation, spiritual violation results in a physical problem, physical violation results in a spiritual problem.

When there is no connection to the unconscious, then psyche goes wrong, and if there is no connection to the land then matter goes wrong. The manic, grandiose illusion that is the global economy omnipotently assumes that we have broken free of our relationship

28. CW 8, *Synchronicity: An Acausal Connecting Principle.*
29. CW 8, par. 45

with, and are self-sufficient from, the land that feeds us. We are separate from the elements of air, earth, fire, and water that support us, and the Minerals, Plants, Animals, and Ancestors, who are Our Relations, are our servants and slaves, and we have assumed dominion over all. As a result we are under the spell of a perverse and contrary participation mystique—a dissociation mystique so to speak. Like Faust, we do not acknowledge Care and are unable to tend that which gives us life. The ecology is dismembered, nature is carved at her joints, and we have lost our spiritual relationship with the world of matter.

Like Faust, in his lust for land and his turning away of the grey women, the Western psyche has ignored its obligations to the natural world, and as a result is heir to an archetypal guilt arising from the betrayal of what gives us life. Indigenous cultures have not severed their relationship with the sacredness of the natural world. Like Philemon and Baucis they have given shelter to the gods. Therefore, guilt in indigenous cultures is less archetypal. There never was any expulsion form the Garden of Eden. It is a human, everyday ledger of obligations toward, and transgressions against, one's family and community. Western culture defends against this archetypal guilt with a catastrophic dissociation and psychotic denial of the reality that the planet we live on is alive and has consciousness.[30]

The heroic world economy is unsustainable, in spite of the defensive and euphemistic rationalisation of "sustainable development." Were it not for the severe breakdown in reality testing, even a single statistic would be enough to confront us with our destructiveness. But let's pick some examples at random:[31]

- Since 1970 nearly 80 percent of the world's indigenous forests have been destroyed. In the USA 95% of old growth forests are gone. Seventy countries in the world no longer have any intact or original forests.

---

30. I use the terms "dissociation" and "psychotic" here in their clinical sense. Dissociation meaning a pathological alteration of consciousness as a defense against the awareness of trauma. Psychotic meaning a severe distortion in reality testing.
31. www.fertilegroundinstitute.org/indicators-of-ecological-collapse.html

- In 1992 the Grand Banks fishery off Newfoundland, the richest fishing ground in the world that fed Europe for centuries, collapsed. It has not recovered.
- Since 1950 more resources have been consumed by humankind than in the whole history of the human race.
- Zooplankton (the basis of oceanic food chains) populations have dropped 70% in the last four decades.
- For the past 300 million years, excluding this century, approximately one species went extinct every four years. In 2017 one species went extinct every 15 minutes.
- Species extinction has increased to rates of 10 to 100 times greater than that of 30 years ago. At current rates one-half of all species will be gone by the end of the century.
- Climate models predict that the average temperature of the Earth could increase up to about 7 degrees Centigrade by the year 2100.
- Male sperm counts have dropped more than 30% in the past 60 years.

This dissociation and its sidekicks—heroic activity and the flight into hope—can perhaps be understood by listening to some of Melanie Klein, the child psychoanalyst. She observed that, from the very beginning of infancy, there is a splitting between negative experiences which are attributed to the hated "object", and positive experiences which are attributed to the good "object". Because the infant does not have the mental capacity to view these things as the same, they are split and the idealised experiences are separated from the persecutory ones. The infant feels that the hated object is also hate-ful and persecutory. TheIf this is not modified during later development this persecution-hatred axis comes to have two ends. Persecution must seek out hatred and hatred must seek out persecution. This developmental phase is called the "paranoid-schizoid" position.[32]

As the infant matures it becomes aware of his or her ambivalence;

---

32. This is not to be confused with the psychiatric diagnoses of bipolar disorder (manic depression), schizophrenia, or schizoid personality disorder.

and the mother is perceived as a whole not a part object, in other words as a person who both satisfies and frustrates, one who is both loved and hated. Ambivalence means that the infant is concerned and feels guilty that its aggression (read distress, anger, neediness, demandingness) will damage the the mother in some way (read drive her away, make her angry, stop loving). This brings about the capacity for love and gratitude as well as the wish to repair and restore any damage done (real or imagined). This phase is called the depressive position because awareness of one's ambivalence brings with it the threat of the loss of what is loved and loves.

For the infant (and the adult in later form) fear of losing the loved one (or having sent them away, disappointed them, incurred their disapproval, or made them angry) initiates an important developmental change. Feelings of guilt and upset now become part of attachment and love. (Mummy, I'm sorry. Don't be angry at me. Please don't.... I'll be good. I'll make up for it. All this may be verbal or non-verbal) From this emerges a capacity for empathy, the ability to identify with the experience of others, and responsibility toward, and a concern for, others whom we care about. When the person begins to integrate their aggression as opposed to projecting it into others, a healthy depression ensues, leading to a tolerance of goodness and badness within the other. It also leads to the desire for reparation, to feel remorse, to apologise from the place of feeling and knowing the hurt given and received (Twitter doesn't count), and to make good. In other words, the depressive position leads to a truly fundamental re-orientation towards reality and we begin to take responsibility for our own impulses. On the other hand, any flight from ambivalence brings about a regression to the paranoid-schizoid position. All this is a psychological road map of how to repair our relationship with the Earth.

Our global dissociation is akin (and this is more than a metaphor) to Klein's notion of manic defenses against the depressive position. Manic activity (aka business growth and development) or mentation (aka the idealisation of intellect) defends the person against the depression inherent in realising his or her own destructiveness. Put less starkly, doing keeps me from not seeing and not knowing the effect I have on others, good or bad. Doing keeps me from feeling the shame and humiliation, or the pride and self-confidence, that comes with that knowing. It is a position or pattern that can emerge at any age and stage when we get above, beside or below ourselves and don't live within our limitations or live up to our capabilities.

When the depressive position is achieved (although it may be lost again and again resulting in the re-emergence of the paranoid-schizoid position) others can be allowed a more separate existence with their own needs, omnipotence is lessened, and there is a decrease in guilt and the fear of loss.

Hanna Segal (1918–2011) was one of Klein's foremost students. Unbeknownst to her, a quotation from her paper 'A psychoanalytical approach to aesthetics' was used as a rallying call for the World Trade Center Mural Project. The project was set up following 9/11 with the aim of creating a mural, 70 feet high, on the Equitable Building in New York as a symbol that life could survive destruction.[33] "It is when the world within us is destroyed, when it is dead and loveless, when our loved ones are in fragments, and we ourselves in helpless despair—it is then that we must recreate our world anew, reassemble the pieces, infuse life into dead fragments, recreate life."

But what if the life that has supported us without complaint or question, the Earth itself, what if it cannot reassemble its own dead fragments and recreate life? Have all the apocalyptic writers foreseen this? Is the Christian story of finding a post-Armageddon home in heaven at the side of the Lord just a spiritualised version of let's colonise Mars? For all its so-called advances, Western civilisation has regressed to to the paranoid-schizoid position in its relationship with the Earth. It is infantile. Departed are the capacities for gratitude and concern for all of creation. Returned are grandiosity, neediness, exploitation and neglect.

Here we might listen, with a different ear, to the apocalyptic warnings that abound at the end of the millennium. When this inflation, the mark of our Western and now global culture, undergoes an *enantiodromia* and the awareness of the previously inflated state and its destructiveness, together with the accompanying guilt, reaches

---

33. https://melanie-klein-trust.org.uk/writers/hanna-segal.

consciousness, then the collective ego will be overwhelmed.[34] The collective unconscious symbolises this in apocalyptic imagery such as Zeus' flooding of the land as punishment for the inhospitality of the inhabitants, as we shall see in Ovid's story of Philemon and Baucis.

When the *enantiodromia* comes about it will not be a pretty picture. The global omnipotent ego is in thrall to its histrionic anima—the stock market. In the psychological underworld of the global economy the libido-laden words of interest, credit, account, inflation, depression, and exchange, carry great weight. Like Faust's being blinded (a loss of consciousness) by Care, the unacknowledged feminine may take revenge by insinuating the feminine elements of chance and chaos. (The commingling of order and chance accounts for the archetypal fascination with gambling and sports). The stock market, as the moody, unpredictable, irrational anima, may compensate in some way.

I wrote the passages above in 1999. Some time afterward, the terrible events of September 11, 2001 took place. Given the inflation of Western culture, a compensatory deflation was inevitable. I thought it would have been the stock-market or the economy. No-one could have imagined it would happen in such a tragic and graphic way. Deeper and broader learnings seem unlikely to flow from this event, as it is viewed simplistically as a battle between good and evil. It has also gone unnoticed that a similar structural collapse followed hard on the heels of 9/11. In what was at that time the biggest bankruptcy in U.S. history, the energy corporation Enron collapsed barely two months after the terrorist attacks.

From the vantage point of 2023 we can see that life has upped the stakes. The dominoes have gotten larger. From the fall of the World Trade Centres in 2001, to the Global Financial Crisis in 2008 then in 2020 matter, not content with world trade or money markets, and with lessons not having been learned, introduced us to a virus, Covid-19. A virus indeed, the smallest living thing, with not even a nucleus, that brought world trade and global economies to a standstill. There is more to come. We have gone from world trade to money to viruses. What's

---

34. *Enantiodromia* (Greek, meaning "running counter to"): The emergence of the unconscious opposite in the course of time. CW 6, par. 709.

next? If we follow the progression "downwards" then "non-living" matter is next in line. Covid-19 was managed with ventilators, vaccination, protest, and masks. Now the weather—the elements of fire, air, water and earth—does not submit so readily to our efforts. In other words, climate change.

Clearing the Highlands

Out back beyond the dry-stone wall of understanding and the creaking gate of firm belief, the croft of cold air, thin and hollow, hung its knife-edge sharpness over the tart juice and the dark orchids. The fruitful seeds of memory dropped from her tears and their joy as they struck the heel-worn stone floor.

"Weesht, noo," she said, drawing in air as blue as her lips, Thin lips, tight as a purse, as if air was in short supply and not to be wasted, stretched taut against all time, a rictus in the teeth of the northwesterlies that threw rain and fish and rabbits up against the single door.

She sat, briefly, permitting herself the sparse luxury of a small exhale—a secret indulgence, an easing, a letting down, a wee dram of the last great exhale when she could finally be at rest. The horizon-thin lips shut again—disapproving sentinels of her heart, inspecting all for hidden pleasure—they nipped the shirttails of the escaping exhale, fleeing like a degenerate on day parole. Set firm against the insolent heat of urgent flowers, pale and spared of blood as oatmeal, they denied, for all to see, the secret war on life she carried and the exhaustion of a living death. And down below, in a minor corner, lay careless orchids, tumescent, engorged in silent pleasure, their purple darkness dividing wind and rain, fish and rabbits.

Hot in the evening, dresser drawer-cold at night, fried for breakfast, a slab for lunch: the oatmeal, wan sister that she was, barely kept body and soul in begrudging friendship. Like oatmeal, like warmth for the heart, peat for the fire, shoes for the feet, rags for the cracks—there was never enough. Now that the lairds had come and the land was gone, love was a cruel extravagance. Now the land grew only trees, dwarfed and horizontal as the wind. Now the land grew only hardness of heart, hardness of hand and hardness of drink. Be frugal, be sparing, tighten the belt; not needing, not having, not wasting was better than living—or dying.

"Och, I must be awa' to ma chores," she muttered, pulling upwards from the gravity of the fire and the faint glint of a possible warmth inside her. Like the broken knuckles of the bens and the trampled thighs of the glens, glacier-ground, she had been scoured by life, scarred by living with the corpse of a land that once held her people dear, the bones of a body that she could neither leave nor grieve, that gave still birth to a sullen, secret hate that shuttled down the loom of time, unweaving what had been woven and what would be woven.

The bones of her hand tightened on the corner of the table as she stood from the chair and took the half-dozen steps that full-spanned the single room. With her man and the boys still yet an hour in the field under the eyebrows of gathering twilight, she stood at the table and sank, with hardly a ripple, into the merciful pool of forgetful routine, suspended, drowned and weightless, between two worlds. And so it was that she made herself busy and got on with her chores.

2

———

A FEW ROUGH BEASTS
SLOUCHING

Let's start at the end. That always determines the beginning. Yes, the rough beasts are an allusion to Yeats's poem "The Second Coming" (and further on, David Bowie's "All the Young Dudes/Carry the News," sort of). Yeats's poem has snagged something in the collective imagination with oft-quoted lines such as "the centre cannot hold" and "the worst are full of passionate intensity." Now everyone is passionate about something. The poem contains so much that it's worth repeating here:

> Turning and turning in the widening gyre
> The falcon cannot hear the falconer;
> Things fall apart; the centre cannot hold;
> Mere anarchy is loosed upon the world,
> The blood-dimmed tide is loosed, and everywhere
> The ceremony of innocence is drowned;
> The best lack all conviction, while the worst
> Are full of passionate intensity.
> Surely some revelation is at hand;
> Surely the Second Coming is at hand.
> The Second Coming! Hardly are those words out
> When a vast image out of Spiritus Mundi

Troubles my sight: somewhere in sands of the desert

A shape with lion body and the head of a man,
A gaze blank and pitiless as the sun,
Is moving its slow thighs, while all about it
Reel shadows of the indignant desert birds.
The darkness drops again; but now I know
That twenty centuries of stony sleep
Were vexed to nightmare by a rocking cradle,
And what rough beast, its hour come round at last,
Slouches towards Bethlehem to be born?

Yeats wrote the poem in January 1919 and it was first published in 1920.[1] This situates it within the context of his 1925 work, *A Vision*, a complex description of the rhythms of historical cycles, extensively revised in 1937. He said, "I dare say I delude myself in thinking this book is my book of books".[2] It was the product of his wife Georgie's automatic writing beginning in 1917. Yeats spent over ten years elaborating the material and said it provided him with the impetus and security for his later work.

More poetic and allusive than exact regarding dates, *A Vision* deals with historical periods of 1050 years—as did Jung in *Aion*—or about 2,200 years which were marked by gyres, thus the opening line of the poem. Gyres are cones or vortices of increasing or decreasing influence. As each gyre wanes so the opposite or antithetical gyre waxes. With regard to the current gyre, beginning around the birth of Christ, Yeats suggests that this will give way in the near future to the second coming not of Christ but of his antithetical opposite. Yeats portrays the antithetical Messiah as Oedipus, "an image from Homer's age, who lay down upon the earth and sank down soul and body into the earth. I

---

1. www.yeatsvision.com/SecondNotes.html
2. Letter from W. B. Yeats to T. Werner Laurie, July 27, 1924.

would have him balance Christ who, crucified standing up, went into the abstract sky, soul and body."[3]

Although gyres, moon cycles, and aeons describe the great archetypal rhythms of time, to explore them here would take us too far from our theme.

Beastly archetypes

One of the great contributions to the psychology of this century is the theory of the complexes, which says that a complex (a slice of history) which is not reflected upon and made conscious, repeats itself in a potentialised and hypertrophied form.[4]

Forms within the collective unconscious are called archetypes, from the Greek *arche-* meaning "first" or "original," and *typos* meaning "form" or "impression"—the original pattern from which copies are derived. Jung said, "An archetype is like an old watercourse along which the water of life has flowed for centuries, digging a deep channel for itself."[5]

Just as the laws of physics and chemistry order the material world, so archetypes are the psyche's natural laws. They are our non-physical DNA.[6] Like physical laws, they are impersonal and are not limited to any particular time, place, culture or race, any more than the law of gravity is. These archetypal patterns and deep structures of the psyche manifest themselves in images, symbols, dreams, mythology, fairy tales, religions and repetitive patterns of behaviour. All humans are born with potentials for sexuality, love, spirituality, violence, work, compassion, exploration, to name a few. In animals, we call these inner laws instincts.

Archetypal forces can remain dormant until cultural conditions permit, like dry river-beds that fill when it rains. Just like gene-environment interactions, the expression of an archetype changes from culture

---

3. "W. B. Yeats and 'A Vision': The Historical Cycles." www.yeatsvision.com/History.html
4. Lopez-Pedraza, *Cultural Anxiety*, loc. 1483.
5. CW 10, *Civilisation in Transition*, par. 395.
6. See Owen, *The Maya Book of Life*, Chapter 8, DNA.

to culture but the drive behind it remains the same. The desire for sexual pleasure—insatiable, raunchy, tender or sanctified—was the same for the Scythian nomad as it is for the Chicago street kid. Falling in love was the same in the Shang dynasty three thousand years ago as it is in Argentina today. The Pitanjara mother who walked the Australian bush 40,000 years ago loved her child in the same way as the Muslim mother living in south London. The warring of Maori iwi (tribes) with one another five hundred years ago was the same warring as the Serb-Croat conflicts in the Balkans. The urge to pray was the same for a Maya *ajk'ij* (priest) 1,500 years ago as it is for a modern Afrikaans *dominie* (pastor). Love, motherhood, war and spirit—all are archetypes and we are in their thrall.

An archetype cannot be experienced directly—it is too powerful and has the weight of millennia of human experience within its bones. The closer we get to its power the more we get swept away by its collectivity and we lose our individuality and our humanness. Only if we are equally organised within ourselves—that is, if we have a functional connection with the archetype of wholeness, inside or outside—can we hope to keep our head above water when we are swamped by archetypal passions or beliefs. Just as the ego is the centre of consciousness, so the Self is the organising centre of the whole psyche, both conscious and unconscious. The Self is what Jung called the objective psyche, in the sense that it stands outside the ego, is independent from it, and can see the ego and reality as-they-are. It sees reality unclouded by the beliefs, feelings, desires, complexes and distortions of the ego. In other words, our conscious viewpoint is not the only one we have. The Self has a mind of its own and functions according to its own laws.

There are as many archetypes as there are typical human situations —mother, father, lover, hero, wise man, paradise, the perilous journey, the helpful animal, the crucified and resurrected god. When we experience an archetype it will take its colour and form from the individual or cultural consciousness in which it appears.[7] For example, the archetype of the sun is expressed by images of the lion, the king, the gold guarded by the dragon, or the power that gives life and health.

---

7. CW 9i, par. 6.

When we experience an archetype directly it produces what religions call a spiritual experience, and what Jung called a numinous experience of the archetype. This can lead to the ego identifying with the archetype and losing its identity. The person thinks that the experience is special and something that they have, rather than something that has them. Possession by an archetype leads to either a positive inflation such as believing we are the next Messiah, or that we have the one and only secret to wealth, weight loss or enlightenment, or a negative inflation such as debasing ourselves as "a poor, miserable, hell-deserving sinner conceived in lust, delivered in evil and slave to every loathsome appetite the flesh is heir to."[8] Both are puffed-up. On the other hand, the ego may dis-identify with the archetype and project it onto someone or something else that is then worshipped as the saviour or hated as the devil.

The ego is what we usually refer to as "I" or "me." Our conscious awareness thinks that it knows all there is to know about itself and sees itself as whole, undivided and obvious. But the total psyche is made up of many different parts of which the "I" is only one. When the psyche is undeveloped, a person doesn't know about the whole personality and doesn't know they don't know. Accordingly, the individual is largely under the influence of the archetype, though they will think they are in control and behaving "rationally."

If we develop a healthy, functional ego, then we have a sense of identity, we can tolerate a degree of stress without collapsing, we can tolerate painful and pleasurable feelings without losing ourselves, we know what is inside and what is outside, we can tolerate ambivalence and contradiction, and we can be separate and connected at the same time. The process of becoming conscious and developing an ego is the hero or heroine's journey that is told in many myths and legends.

The ego must neither cut itself off from the blessings of the archetypal forces nor lose itself in their numinosity. It must try to develop a relationship with the archetype, a unique, personal standpoint from which it can treat with these impersonal powers. Then something unique happens—both the ego and archetype become transformed in a

---

8. Calvinist prayer, 18th century.

profound way. From the efforts of the ego the DNA of the archetype is transformed. History, both past and future, is changed. The collective both loves and hates the individual who does this.

Human descriptions of gods and goddesses, as in Greek mythology, are an attempt to speak about archetypal forces by personifying them, giving them names, and telling stories about them. The attributes of a god or goddess always describe archetypal forces such as birth and death, law and order, art, fertility, or the movement of the heavens. The monotheistic brother-religions of Judaism, Christianity and Islam have gathered up the archetypal functions of the many earlier gods into one God who put himself in charge of everything. Intense and hostile competition for top spot between the brother religions has been the result.

Jung called mythology the "textbook" of the archetypes. In myths the unconscious presents itself as a story not as a didactic lecture or an infomercial. Myth and fairy-tale are the native languages of the psyche and no intellectual formulation comes close to their colour and depth. The story of Cinderella, for example, is a household tale on every continent and takes different forms according to the culture. The name Cinderella means stars in the cinders.[9]

The story is about the light of the soul almost extinguished in the darkness of matter, its exile because it has forgotten its divine origin, and its transformation from a sooty drudge to a radiant bride.[10] After descending into the material world, the soul journeys to find herself and regain her relationship to the divine world from which she came, so she can return with the knowledge of who she really is. Cinderella's fairy godmother is actually Sophia, or divine wisdom, who guides the soul in her quest. At the end of the story, the masculine and feminine potentials of the soul (Cinderella and Prince Charming) unite in a sacred marriage. So it's not just a Disney movie.

I will use myth and archetype as ways of talking about slouching beasts woken from a long sleep.

____

9.   Bayley, *The Lost Language of Symbolism*.
10. Baring, "Cinderella: An Interpretation". In Stein and Corbett, *Psyche's Stories: Modern Jungian Interpretations of Fairy Tales*, 49–62.

Archetypal beasts

The larger culture, the other children, our brothers and sisters who share the body of this small, green planet, know who they are. A rose is a rose is a rose, it knows its gift. A rock cannot be anything more or less than a rock. The buffalo doesn't wake up in the morning and think "Today, I will move to Florida".

Jung said, "When God made animals, he equipped them with just those needs and impulses that enable them to live according to their laws".[11] "The only true servants of God are the animals".[12] And "Too much of the animal distorts the civilised man, too much civilisation makes sick animals".[13]

Along with the gift of free will two-leggeds got leadenness and flightiness. We are free to be in tune or out of tune with ourselves and the world around us, human or natural. We can be more or less than who we are. Unlike animals, we have free will choice that enables us to break the bonds of fate and instinct. A Hebrew saying reminds us that "Man was created for the sake of choice". But here's the rub—it is only by choosing at the fork in the road, and encountering our limits, our chains, knowing what we are not and cannot be, that we can then find ourselves and enter into an authentic relationship with world around us.

Humans have always looked to the natural world of weather and plants and animals to guide their behaviour and bring themselves back into balance. So, as well as being beastly and instinctual, animals are also a source of wisdom. In all their forms they are both spiritualised instinct and instinctualised spirit. They span both earth and sky. Chief Letakots-Lesa said: "In the beginning of all things, wisdom and knowledge were with the animals; for Tirawa, the One Above, did not speak directly to man. He sent certain animals to tell men that he showed himself through the beasts, and that from them, and from the stars and the moon, man should learn. Tirawa spoke to man through his works".[14]

---

11. *Letters 1*, January 8, 1948, 486.
12. *Letters 2*, June 27, 1947, xxxix.
13. CW 7, par. 32.
14. Chief Letakots-Lesa, Pawnee, as told to Natalie Curtis, c. 1904. In Joseph Campbell (1983) *The Way of the Animal Powers*.

So sayeth the Book of Job: "But ask now the beasts, and they shall teach thee; and the fowls of the air, and they shall tell thee: Or speak to the earth, and it shall teach thee: and the fishes of the sea shall declare unto thee.... Who teacheth us more than the beasts of the earth, and maketh us wiser than the fowls of heaven?".[15]

The beasts of the earth and the fowls of the air are the carriers of prophecy. But the word prophecy and its cognates have too many layers and associations. I look at the thesaurus and get foretelling the future, fortune telling, crystal-gazing, prediction, second sight, clairvoyance, prognostication, divination, soothsaying, augury, haruspication—all words that are rarely used in polite company and are in need of rehabilitation and restoration to their rightful place in a functional culture. I want a word that is simpler, less freighted but I don't have one so I will stick with prophecy. This is the "seeing"—although it may occur in other than visual ways—of potential events as they move from spirit into matter. But, and this is a big but, the seeing is always influenced by who the seer is. So with all oracles, the seer prepares themselves through some form of withdrawal from the doings of the world (fasting, prayer, ceremony) so their vision may be clearer.

The prophetic, apocalyptic, eschatological and millenarian literature is immense and I shall steer well clear it. But there is a body of Western end-of-the aeon literature that includes texts such as Nietzsche's *Thus Spake Zarathustra*, Spengler's *Decline of the West*, Toynbee's *A Study of History*, and Jung's *Aion*. Such works couldn't be written except at the end of an age—in the middle you can't see the age in its totality.[16] I have also intentionally omitted mention of the many so-called indigenous prophecies of the future. Extraordinary discrimination is needed to separate the wheat from the chaff but the Hopi prophecies would be a trustworthy place to start for the interested reader.[17]

So it's a rough beast, in all its wisdom and instinct, that slouches toward the birthplace of Christ to bring balance to the last two thousand-year gyre. Yes, it's an apocalypse but old-fashioned apocalypses are

---

15. Job 12:7-8, 35:11.
16. Edinger, *The Aion Lectures: Exploring the Self in C.G. Jung's Aion*, 98.
17. www.theshamanictimes.com/indigenous-prophecies.html

out of style and a little too dramatic and removed in time from modern sensibilities. The Whore of Babylon, the Four Horsemen of the Apocalypse, or the Rapture, in the Book of Revelation don't capture the attention of a rational and technological culture. We will need something even more dramatic—like the destruction of the planet.

Culture as beast

The beast is a symbol of our animal nature, of nature red in tooth and claw, of all the traits that culture has worked so hard to civilise. But it is two-faced, duplex, having a front end and a hind end. Evolution tells us that life evolved from a radial pattern to a symmetrical one. With that we got a head and a tail, front and back, light and shadow, dorsal and ventral, topside and underside, clean and dirty, right and wrong—all the opposites.

On the one hand the beast is brute force, strength, bellowing bravado, alpha-male, dominance of the individual, and the survival of the fittest. It's the archetype of the hero—of any gender. It is the enemy of collectivity and socialism. No Big Government. Don't fence me in. I want competition and victory, Hemingway death-and-dust in the afternoon sun. No placid, white light, temple-oneness for me. I ride the range, open carry, and answer to no man. And, er, I also wear big hats indoors.

But on the other hand, as much as this psychic position, culture, stereotype, archetype, call it what you will, fawns over individuality and free will, it is a collective individuality. The right-wingers all sound the same. Just like the left-wingers. The individuality of the hero—read patriot, soldier, cowboy, thank-you-for-your-service—looks highly individual but is, in truth, highly collective. He is welded and wedded to the anonymity of the collective and shares beliefs, opinions, and history with millions of other individuals. He has never had the courage to be different.

So what might an authentic individual look like? Jung said, "I term collective all psychic contents that belong not to one individual but to many, i.e., to a society, a people, or to mankind in general…. The antithesis of collective is individual."[18] The psychic contents that belong only to an individual are, by definition, not found in the collective. They are unique and rare as hen's teeth made of gold and found in only one place in the whole world. Bagger Vance said:

> Yep, inside each and every one of us
> Is one true, authentic swing.
> Something we was born with,
> Something that's ours and ours alone.
> Something that can't taught to you or learned.
> Something that's got to be remembered.[19]

If too few take up the challenge of finding their own swing, what Jung called individuation, then the task is left, as David Bowie sang, to all the young dudes to carry the news. Their age demands that they push up against the walls and boundaries so they don't need to carry the unfinished business of previous generations.

The collective is the group, the iwi, the hive, the pack, the clan, the tribe, the herd. Twitter and Facebook feed the beast with fast food, giving an illusory feeling of belonging and friendship to millions who have never breathed the same air or stood on the same ground. The more we strive for a false individuality the more collective we become. Patriotism, the flag, and the anthem become unquestioned. It's the mythology that built the US of A.

Culture is always a cult—one that's acceptable at that time and in that place. We identify with the our culture be it Romanian, Japanese, American, Maori, Canadian, Jewish, Cheyenne, or Maya. Or Christian, Hindu, Islam, or Buddhist—the big four religions accounting for 77% of the world's population. But the warmth and safety of their collectivity deprives us of free will. Not our conscious, ego-driven free will that's on social display but the hidden voice of the deeper will that is our

---

18. CW 6, par. 692.
19. *The Legend of Bagger Vance* was a 2000 film directed by Robert Redford. Captain Rannulph Junuh meets a mysterious caddie who teaches him the art of mastering the perfect golf swing and finding meaning in one's existence. The plot is loosely based on the Bhagavad Gita.

own, that comes out of hiding if the climate is right, if we are listening, if we pay attention. It talks to us unceasingly through dreams, coincidences, feelings, animals, weather, and relationships. It hides from concrete, diesel, rap music, bigging-up, smalling-down, CNN, Fox News, major highways, smelters and plastic. Mostly it hides from us. We are not fertile ground yet for this seed to blossom. Any collective idea, religion, movement, science, world-view, culture or society (as necessary as they are for the collective) is too bright, too loud, too quick.

Approaching culture is a delicate matter. Its closely-held "values" are easily insulted and brook little questioning whether it be black culture, white culture, Islamic values, Christian values etc. Like Trump, cultural values are narcissistic and thin-skinned. They are easily bruised resulting in a "moral injury". But we also need prohibitions against hate speech and sadistic verbal aggression.

Culture is a beautiful necessity and a confining container. It provides refuge for those seeking refuge from themselves. I will not belabour the reader with the more popular stories of beauty, history, persecution, art, war, achievement, and integrity that all cultures have. That story is the visible shining, golden head of culture worthy of admiration. Rather, I point to the tyrannical underbelly of culture, its collective bullying, its animal nature.

The dislike of eating anything that has a face

Chefs know that whole fish, with the eyes staring up at you, are less popular with customers. It's called the Bambi effect. It used to be that celebrities would fly from Europe to the Arctic in spring time to protest against the clubbing of whitecoat seal pups for their fur (Ohh! Those big sad eyes. Poor things!). Fair enough, I am on their side—the seals that is. Or how about those folks who throw paint at fashion shows to protest against the fur trade, or become animal activists and bomb research laboratories? The majority of such protesters are young, overly-burdened with principles, and live in cities.

Fundamentalist activism on behalf of the environment are modern forms of white saviour colonisation and paternalism in a different guise. Was it not just a few generations ago that we thought women needed protection by someone bigger, wiser and male? Now the animals supposedly need our protection. Let's notice that plants are considered a lower form of life than animals. It's OK to eat one but not the other. Don't slaughter the lambkins but it's okay to kill the carrots. Please explain this to my cat.

Greenie protests are often committed by city dwellers or people from highly urbanised countries who are passionately principled. Long separated from their own red-bloodedness, it is their own animal soul that is in need of liberation. Having abandoning their own unique nature for the security of subculture beliefs, they are driven to sentimentally rescue in the outer world what they have lost in the inner world. Capitalist, communist, right-wing, left-wing—they all look the same through from underneath. The Earth looks up and sees the sphincter of things.

As a psychologist I wonder, in their fevered prevention of suffering, what the activists' relationship is to their own suffering. Am I being fervently sold a philosophy consciously or (more likely) unconsciously motivated by their own complexes, and unresolved pain, victimisation, trauma, or suffering? Or unresolved matters of power and authority? Like any medical or scientific paper nowadays, authors are required to declare any conflicts of interest, personal, commercial, political, academic or financial. Let's have an activist declaration of psychological conflict of interest as well. Perhaps vegans and vegetarians are incapable of bringing about death and change in their own psychological backyard, so they export it packaged as a principle.

I don't only mean external or historical trauma, that's too concrete and simplistic. Trauma is never a cause and effect, one-to-one traumatisation. Trauma always happens to a person who, consciously and unconsciously, digests the external experience in a unique way, just as no two trees of the same species ever grow exactly the same shape. In addition, because no human being had perfect parents and because life is not perfect (meaning trauma-free) we are all traumatised. We all have our unique sensitivities, neuroses and quirks. Much of this is subsumed under "normal" and so goes unrecognised.

Much activist polemic has an overt or covert whiff of censure, either-your-part-of-the-solution-or-your-part-of-the-problem, heated drivenness about it. Yes, the planet is dying. (If she dies would we be guilty of murder or manslaughter?). But thinking that action (as in "activist") is the only solution is the same concrete, mechanistic, stimulus-response, cause-effect thinking that got us into the mess in the first place. It gives no room for nature and spirit to work. I think of Yeats' "And the worst are full of passionate intensity" and roll my eyes every time I hear another person say, or I read one more website that tells me, "I'm passionate about…" And You've probably heard this one but… How do you tell if some is vegan? Just wait, they'll tell you.

My thoughts about veganism or vegetarianism are neither for nor against. I do not argue the health benefits for a particular individual, nor the sense of physical well-being it may bring, nor the more economical use of the Earth's limited resources. Nor do I turn a blind eye to the blood on the killing floor, or the chain line at the meatworks, or the force-fed pigs unable to move in their pens. But I also see that humans have eaten meat for millennia. Plants-only is the purer-than-thou new kid on the block. I take issue with vegetarianism-by-principle when our distaste of eating animals is driven by mass-minded psychological motivations where the red-blooded animal of one's body is not consulted. I could count on the fingers of many hands the vegetarian friends who crave a good steak once in a while.

People for the Ethical Treatment of Animals is a charity dedicated to establishing and protecting the rights of all animals. Hmm, ethics and rights are human inventions, aren't they, so how come we think animals should have them too, or have ours imposed on them. And why is it our duty to see that they are protected? Why all the high-sounding philosophy? Just don't be mindlessly cruel to your cat, your dog, or your next food item. If you do you get dealt to. Simple as that. The wisdom of sacred slaughter for kosher or halal meat is apparent.

The dividing line apparently is "Do they suffer?" Sounds like flagrant mammalianism to me. And out-and-out anti-phytism or anti-mineralism. Plants and rocks clearly don't suffer so we can forget them. And by not eating meat we secretly collude with all the herbivores by allowing them to continue their cruel massacre of helpless vegetation. Yes, cows murder the grass. Almost all the meat we eat is from herbivores—a cow is a walking plant—and very rarely, if ever, from carni-vores. Lions take much more effort to catch and kill.

Take a look at the PETA website. If you scroll past the home page offering pics of the "20 Sexiest Vegetarian Celebrities," and mosey on down to "PETA's Vegetarian/Vegan Starter Kit" you will see pics of Natalie Portman and Paul McCartney.

He says "If anyone wants to save the planet, all they have to do is stop eating meat." Straight up. I like this.

She says, "I am a very strict vegetarian... I just really love animals, and I act on my values. I really am against cruelty to animals..." I don't like this.

Hear the difference? In Portman's statement you get: two "reallys" —an adolescent and unneeded emphasis betraying its hollowness; one "I love animals"—meaning she doesn't eat what she loves, therefore she must have plants; one "strict"—a school-marmish intimation of self-inflicted punishment if she strays from the straight and narrow; and a reminder that one is morally lapsed if one has values but does not act on them. I support her action but not the motivation. If the motivation is not true to our own inner nature and has not paid its dues, has some life experience underneath its belt, then the outer-seeming is all hot air and passionate beliefs. Or, if it is proselytised, crusade-ified, preached and converted, then it becomes actively destructive.

Yesterday, a woman on the beach offered to share her lunch of crickets and rice with me. Are crickets counted as meat? If I was vege-tarian should I have declined? Should I have asked how the crickets were killed? I wouldn't have thought to ask about the rice, it's just harvested not killed. Would fish have been OK? Perhaps they don't "suffer" as much as insects. But what about ugly, pestiferous mammals like rats? Where are they on the scale? How about rat pie? Then there's reptiles. Snakes don't scream or bellow. Would gecko meat be OK?

So let's follow this down the phyla. Vertebrates are clearly afforded special attention, at least the ones with big eyes and four legs, because they look like us. That's specism which is a close cousin of racism. But those poor invertebrates are fair game for a meal. What about nema-todes—the most common multi-cellular animal on the planet? Bacteria? Viruses? And what about cells, do they suffer when we cut them? All in all, modern vegetarianism is the same vertical, evolution-as-a-line-not-a-circle, nature-killing, Darwinian, specist, Western consciousness in different garb.

We find, in the history of vegetarianism, that the further removed a culture was from nature, and the more spiritual it became, the more vegetarianism arose as a practice. Industrialisation and vegan-by-principle go hand in hand. The Three Sisters (corn, beans and squash) have fed the tribes of the southwest for millennia but please find me an indigenous culture that is exclusively vegetarian.

The earliest records of vegetarian practice are found in Hindu and Buddhist records around the sixth century BCE and with Pythagoras in ancient Greece around the same time. A vegetarian diet was "abstinence from beings with a soul."[20] Apparently, some beings have souls, some don't. Oops, another hoop of creation is broken. Too late now to get our Palaeolithic ancestors, or the hunter-gatherer peoples that are left, to see the error of their ways. Early Christians sects were often vegetarian. The Rule of Saint Benedict drew the line at quadrupeds—fish and fowl were OK but not four-leggeds. The Renaissance and particularly the 1700s and 1800s saw a rise in the popularity of vegetarianism particularly in England, ironically the birthplace of the Industrial Revolution.

And this about democracy for a moment. From the point of view of the planet it is a form of specism invented by two-leggeds. Fro humans, it's best we've got. As Churchill said, "Democracy is the worst form of Government except for all those other forms that have been tried".[21] Whether by autocracy or democracy the majority of humans live their lives asking governments—and religions, sports stars, and entertainers—to carry the burden of their own successes, failures, and unlived lives. Democracy is rule by the people for the people. But it is the lowest common denominator. The masses are always swayed by the tides of public opinion, by the mob, by populism. We have gone from spiritual kings, to secular kings, to secular masses. The secular king always had his advisors, viziers and wise men on hand to give advice. The early English Parliament until was divided into the Lords Temporal and the Lords

---

20. https://en.wikipedia.org/wiki/Vegetarianism#History
21. Winston Churchill, House of Commons, November 11, 1947.

Spiritual. But democracy is all too human. Oren Lyons asked the United Nations, "Who speaks for the plants, the animals and the earth itself?"

We lost the golden thread starting with the ancient Greeks and the sprouting of rationality. There is an early Christian tradition that when the heavenly host told the shepherds at Bethlehem of the birth of Christ, a deep groan, heard through all the isles of Greece, told that all the royalty of Olympus was dethroned, the deities were sent wandering in cold and darkness, and most significant of all, the great Pan—the god of nature—was dead.[22] The voice of the other children of the Earth were silenced and balance—not equality but balance—was lost, given over to the tyranny of humans.

So we have the narcissistic, species-arrogant notion that the more human something looks the less we should eat of it. In this hierarchical view, many unthinking and overly principled vegetarians feel better off eating eat fruit and grains and root vegetables than being reminded of the bellows and blood of the killin' floor. Death to wheat and pineapples is fine. Death to cod is maybe fine. Death to mammals is not fine. Sounds like a death-denying, holier-than-thou, convenience to me, a privileging of our human consciousness as the arbiter of what we are allowed to kill without too much bother.

If we are going to kill then let us do so consciously rather than hiring contract killers with stun guns to do our dirty work, or mechanical harvesters to pull up the carrots. Having to go out and kill and dress the hamburger you're going to have for lunch would put a bit of a crimp in the currency trader's day and bring him back to reality of a mid-morning.

Vegetarians are deaf to the screams of carrots as they are torn from their womb of soil, or are cruelly insensitive to the battery-like conditions in which potatoes have to live, all lined up in rows. I see no "lettuce liberation movement," "potato protesters," or "onion activists," keen to free said vegetables from their market garden incarceration, or assault those unprincipled pensioners who keep the lettuce, unable to move, staked to the grounds of their allotment.

They draw a line that differentiates "sentient" from "non-sentient"

---

22. Bullfinch's *Mythology.*

life. But how about this? Acacia trees in the Transvaal get browsed by antelope and produce leaf tannin in quantities lethal to the browsers if they keep browsing. They also emit ethylene into the air which can travel up to 50 yards and warns other trees of the impending danger, and they then step up their own production of leaf tannin within just five to ten minutes.[23] Or the ongoing shock and surprise of scientists who "discover" that plants or animals are conscious.[24]

In the circle of life, there is no hierarchy and an indigenous consciousness does not privilege animal over plant, or human over animal nor even (and this might be a real stretch for the irrationally-challenged) human over mineral. All matter is holy and when life or place or livelihood is taken it must be done in a sacred way to feed the other world so that it may feed us. So I offer a veggie garden prayer for the carrot-people.

"Sacred Ones, you who have long rested in the darkness, taking water, taking food from this soil in the mystery of growth and life. I ask that you now come into the light, bring your bodies out of the place of your moistness, so that your bodies may feed our bodies. To you and your Sister Plant Nations, I give thanks for the gift of this life that you unceasingly offer in your death. I now take your life and in its taking I offer you this gift made from the beauty of my word-flowers and the labours of my own hands. I too one day will return to this earth and live by your side, so completing the sacred cycle of life and death as it has been since always. I have spoken".

---

23. Sylvia Hughes, *New Scientist*, 29 September 1990, www.newscientist.com/article/mg12717361.200-antelope-activate-the-acacias-alarm-system
24. Are plants conscious? Radical new experiments suggest they could be. Natalie Lawrence, 24 August 2022, www.newscientist.com/article/mg25534012-800-the-radical-new-experiments-that-hint-at-plant-consciousness

3

ORACLES ANCIENT: OVID AND THE MAYA

METAMORPHOSES

EVERY THERAPY in depth involves an anamnesis (*an*, without; *amnesis*, absence of memory), a re-collection and remembering of what has gone before, the pattern that is ourselves. First, the individual explores their personal history which reveals the personal unconscious. Crudely put, this is the cure of our symptoms. Then, if they are meant to proceed deeper, their dreams lead toward the collective unconscious, the archetypes, and the Self. This is the discovery of, objectively, who we are from a standpoint outside the conscious ego. In this book, our rough archetypal beasts are our anamnesis.

They are our oracles both ancient and modern, the signs, the prognostications, of the illness we've missed, forgotten, and forgotten we've forgotten. I will speak first of ancient oracles such as Ovid's *Metamorphoses* and the Maya Long Count. When there are no seers, wise women with long eyes, no oracles who speak, then hard matter is forced into its unaccustomed role of being the mouthpiece of the things to come. So later we shall come upon modern oracles—Goethe's *Faust*, Jung's *Aion*, the Titanic, and 9/11.

Bur first I will take a long detour—not a detour really as it sketches the whole story as told in *Metamorphoses*—because two thousand years ago Ovid spoke of things to come. A great leveller, a great antidote to the torment of progress and improvement, is to realise that not much has changed.

Ovid (43 BCE–17 CE) is considered, alongside Horace and Virgil, to be the greatest of the Latin poets. He was the most read of all the classical authors during the Middle Ages and greatly influenced Chaucer, Marlowe, Shakespeare, Milton and, in the twentieth century, James Joyce. Both Rubens and Rembrandt painted Philemon and Baucis, and other stories of Ovid's were painted by Titian and Breughel.[1] Jonathan Swift, the author of Gulliver's Travels, wrote an imitation of the Baucis and Philemon story from Metamorphoses: "On the ever-lamented loss of the two yew-trees in the parish of Chilthorne, Somerset." In medicine the Philemon and Baucis Syndrome refers to the natural death of a married couple at the same time. Later we shall come to the importance of the Baucis and Philemon story.

Metamorphoses was Ovid's major work.[2] It was completed in 8 CE and described the history of the world from its creation to the deification of Julius Caesar, who had died a year before Ovid was born. It was told in heroic hexameter, as were Homer's *Iliad* and *Odyssey*, against a mythological and historical background. Unlike Virgil's *Aeneid* written twenty years earlier, which told of the heroic journey of an individual hero, Aeneas, in his wanderings after the Trojan War, in Metamorphoses it is the story itself that wanders, on a collective journey not an individual one. It is not bound by the three-dimensional specifics of time, place and person but to the five dimensional world—the three-dimensional physical world, the fourth dimension of historical time or *kairos*, and to the fifth dimension of the dream or spirit.

Metamorphoses is divided into 15 books with a total of 108 stories which have no discernible connection or narrative flow. Ovid begins with the words, "I intend to speak of forms changed into new entities [and] spin an unbroken thread of verse, from the earliest beginnings of the world, down to my own times." Metamorphosis (Greek *meta-*

---

1. www.nga.gov/collection/art-object-page.1204 and www. eclecticlight.co/2016/04/27
2. Quotations are taken from Ovid, *Metamorphoses*. Translated by Brookes More. Boston, Cornhill Publishing, 1922. And from www.theoi.com/Text/OvidMetamor phoses8.html

meaning beside, beyond or about; *morph-* meaning shape or form) is about the process of change into a radical new form just as a caterpillar in its chrysalis changes into a butterfly. It's not about changing the game —the players, the stadium, the teams—it's about changing the rules of the game itself.

The stories tell of human beings transformed into trees, rocks, animals, flowers or constellations—or the reverse. Before the rise of modern consciousness the world was a more fluid place, the relationship between the visible and non-visible worlds was closer, the crack-between-the-worlds was real, the veil was thinner, and beasts and humans could be magical beings changing form, or not.

The abundant flow of death, change, and rebirth—in other words, metamorphoses—from form to form ensures that the balance between this world and the other world is kept. Matter and spirit are held in good relation through the intercession of humans. It is only when we recognise the reality of the gods and goddesses (which Jung called archetypes) that we can bring their colour into the greyness that exists between the blacks and whites of religion and science. We can negotiate with them properly and hold our very human place between the irresistible seductions of the body, instinct and matter, and the irresistible compulsions of belief, conviction, creed and faith. The monotheistic resolution of this tension has swing too far toward the latter.

Although there is no discernible connection between Ovid's stories we might suspect that there will be a pattern, albeit not an obvious one. The bare-bones expression of pattern is number. Jung remarked that if more years were granted to him he would have worked on "the problem of numbers." Marie-Louise von Franz said: "Number, as it were, lies behind the psychic realm as a dynamic ordering principle, the primal element of which Jung called spirit. As an archetype, number becomes not only a psychic factor, but more generally, a world-structuring factor. In other words, numbers point to a background reality in which psyche and matter are no longer distinguishable."[3]

We shall concern ourselves mostly with Book VIII of

---

3. Von Franz, *Psyche and Matter,* 216. Von Franz was one of Jung's closest colleagues and worked with him for almost 30 years.

Metamorphoses as this tells the story of the fate of the feminine, and the man who ate himself. Let's note the shift between the numbers eight and nine in Roman numeration. Eight is VIII and nine is IX. But why is nine not VIIII? I suggest that this signifies the shift between the harmony and balance of eight and the chaos of nine. As we shall see, the beginning of Book IX is the story of Heracles, the patriarchal hero and his downfall. So understanding what happens in Book VIII is our anamnesis, our remembering, our following the crumbs that lead to the death of the Earth. But first, we need to understand the importance of the number nine.

The nature of nine

Psychic energy, or any energy, moves in ten movements or transformations. This is implicit in our Western decimal system (10) or the Maya duodecimal (20) system. Energy starts at 0 (the void, the nothingness that gives birth to all things)[4] and moves outward in all eight directions 9 times before returning to the source (10) to begin a new cycle. Note that 0 to 9 is a ten-step movement (0-1-2-3-4-5-6-7-8-9) just as, more conventionally, we might count from 1 to 10. Each form is born at 0, transforms itself 9 times, and at 10 becomes the zero at the beginning of the next cycle. This is not the same zero that it started from but a metamorphosed zero plus one movement, $1 + 0 = 10$. At 8 the movement has gone through 7 successive changes and attains physical form and pattern. In other words, it has become perceptible by the five senses (form) and the sixth sense, intuition (pattern). At the 9th movement the form breaks apart, creating a new pattern (chaos) that is perceptible only by the Creator. This chaos (as consciousness might see it) is the Creator's way of destroying old forms so that it can return to the source and re-create itself anew. Genesis is a creation story happening in every moment.

The number 9 then is about how to live when there is no perceptible pattern. Western consciousness cannot surf the wav, flails and stiff-

---

4. "Only absolute totality can renew itself out of itself and generate itself anew." CW 9i, par. 221.

and drowns. This ossification of Western consciousness over the centuries has created its compensatory opposite, a disruptor, a guy who likes a fight, drains the swamp, doesn't follow the rules, and who creates chaos because he can't stand being beaten. Welcome, Donald Trump.

Nine is about timing, knowing when to stop, when to start, when to watch and when to act. It is the ability to use our energy efficiently ("A stitch in time saves nine") and catch the opportunities and "lucky breaks" offered by the chaos of life. Nine is the highest single number and is the last number before the return to the unity of the 10. It is the maximum that is imaginable as in, "dressed to the nines," "on cloud nine," "the whole nine yards," "nine times out of ten," "a nine-day wonder," or "possession is nine-tenths of the law." Tiresias the seer told Zeus that a woman had nine times as much sexual pleasure as a man. In medieval Wales, a dog that had bitten someone could be killed if it was nine steps away from its owner's house, and nine people assaulting one constituted a genuine attack. In German law the ownership of land is terminated after the ninth generation. In Mayan the number nine means "to stop, to detain, to limit."

Franz Schubert completed his Ninth Symphony and started work on his Tenth shortly before he died. Anton Bruckner died in the midst of writing his Symphony No. 9 in D minor. Antonin Dvorak's last symphony was his Symphony No. 9, likewise Ralph Vaughan Williams. Gustav Mahler completed his Ninth Symphony but died two years later with his Tenth unfinished. In an essay on Mahler, the composer Arnold Schoenberg wrote: "It seems that the Ninth is a limit. He who wants to go beyond it must pass away. It seems as if something might be imparted to us in the Tenth which we ought not yet to know, for which we are not ready. Those who have written a Ninth stood too close to the hereafter."

The number 9 represents both the end and the beginning of a new cycle. We see this in pregnancy. The mother has the potential to become pregnant (0), she then receives the seed (1), becomes pregnant (2), gives birth after nine months (9), and then returns to 0 again but with a separate other, the baby (1 + 0). After 9 months in the womb, we start at the 0 of 10 again.

Nine is a recursive number, in other words it always returns to itself.

All nine digits add up to nine ($1 + 2 + 3 + 4 + 5 + 6 + 7 + 8 + 9 = 45 = 9$). Nine added to itself is nine ($9 + 9 = 18 = 9$). Nine multiplied by itself is nine ($9 \times 9 = 81 = 9$). Nine multiplied by any number always equals nine ($9 \times 7 = 63 = 9$; $9 \times 26 = 234 = 9$). In a circle there are four cardinal and four non-cardinal directions plus the centre which equals nine. In Hinduism the number 9 is revered and considered a complete, perfected and divine number. Nine symbolises completeness in the Bahá'í faith. In the Christian angelic hierarchy there are 9 choirs of angels. Christ died on the cross at the ninth hour. Ramadan, the month of fasting and prayer, is the ninth month of the Islamic calendar. The initiatory Eleusinian Mysteries took nine days. The Romans buried their dead on the ninth day and held a feast, the Novennalia, every ninth year in memory of the dead. Yggdrasil, the World Tree, had nine roots plunging into nine springs, and the nine branches reached toward the nine heavens. Odin hung from the World Tree for nine days and nine nights before he received the wisdom of the Runes. There were nine hells in Dante's Inferno. The River Styx encircled Hades nine times.

Robert Graves gives many instances of nine in Greek mythology, for example: Tartarus, a gloomy place in the Underworld, lay so far from the earth that it would take a falling anvil nine days to reach its bottom. Zeus fathered the Three Muses with Mnemosyne, with whom he lay for nine nights. Hephaestus spent nine years in a grotto show his subservience to the moon. For nine days and nine nights Niobe bewailed her dead. A tribute of seven youths and seven maidens were sent every nine years to Crete as prey for the Minotaur. A charm used by witches to curse a house, field or byre is to run naked around it nine times, widdershins or counter-sunwise, during menstruation. At the annual festival of the Cabieri, the hearth-fires are extinguished and offerings are made to the dead for nine days. And the siege of Troy lasted nine years.[5]

There are nine planets. A cat is pregnant for nine weeks and has nine lives. There are nine months of human pregnancy. At the age of eighty-one we enter the Big East Moon, the Big Moon of Illumination and Enlightenment. The age of eighty-one represents the beginning of

---

5. Graves, *The Greek Myths*.

wisdom, the consciousness of pattern (pattern 8 + 1 consciousness = 9 movement), and is nine cycles of nine (9 x 9 = 81).

Finally, Jung described nine this way: "Unless the conscious mind intervened, the unconscious would go on sending out wave after wave without result, like the treasure that is said to take nine years, nine months, and nine nights to come to the surface and, if not found on the last night, sinks back to start all over again from the beginning".[6]

So why all the fuss about 9? Because 9 is the limit, the furthermost extension of something, the end of pattern and form, and the chaotic transition into a new form. We might then think about the end of Book VIII in Metamorphoses as a story about what occurs in the chaos and transition just before the end represented by Book IX.

Ovid's dream

A dream is a private myth. A myth is a collective dream. The human psyche has two layers, so to speak. The top layer is personal—an accumulation of our personal experiences over time. It is both conscious (thoughts, sensations and feelings that we are aware of) and unconscious (painful or unintegrated experiences that have sunk into the unconscious, or capacities that have not yet emerged from the unconscious).

The barque of consciousness is carried by currents and eddies of the unconscious, of which we are unaware just as we are oblivious to the workings of our mitochondria. All the while Captain Consciousness believes he is master of his ship. Jung said, "Dreams are impartial, spontaneous products of the unconscious psyche, outside the control of the will. They are pure nature; they show us the unvarnished, natural truth, and [they] give us back an attitude that accords with our basic human nature when our consciousness has strayed too far from its foundations and run into an impasse."[7]

Underneath the personal unconscious is an archetypal layer which is not formed from our personal experiences but is composed of the innate psychological structures of the archetypes, which have evolved over

---

6. CW 12, par. 111.
7. CW 10, par. 317.

millennia. They are ways of behaving, thinking and feeling that we are born with just as we are all born with the same human anatomy and physiology. Archetypes have been recently re-discovered as "intergenerational transmission" although this concept only extends back a few generations not millennia.

Most of us going about our daily business are not too fussed with the archetype we might be living out. We live, love, work, struggle, succeed and take it all personally. The paradox is that these life-stories of love and loss are unique but also as common as potatoes. They have been lived before by millions over millennia. The images and stories held in myths are the timeless record of these archetypal patterns. Like plankton living and dying on the surface of the ocean and falling into the depths, like sediment being transformed by pressure and movement and time into rocks, so we walk on the living and dreaming of our ancestors. And I don't just mean our human ancestors. The animals, the plants, the bacteria, the rocks, the elements and the stars are our ancestors. Their dreamings are our archetypes.

But we get into trouble when we over-identify with, or are possessed by, an archetype and we take ourselves, our pursuits, and our culture, way too seriously. Retaining the discipline of humour requires some objectivity. We take the archetypes for granted, confuse them with reality, and get all precious, losing our objectivity and our unique human identity. Archetypes are our non-physical ancestors and like our physical ancestors they evolve—and wish to evolve, just like we want a better world for our children—but not through so-called random genetic mutation and natural selection, untouched by human hand. They do it through the exact opposite—the conscious, but fallible, free-will choices and decisions of humans. They want to be lived and impress themselves on us because we are their DNA.

We can't avoid the archetypes, any more than a swimmer can avoid the water, and the best we can hope for is to tread water once in a while or reach dry land. To do this we must make a deal, negotiate, take a stand with the archetypal forces, stand on the ground that is uniquely ours, and do something different than what has been done before.

What do we get when we do this? We get consciousness, aka inner freedom. Inevitably our culture confuses outer freedom with inner free-

dom. The diamond beauty of individuation is formed from the heat
and pressure that attends the heroic acts of, first, standing outside our
personal psychology and, second, standing outside the archetypes that
rule our lives, our culture, and our historical time. A little bit, anyway.

We want stability, sameness and familiarity but everyone secretly
likes a rebel. The increasing certainty and rigidity of Western consciousness over the centuries has created its compensatory opposite, a disruptor, a guy who likes the heat, doesn't follow the rules, and does things
his way. Donald Trump is an archetypal necessity. He wants to drain the
swamp and change the rules. He carries the projections of the collective
for individuation and archetypal deal-making. But the fact that
someone like Trump was given this necessary job is an indicator of how
concretised and collective things have become. He is but a pawn of his
personal psychology, and of impersonal archetypal forces, as are 49% of
the US population who voted for him.

Our idealisation of outer freedom is matched by our denial of the
inner chains that bind us. We are not as free as we think. Trump may be
partially aware of the personal forces that drive him: in a moment of
partial insight he said in his 2007 book, *Think Big*, "That's why I'm so
screwed up, because I had a father that pushed me pretty hard."[8]

But he is totally unaware that he, the USA, and our global culture
are occasions for the living and dying of an archetype whose time has
come to an end. This end was dreamed by Ovid two thousand years ago
in Metamorphoses.

Dreams sense

Dreams make sense. They are not non-sense. We can begin to understand their structure and rhythm if we are willing to learn their language
—not only the night-language that whispers to us in the asleep-dream
but also the day-language that shouts at us in the awake-dream. There is
no single defining theory of dream structure and such a thing would be
neither possible nor desirable. Our thinking function irritably reaches

---

8. www.politico.com/magazine/story/2017/11/03/mary-macleod-trump-donald-
trump-mother-biography-mom-immigrant-scotland-215779

after fact and reason, as Keats put it, but dreams walk a different path. Nevertheless, theory—if it is not saddled with the baggage of truth or heavily addicted to belief and evidence—can be useful in making visible some dream patterns that, at first, are invisible to consciousness but can bring understanding and a widening of consciousness. Like morning dew on a spider web, they bring to light something present but unseen. But, like all theories, it may eventually lose its usefulness, live past its expiry date, and become dogma.

Nevertheless, let's roll with a theory about dreams which goes like this: most dreams are composed of four acts or scenes, as in a play in which your current predicament is on stage, and you are the director, actor and witness. In the first act or exposition, the dream shows a central conflict or problem—an opening scene which introduces the place, characters, and situation that the dreamer is facing. The second act is the plot or unfolding story that contains something new. In the third act, the culmination, the dream reaches a climax, something critical happens and the dreamer responds. In the fourth and last act, the lysis or resolution indicates how the dreamer might respond to the issue that was portrayed in the first act.

Jung attributed particular significance to the end of a dream because we cannot consciously influence it and so the dream reflects the situation as it actually is, as opposed to how we would like it to be. He said: "Nature is often obscure or impenetrable, but she is not, like man, deceitful. We must therefore take it that the dream is just what it pretends to be, neither more nor less. If it shows something in a negative light, there is no reason for assuming that it is meant positively.... The dream itself wants nothing; it is a self-evident content, a plain natural fact like the sugar in the blood of a diabetic or the fever in a patient with typhus."[9]

Metamorphic dreams

With these notions in mind, we could look at Metamorphoses as having a dream structure of sorts. Book VIII has, in essence, six main stories:

---

9. CW 7, par. 162.

Scylla's betrayal of her father; Theseus and the Minotaur; Daedalus and Icarus; the Calydonian Boar Hunt; Philemon and Baucis; and Erysichthon.

As with a dream, the opening story of Scylla is the problem or issue confronting collective consciousness at the beginning of the Christian era when Ovid was writing Metamorphoses. This period marked the beginning of two thousand years of what we might call Western consciousness, at least in Europe and then North America. The main protagonists are Scylla, the daughter of King Nisus; the King himself; and his antagonist (but also his shadow ally in war) King Minos. But there is no Queen. Marie-Louise von Franz, commenting on the fairy-tale "The Three Feathers" said:

> So you see the close connection between the king and the queen, the
> Logos-principle dominating a certain civilisation and collective attitude
> and the Eros-style accompanying it in a specific form. That the Queen
> is lacking means that the latter aspect has been lost and therefore the
> king is sterile. Without the queen he can have no more children. We
> must assume, therefore, that the story has to do with the problem of a
> dominant collective attitude in which the principle of Eros—of related-
> ness to the unconscious, to the irrational, the feminine—has been lost.
> This must refer to a situation where collective consciousness has
> become petrified and has stiffened into doctrines and formulas.[10]

The missing queen is a common theme in fairy tales where the queen cannot have children, or the queen has died and only the king and his daughter remain, or the king has remarried and the new wife becomes the wicked stepmother who persecutes the daughter. In other words, he is infertile and the land is laid waste. The king symbolises the dominant collective attitude that has had its day. It is the death-that-gives-death not the life-that-gives-life, the life-that-gives-death, or the death-that-gives-life.

Two thousand years later—after the rebirth of the Renaissance from the so-called Dark Ages, under the blinding weight of the

---

10. Von Franz, *An Introduction to the Interpretation of Fairytales*, 39.

Enlightenment, and with the rise of scientific progress—Western consciousness has ever believed its own press and become entranced by its own reflection. The problem has become not only the loss of relatedness to the feminine and the unconscious but the loss of our relationship to matter itself, the very planet we live on. However, what is supposedly lost hides in out-of-the-way places. Von Franz said:

> [T]he psychic experience of the antique mysteries disappeared almost completely in the seventeenth century. They were superseded by the Enlightenment, the rationalism and scientific and technical development with which we live today. But since archetypal values cannot die, in our day they reappear everywhere in the proliferation of sects, in drugs, in an infatuation for the esoteric in all its thinkable forms. At the same time these irrational values, which nowadays have disappeared from collective consciousness, live again in an unexpected form in Jungian psychology."[11]

Holy matrimony

But back to Minos and Nisus. They are at war with each other but this is war as an end not a means. It is the archetype of war at work, having its way with the leaders, dictators and slaughtered millions. As James Hillman said, war is normal. Minos wants war for the sake of war and is contemptuous of Scylla's thought—silly girl—that he wants an end to war and that love and relatedness will overcome all.

After the exposition of the Scylla-problem—the absence of the mature feminine—there are five further stories. The dream story develops with the rise of the masculine hero, Theseus, who slays the Minotaur. Then comes the idealisation of the intellect—Daedalus constructs the Labyrinth that held the Minotaur. But with the inflation that inevitably comes with achievement, success and flying too high, there comes a deflation. Daedalus' son Icarus flies too close to the sun, his wax wings melt, and he plunges into the ocean.

We then read of a compensation, a swing to the opposite of this rise

---

11. Von Franz, *The Golden Ass of Apuleius: The Liberation of the Feminine in Man*, 229.

of the masculine, with the return of the repressed in the Calydonian Boar Hunt. This compensation is brought about by a woman, Atalanta, the protegé of Artemis, the most virginal of goddesses. It is Atalanta who kills the boar and then the boys start to fight amongst themselves. What started out as a regular ol' pig hunt ends up with three dead, not including the boar.

With the next story of Baucis and Philemon there is the possibility of resolution. The old couple who provide hospitality to the gods are an archetypal image of the masculine and feminine in good relation. When this comes about internally or externally, the Earth can continue to be a fertile planet. In other words, the union of the horizontal opposites of the masculine and feminine allows the vertical opposites of spirit and matter to come together.

Without a conscious marriage between the masculine and the feminine within and between humans, spirit and matter cannot touch. The Great Grandfather Stars and Great Grandmother Void cannot make love and give birth to the worlds, and Grandmother Earth cannot receive the seed of Grandfather Sun and continue to be a fertile planet unless the masculine and feminine on this planet are in balance. This is why in its truest essence matrimony is holy.[12]

Two thousand years ago the opposite happened. Spirit and matter were forced together by the masculine Yahweh who had begun to show an unhealthy interest in human affairs. This drove the masculine and feminine, men and women, apart. The result was the emergence of the monotheistic sibling triad of Jewish ethics, Muslim mercy, and Christian love as a compensation for the inhumanity of Yahweh-God-Allah.

The Christian God, who was male, sent the Son of God down to Earth. Let's notice there was no Daughter of God, and no mention of a sister of Jesus in the Bible. He came down through an asexual virgin birth, and left through a bloody death impaled upon wood set into the Earth, with all sorts of miracles in between. This suggests that something must have been desperately wrong two thousand years ago in

---

12. Owen, *The Maya Book of Life*, 333.

spirit or matter or both. More of this later when we come to Jung's *Answer to Job*.

So we must ask what archetypal forces were at work at that time (and are still at work today robed in literalness and fundamentalism)? Without the moderation of conscious humans, the spiritual power of an archetype appears in matter in full force, in raw form, as dogma and certainty, passionate intensity, direct action, and fundamentalism, whether Judeo-Christian-Islamic, Buddhist, Communist, capitalist, feminist or vegan. In indigenous consciousness, the archetype is made functional by a living relationship with the Earth, and does not loom so large or take on such extreme values. The relationship between spirit above, earth below, and humans between, is kept in balance.

The time in which Ovid lived was at the junction of two great archetypal ages, crossing from the Age of Aries to the Age of Pisces, and replete with revelation, prophecy and prediction. As we now cross from the Age of Pisces into the Age of Aquarius let us not repeat the pattern. Before we regress to a Scylla-like state of starry-eyed innocence, hope and rigid optimism, let's heed the lysis or possible outcome suggested by Ovid in the last story in Book VIII—the story of Erysichthon, a man who eats himself.

$$4$$

BULLS AND PURPLE HAIR
DEATH BY DAEDALUS

Let's look at the action in Ovid's dream in more detail. Scylla's father, King Nisus of Megara, and King Minos of Crete were at war. The war had lasted for "six new moons" and, watching the drawn-out conflict from the city walls, Scylla fell in love with King Minos. Her father was protected from harm and made invincible by a lock of purple hair. Scylla resolved to cut her father's lock and bring it to King Minos as a token of her love. But when she did so, she was spurned by Minos: "[S]he held out her gift in her sinful hand. Minos recoiled from what she offered him and, shaken by the thought of this unnatural act, he answered: 'May the gods cast you out, and earth and ocean reject you, infamous daughter of our time!'" Minos forthwith sailed back to Crete.

Scylla had spiritually emasculated her father. But it is the feminine within all things that gives birth to change when change is needed. The head is the sacred seat of intelligence and the power of the soul. We are reminded of the violet colour of the seventh chakra which is at the top of the head, and the topknot of the Hindu sikha or Maori tikitiki. When Delilah cut Samson's hair he lost his strength. When Nisus lost his lock, he lost his power. Nisus was now "weak" so for Minos it wasn't fun anymore. He threw a hissy, packed up his war toys, and sailed home.

Scylla was beyond distraught, her beloved Minos was leaving. She threw herself into the sea after the receding ships and was turned into—accounts differ—a rock dove (a pigeon) with purple breast and red legs, or a ciris (from the Greek *keiro*, I cut), a cutter or shearwater. Her father though changed into a hawk and followed her in vengeful pursuit. Various translations write of the "impious gift... the parricidal present... a deed so base" that Scylla should be banished from earth and sea. In other words the feminine presence in the story has not only been regressed to a love-struck, impulsive, suicidal adolescent but has been driven into the sky, the dream, the unconscious, and denied any existence in the material world of earth and water.

However, the archetypal drama does not disappear—it continues in the collective unconscious with the vengeful hawk up high pursuing the ciris that skims the waves. Like Delilah, Scylla is cast as the dangerous temptress who brings men to ruin. Like Eve, she is the rebellious woman who disturbs the stagnant paradise of the Garden of Eden (or in this case, the comfy state of war, as with Troy). But unlike Eve she betrays her father not for knowledge but for love.

Any masculine state that is not creative, that is sterile, that cannot birth new life, that is not in good-enough relationship with the feminine and able to procreate, will not be tolerated for long. It will bring upon itself a state of affairs where the feminine births new life at whatever cost to the old order, even if this requires the feminine to impregnate itself with itself—a parthenogenetic birth. An explanation never considered as to how Mary became pregnant with Jesus.

Already, at the beginning of this eighth book, the mature feminine is absent. All that remains is a young girl/woman who is smitten with King Minos. Robert Graves translates her name as the opposites "she who rends" (aka the cutter) and "puppy" (aka the rock dove). The latter is embodied by Scylla's puppy-love for Minos whereas her opposite is the much older and more dangerous sea monster of the eponymous Scylla and Charybdis in Homer's Odyssey (c. 8th century BCE).

Scylla's father has a lock of purple hair that protects him from external but not internal harm. He is protected from everything except his own daughter. She is the feeling function, albeit young and undeveloped, the capacity for relatedness over separation, for pattern over discrimination, for similarity over difference, for foolishness over wisdom, which brings, let's note, an end to the stalemate of war. But the feminine does not appear in its fullest form. It has already been side-lined, diminished, infantilised, and rendered starry-eyed and foolish. This sets the tone for the stories to come.

Theseus and the Minotaur

The second story of Ovid's eighth book was well established by at least the 7th century BCE. It tells how, after he had ascended to the Cretan throne, Minos competed with his brothers to rule. This continues the Scylla story but the messy feminine is now out of the way.

Minos prays to Poseidon, the sea god, to send him a snow-white bull as a sign of his favour. But he has to kill the bull immediately to honour the sea god. Note the materialisation of something from spirit into matter as the result of the desires and intentions of humans. Western consciousness lamely calls this magic—unless it is the Christian God who has answered your prayers in which case it is the power of the Lord, or something like that. But, as in human affairs, a gift is a debt that must be repaid, the ledger must balance.

His prayers are answered but instead of sacrificing the bull immediately he decides to keep it because of its beauty and sacrifice one of his own. Poseidon is offended and to punish Minos he makes Pasiphae, Minos' wife, fall passionately in love with the bull. So in lust is Pasiphae that she has the inventor and craftsman Daedalus make a hollow wooden cow, and she climbs inside it in order to mate with the white bull.

Minos returns to Crete from the war with Nisus, pays his dues to Zeus with the sacrifice of a hundred bulls, and hangs up his war trophies. But he is disturbed by the scandal concerning his family and Pasiphae's union with the bull, which becomes public when she gives birth to a strange hybrid monster, the Minotaur, with the head of a bull and the body of a man. Minos resolves to remove this shame from his house, and, after consulting the oracle at Delphi, has Daedalus construct a labyrinth near his palace at Knossos to hold the Minotaur. Its common name means the Bull of Minos but its proper name is Asterion meaning "starry one". So the stars and fate might be at work here.

While visiting Athens, Minos' son Androgeus defeats Aegeus, King of Athens, in every contest during the Pan-Athenian Games. This angers Aegeus who has him killed (some versions tell that he sends Androgeus to fight the Minotaur, which kills him). Minos, in turn, is angry at this and declares war on Athens, but offers peace on the condition that Athens sends seven young men and seven young women every nine years to Crete to be fed to the Minotaur. After 27 years, when the time of the third sacrifice comes round, Theseus, Aegeus' son, volunteers to slay the monster. The number one represents unity and undividedness, the number two is division, opposition and conflict, the number three is change and movement toward resolution of the conflict. The completion of three cycles of nine represents a significant shift and a chaotic movement into a new cycle.[1]

Minos' daughter Ariadne falls in love with Theseus at first sight. "I will help you to kill my half-brother, the Minotaur," she secretly promises him, "if I may return to Athens with you as your wife." Theseus gladly accepts and swears to marry her. Ariadne helps him navigate the Labyrinth by giving him a ball of thread, allowing him to retrace his path. Theseus kills the Minotaur with the sword of Aegeus and leads the Athenians out of the Labyrinth.[2]

Sex with a bull

Sex with a bull seems to have been a tradition in the Minos family. Minos himself was the offspring of Zeus who had lusted after the beautiful Phoenician maiden Europa. Zeus changed into a white bull and hid amongst her father's herds. Fascinated by the bull, Europa was carried off to Crete on its back. There Zeus revealed his true identity, breathed from his mouth a saffron crocus, and impregnated her. Europa gave birth to three children by Zeus, one of whom was Minos, and she became Queen of Crete.

Although seen as an involuntary seizing and carrying off (as depicted

---

1. For a further discussion of the significance of the number 27 see Owen, *The 27 Club: Why Age 27 Is Important*.
2. https://en.wikipedia.org/wiki/Minotaur

for example in the Rape of Europa painted by both Titian and Goya) we don't know if she gave consent, to use a modern term. And what greater "power imbalance" than to be raped by Zeus himself, the most powerful god of the pantheon. But willingly or unwillingly, through pain or pleasure, the result of the union was that Zeus gave her four gifts: A necklace made by Hephaestus, blacksmith to the gods; the eponymous Talos, a giant bronze man also made by Hephaestus who circled the island's shores three times daily and protected Europa and Crete from abductors and pirates; Laelaps, a dog who never failed to catch his quarry; and a javelin that never missed.

Hephaestus was the earthiest of the gods. He was a blacksmith, a craftsman, a worker of metal, an inventor of things both artistic and practical, and a creator of beauty from matter. He was rejected at birth by his mother Hera because he was crippled, was cast out of Olympus, and fell to Earth. Similarly, Norse mythology has Weyland Smith the lame bronzeworker. Hephaestus is the archetypal artistic and creative principle which has entered the earthly realm. His lameness, deficiency, weakness, or defectiveness suggests that creativity and woundedness are linked—our greatest wound becomes our highest gift. As Rumi wrote (and latterly Leonard Cohen sang), there is a crack in everything—that's where the light gets in

As well as physical children and magical protections, Zeus also gifted Europa with saffron, the spice long prized as a dye and a medicine, derived from the saffron crocus which was originally cultivated in Crete. The flowers are male, sterile, and the plant requires the assistance of humans to propagate. Zeus' gifts to Europa all had masculine qualities. We might think of these gifts as the qualities that bestow full queenship upon her so that she has no need of the outer masculine and is complete unto herself.

The masculine (as experienced by all humans, independent of sexual orientation) wants to act on the world so it can change what is. The feminine (also a universal gift) wants to absorb the world so that it can understand what is. It is the instinctual nature of the feminine to receive the projections of those around her and mould herself to them, not as an act of inferiority and submission but as a way of getting inside things, feeling them, relating, joining, and knowing them in a different way from the masculine. Behaviourism is masculine, depth psychotherapy is feminine.

The light side of Europa and Pasiphae is the capacity to receive knowledge and illumination by joining with the masculine power of the bull. What comes of this union is what monotheism refers to as wisdom or Sophia. The light side of the bull is the positive masculine like the Celtic Dagda (In Daghda, the Good God, or All Father); the Gallic Cernunnos, the Horned God; Shiva's bull, Nandi; Osiris in his bull form, or the Vedic Rudra who fertilises the world with his semen.

Brinton-Perera describes the positive masculine as follows: "The Dagda is himself a beast, a very earthy bull with all of the primordial energies and fertility potential that make him lord of animals and the harvest. But he is also more. He is an Irish shapeshifter. Thus he appears also as a mighty warrior, rousing terror in his enemies. He is a potent lover and the respectful partner of three Great Goddesses. He is a just and generous king who can bear and contain the opposites and all that is dished out to him. He is a builder and musician, a wise magus from time immemorial. He is an image of the archetypal Anthropos, a 6,000-year-old, ever-living ancient".[3]

But monotheism and religious colonisation (aka spreading the gospel and evangelising) have had their way with the bull and its sacred power was degraded into "idolatry" and "worshipping graven images" and only its dark side remained visible. The shadow side of desiring and receiving the bull is zoophilia or bestiality, apocryphal stories about Catherine the Great, or modern pornography.

Aside from its individual psychopathology, mythologically the union with the bull represents a ritual union between the priestess, wearing cow's horns, and the priest, wearing a bull's mask.[4] This sacred marriage of the Sun and the Moon was enacted to ensure balance and harmony between above and below and to bring fertility to the land. So it was with Europa and Zeus whose union brought great gifts. But not so with Pasiphae and the bull—a profane marriage which produced monsters.

---

3. Brinton-Perera, *The Irish Bull God*, 14.
4. Graves, *The Greek Myths*, 297.

The bull was worshipped in Crete and Minoan frescoes and ceramics depict participants of both sexes somersaulting over bulls by grasping their horns. The sacred bull was important in ancient Egypt, where he was worshipped as Apis, and later in other cultures from Gaul to Mesopotamia. Fighting with the bull was one of the ritual tasks of candidates for kingship and contact with the moon-horns of the bull enabled the sacred king to bring rain and fertilise the land in the name of the moon goddess. Theseus slew the fire-breathing Minotaur. Hercules' seventh labour was to kill the Cretan bull that was ravaging crops and orchards and had killed hundreds of people. Jason requested the Golden Fleece from the King of Colchis, Aeëtes, whereupon Aeëtes demanded that Jason first yoke a pair of fire-breathing bulls to a plough and sow dragon's teeth in the earth.

We also see the bull in the Mithraic mysteries. Mithraism emerged in the middle of the first century BCE, reached its height in the third century CE and was ousted by Christianity by the fifth century. A typical mithraeum, of which there were hundreds, perhaps thousands, throughout the Roman Empire, was a small rectangular subterranean chamber. At the back of every mithraeum was a representation of the cult's central image: the tauroctony or "bull-slaying" in which the god, Mithras, accompanied by a dog, a snake, a raven, and a scorpion, is shown slaying a bull.[5] David Ulansey has shown that the animals represent the constellations of Taurus, Canis Minor, Hydra, Corvus, and Scorpio, symbolising the slaying, or end, of the Age of Taurus around 2,000 BCE.[6]

The bull archetype is still with us but in a different form. Wherever there are bulls there is patriarchy and its modern worship is epitomised by the "bull market" and the larger-than-life, bronze bull in Wall Street. The Martin Scorsese movie "Raging Bull", modern-day bullfights, Pamplona's running of the bulls, and rodeos are remnants of this archetypal theme. The bull (or boar as we shall see later) is a symbol of the fiery masculine power of nature ("like a bull at a gate") which must be subdued, civilised and brought to heel. We must "take the bull by the

---

5. The frontispiece of Jung's *Aion* is a photo of a statue of the Mithraic lion-headed god.
6. Ulansey, *The Origins of the Mithraic Mysteries*, www.mysterium.com

horns" to accomplish the work of growing ourselves up, or raising a culture.

Wrestling with the bull is the primary developmental task of adolescents and young adults. This suggests that the modern competitive political and business practices are developmentally arrested and have not progressed beyond their teens and twenties. Psychologically, the hero's task is to overcome the monster or enemy and achieve a victory of consciousness over the unconscious. The hero tames the unconscious as opposed to being killed by it. This is why adolescent cultures always need an enemy to fight with. The archetypal bull breathes fire, symbolising that which interests us, attracts us, gives us energy, turns our crank, and lights our fire. We need to find out what excites us, makes us feel alive. It is the rush of running with the bulls. It is getting "horny".

But we also need to develop enough discipline to not let the fire get out of control. This inevitably fails, as it should, and from this "failure" we learn something, hopefully. Fire is the only element that feeds on itself and the bull is destructive to the ego when the ego is not strong enough or falls into identifying with the bull (which the hero unavoidably does, losing himself and so meeting his fate). The bull must be sacrificed, that is, it must be defeated so that it is not lived out in the realm of human affairs and so that we may have the strength to rule wisely in our own inner or outer kingdom.

Edward Edinger says: "In psychological terms, the bull is the primordial unregenerate energy of the masculine archetype that is destructive to consciousness and to the ego when it identifies with it. Therefore, it must be sacrificed, and the sacrifice brings about a transformation, so that the energy symbolised by the bull serves another level of meaning. Seen this way it is not too much to say that the sacrifice or overcoming of the bull symbolizes the whole task of human civilization."[7]

Eating your own

The Minotaur devoured humans for food. With a bull's head and a

---

7. Edinger, *The Eternal Drama*, Kindle 1392-1395.

human body it was an unnatural joining of parts that do not belong together. When the animal is not given its rightful kinship as an equal brother or sister then instinctual behaviour returns in unnatural form and we "let ourselves go to the dogs" or "behave like an animal". Then, like the Minotaur, we eat our own, a theme repeated in the later story of Erysichthon.

The younger, culturally acceptable brothers in the "Eat Your Own" family is seen in "competitive" business practices, or promises of "industrial development" that cannot tidy up after themselves, move on a generation later and leave behind a mountain of tailings, or the Rust Belt.[8]

The older, darker brothers in this family are those who murder, dismember, and cannibalise. We are fascinated by this archetype in the figure of Hannibal Lecter. A psychopathic deficit in empathy, whether it be characteristic of a nation or an individual, increases in direct proportion to the numbers and their distance from the perpetrator(s). The bigger the numbers the easier it is to eat your own. "It's all just unproductive wilderness" (says the real estate developer); "It's terra nullius" (says the coloniser); They're "shithole countries" (says Donald Trump); After the first one it gets easier" (says the serial killer). Or six million Jews as the Final Solution (says Reinhard Heydrich). The further away they are, geographically, racially, or ethnically, the easier it is to eat your own.

In Greek mythology, chimeric crossovers like the Minotaur were lethal to mere mortals. The centaurs, half-human and half-horse, were known for their savagery. Mermen or tritons, and mermaids, half-fish and half-woman, lured sailors to their deaths. The Sphinx, a winged creature with a lion's body and a woman's head, guarded the way to Thebes; she posed a riddle to allow passage and if a passer-by answered incorrectly they were devoured. The gorgon was a creature with a human face, whose body was covered with golden scales, with large

---

8. Just ask, for example, the workers in Saginaw, Michigan where, in the 1970s, General Motors made gearboxes by the millions and employed 26,000 people. Now there are only a few hundred. Or the residents of East London about the benefits of the 2012 Olympic facilities developed in their boroughs. https://www.theguardian.com/uk-news/2022/jun/30/a-massive-betrayal-how-londons-olympic-legacy-was-sold-out?

wings and snakes for hair. If someone looked at her directly they were turned to stone.

Some therapists, Theseus-like, wish to civilise and overcome the monster, lead it out of the labyrinth and restore it to the human fold. This usually fails and the therapist gets eaten.

There is a price to pay when humans, like Minos, take what properly belongs to the gods. Minos lusted after Poseidon's bull and took it for his own. In contrast, the conscious masculine does not attempt to possess the gift, he serves it with grace as and when it appears, and in between stays and does his job. Minos' acquisitive lust gave rise to Pasiphae's sexual lust for the bull which in turn birthed a bull-monster. If the sacred is not honoured and given its due in the other world, it will manifest in debased form in this world. When a culture identifies with an archetype, takes it for granted, idealises it, and has no objectivity towards it, it becomes possessed by it. We then have the cultural equivalent of a personality disorder that characterises whole cultures and ages.

Daedalus doings

The story of Icarus, who flew too near the sun, is well known. Daedalus (meaning "bright" or "cunningly wrought")[9] was a skilled craftsman and inventor, and had been taught by Athena herself. To escape from the island of Crete he fashioned wings for himself and his son, Icarus. He warned Icarus to fly neither too close to the sun or the wax would melt, nor too close to the sea or the feathers would become wet. The middle way—not too much, not too little. But Icarus flew too high, his wings failed him, and he plunged to his death in the sea below. The accepted story is that Icarus was an impetuous youth and just look what happened to him, silly boy. It points to the dangers of expansion, altitude, success and way too much cleverness. Daedalus is cast as the wise restraint on Icarus' impetuousness. But, as we shall see, this is a cover for Daedalus' hubris.

Here's the fuller version of the story.[10] Banished from Athens (we'll

---

9. Graves, *The Greek Myths*, 315.
10. Adapted from Graves, *The Greek Myths*, 311-318; A S Kline www.poetryintransla

get to that later), Daedalus took refuge in Knossos, the capital of Minos' kingdom on the island of Crete. King Minos was delighted to welcome such a skilled craftsman. But, after he built the Labyrinth, Minos locked Daedalus in a tower so that he would not give away its secrets. Another version tells that he lived in Knossos for some time in high favour until Minos, learning that he had helped Pasiphae couple with Poseidon's white bull, locked him up in his own Labyrinth together with his son Icarus until Pasiphae freed them both.

It was not easy to escape from the island of Crete, since Minos kept all his ships under military guard and offered a large reward for Daedalus' capture. But Daedalus made a pair of wings for himself and another pair for Icarus. The quill feathers were sewn in place but the smaller ones were held only by wax. Having tied on Icarus's pair for him, Daedalus said with tears in his eyes: "My son, be warned! Neither soar too high, lest the sun melt the wax; nor swoop too low, lest the feathers be wetted by the sea." Then he slipped his arms into his own pair of wings and they flew off. "Follow me closely," he cried, "do not set your own course!"

But Icarus disobeyed his father's instructions and began soaring towards the sun, lifted by his great sweeping wings. Presently, when Daedalus looked over his shoulder, he could no longer see Icarus, just scattered feathers floating on the waves below. The heat of the sun had melted the wax and Icarus had fallen into the sea and drowned. Daedalus circled around, until the corpse rose to the surface, and then carried it to the nearby island now called Icaria, where he buried it. As Daedalus was burying Icarus, said Ovid, a noisy partridge poked its head out from a muddy ditch and called, cackling joyfully, with whirring wings.[11] But its appearance was a reproach to Daedalus. This final detail about the partridge refers to a lesser known story of what happened to Daedalus before his sojourn in Crete, although in Metamorphoses Ovid tells the story after that of Icarus.

---

tion.com/PITBR/Latin/Metamorph8.php; and A S Kline, *Ovid: The Metamorphoses, Book VIII*, 376-424.

11. Perdix is the Latin name for the genus of true partridges that nest on the ground and only fly short distances. They do not nest in trees and they avoid high places.

Before his banishment from Athens, Daedalus' sister, Perdix, oblivious to the warnings of the Fates, had sent her son, Talos, twelve years old, to be taught by Daedalus. The ingenious child, studying the spine of a fish, took it as a model and cut continuous teeth out of sharp metal, so inventing the saw. He was also the first to pivot two iron arms on a pin, so that one point could be fixed, and the other set at a fixed distance to sweep out a perfect circle. Daedalus was so proud of his own achievements that he could not bear the idea of a rival and to add to this, he also suspected Talos of incest with his mother, Perdix. He grew unbearably envious of Talos and, leading him up to the roof of Athena's temple on the Acropolis, he pointed out the distant sights and suddenly pushed him over the edge.

Daedalus was, in fact, both envious and jealous of Talos. Envy is a two-person dynamic: "I want/hate what he has." Jealousy is a three-person dynamic: "I want/hate what those two have together." Daedalus was envious of Talos' skills and was jealous of Talos' imagined or actual relationship with his sister, sexual or not.

Two translations describe what followed the murder. Robert Graves writes that Daedalus then hurried down to the foot of the Acropolis, and thrust Talos' corpse into a bag, planning to bury it in secret. When challenged by passers-by, he explained that he had piously taken up a dead serpent, as the law required. But there were blood-stains on the bag and his crime did not escape detection, whereupon the Areopagus, the ruling council, banished him for murder. The soul of Talos flew off in the form of a partridge. According to A J Kline's translation, Athena, who favours those with quick minds, caught Talos as he fell and turned him into a partridge in mid-air. His inborn energy was transferred to swift wings and feet and he kept his mother's name, Perdix.

So Talos is the shadow of the well-known story of Icarus. He becomes transformed into the polar opposite of Icarus—a bird that does not fly high but keeps close to the earth. But in this shadow story we also see a mirror-image of the theme of Oedipus, whose story was told by Sophocles in his play Oedipus Rex. Oedipus unwittingly killed his father, Laius, King of Thebes, then married his mother, Jocasta, Queen of Thebes, again unwittingly. The myth was used by Freud, and later Melanie Klein, to illustrate a stage of psychosexual development in young children related to the dynamics of competition, guilt, triangulation, exclusion, inclusion, jealousy and envy. Put crudely and way too literally, the little boy wants to kill Daddy so he can have sex with Mummy. Put less dramatically, the little boy pushes Daddy aside so he can have Mummy all to himself.[12]

With Talos, we have a mirror image of this Oedipal story. While Oedipus kills his father first then commits incest with his mother, all unwittingly, Talos commits incest with his mother first (or so Daedalus believes) and then is intentionally killed by Daedalus, his uncle/father.

Freud and the majority of Freudians (or close cousins thereof) have given so much weight to the child's Oedipal fantasies[13] that the parents' pathology and actual incest or sexual abuse was marginalised or denied. Freud shrank from the enormity of the problem. The story of Talos has the hallmarks of blaming the child for the adult's pathology, punishing him for the adult's behaviour, or for disowned desires (of Daedalus for his sister) projected onto the child.

But to follow Freud's line of thinking, we have here, not the child's (Oedipal) phantasies, but the adult's (Daedalus) phantasies—a mirrored and inverted transform of the Oedipal phantasy. The companion to this is what is called the Jocasta complex where the mother has an over-involved, enmeshed relationship with her son (who is usually the wished-for compensation for that useless man, your father) or, in a not-uncommon variation, an erotically charged, flirty relationship with her daughter's boyfriend.

The story of Talos and Daedalus begs several questions. Where was Talos' father (Perdix's husband) when the supposed incest took place? Was Talos banished from the home by Perdix (fatefully, under the guise of an apprenticeship) for the crime of incest, just as Daedalus would be banished for his crime? Did Talos' father agree that he should be sent to Daedalus? We don't know Icarus' age but what father would risk such danger to their child? The functional masculine, that sets limits, and

---

12. This might seem a bit over the top and too Freudian but spend some time with young children (2–5 years) or highly dysfunctional families, and a version of it will eventually appear in the raw.

13. Sometimes spelled phantasies to distinguish their unconscious nature from conscious fantasies—like phishing is different from fishing.

protects what cannot protect itself, is absent. Psychologically, when a boy has had too much mother/feminine he remains naive and insulated from the world, and is unable to use healthy aggression to protect himself. Or he becomes overly aggressive or macho in an attempt to escape the gravitational pull of the mother-world.

At the age of twelve Talos was crossing over from child to adolescent, from mother-world to father-world. But he could not protect himself yet. Did Icarus pay the price for Daedalus' murderous competitiveness that could not allow Talos to fly higher than he?

This leads us to the Daedalus complex, as I call it. Not long after I wrote this section in 2018 I ran across the website of the Daedalus Trust.[14] The website says: "Dedicated to exploring hubris: There is a growing body of opinion that the exercise of power can distort thinking and create personality changes in leaders that affect their decision making. The Daedalus Trust was founded by Lord David Owen[15] to raise awareness of such changes and understand them better". But I would venture that the opposite process takes place—distorted thinking leads the person to actively seek power and when they gain it, any existing distortions are magnified. They are not a victim of power. And it goes on to say that "The Hubris Syndrome is an 'acquired personality change' i.e. brought on over a period of time. It is sparked by a specific trigger—exercising power." This was not at all "acquired" later in life by Donald Trump. His psychopathic hubris was showing itself in childhood.

As for the choice of name the website states. "In Greek mythology, Daedalus advised his son Icarus to be bold enough to fly but not to fly so high that the sun's heat would melt the wax of the wings he had fashioned for him. Thrilled by his initial aerobatic successes, Icarus ignored his father's advice and paid the ultimate price—a sobering demonstration of unjustified self confidence and the abuse of power." Then why not call it the Icarus Trust? The Trust may have unwittingly got its name right.

I suggest that in fact it was Daedalus, not Icarus, who abused his

---

14. www.daedalustrust.com
15. Medical doctor and ex-British Foreign Secretary, no relation.

power. The issue was not with Icarus, silly boy, who got carried away on his new wings, but a darker motivation of Daedalus'. He had already murdered his nephew Talos who was an ingenious boy—he invented the saw and a geometric compass when he was but twelve—and Daedalus was envious of his creativity. Daedalus was then banished from Athens as punishment for Talos' murder.

For contrast, let me briefly mention its better-known opposite—the Oedipus complex. The story of Oedipus is well known. Oedipus kills his father (patricide) and marries his mother (incest). A favourite testosterone-ish act of aggression is calling someone a motherfucker or muthafucka. This quaint appellative is more common in cultures that have a sentimental attachment to the notion of the mother, or where the father is often absent or violent.

The history of psychoanalysis is shot through with schisms and Oedipal rifts. From 1942–1944 the "Controversial Discussions", as they were politely known and in parallel with the larger conflict of WWII, took place between Melanie Klein and her followers, and Anna Freud and her followers who were loyal to Freud who had died in 1939. This resulted in a split in the British Psychoanalytical Society with the Independent Group occupying the middle ground. Much of the the discussions orbited around what is "true" psychoanalysis (or psychoanalysis as the originalists would have it) and the gravitational pull of Freud, all with a whiff of betrayal and disloyalty to the "father". The Oedipus complex became the defining, and loyalist, theory for Freud and the Freudians.

The fact that there is no accepted name for the Daedalus complex points to its unconsciousness. It better describes the personality disorder of Western culture than does Narcissistic Personality Disorder. With the Jocasta complex—the female counterpart to the Oedipus complex—the mother symbiotically merges with the son. With the Daedalus complex, however, the father has has a hostile, competitive and resentful relationship with his son, and puts him down, demoralises him, nothing is ever good enough, beats him, and otherwise "kills" him. Trump so wanted to be better than his father, a New York real estate developer who, he said, pushed him hard. He both feared and idealised him. What better way to compete with Daddy but to be more cruel and lethal than he was. "Can't we just shoot them?" he said, of the Black Lives Matter protesters.

Either way, physical or psychological death is the result for the son. Daedalus just didn't like the competition from Talos—the boy was way too smart, and rather than the old bull being bested by the young bull, he killed him. Trump, with his contempt for "weak" men, his dysfunctional competitiveness, and his need to destroy the competition, is the modern facsimile. The Daedalus-afflicted person is often narcissistically paranoid about the intentions of others—think Fake News and deep state conspiracies—and cunningly plots to kill before being killed.

And facsimile he is. Although he may look like a unique individual he is blindly living out an archetypal pattern. Millions openly or secretly admire his breaking the rules and doing it his way. A Trump voter said sympathetically, in reference to Trump's July 2019 conversation to pressure Volodymyr Zelensky, the Ukrainian president, to provide information that could be damaging to former Vice-president Joe Biden, which Trump described as "a perfect call" said, "I think he crossed a line but that's the way he is." Trump lives out the stagnant individuation and unlived life of millions of wannabes.

Trump is also driven by another archetypal force—revenge. He was never one to let a good grudge lie down. Loyalty is paramount. All kings and dictators have had demanded fealty. But loyalty inevitably breeds betrayal which is punishable by symbolic or literal death—and the dish of revenge is kept cold for years.

Writ on film, it's a staple theme of Hollywood movies, as in "Ahm goin' to git that man who killed mah daddy". But it's a much older story. Orestes, the son of Agamemnon, avenged his father's death by slaying both Aegisthus, Agamemnon's murderer, and also his own mother Clytemnestra, Aegisthus' lover. But he is pursued by the Erinyes and driven to madness. The three Erinyes ("the angry ones") were also known as the Eumenides or the Furies. According to Hesiod when the Titan Cronus castrated his father, Uranus, and threw his genitalia into the sea, the Erinyes were born from the drops of blood which fell on the earth, Gaia. Alternatively, they emerged from an even more primordial level, older than the Olympian gods and goddesses, as daughters of Nyx (Night), or from a union between Air and Gaia. Their names were

Alekto ("the unremitting one"), Megaera ("jealous rage"), and Tisiphone ("vengeful destruction, the avenger of murder"). They were crones and variously are described as having snakes for hair, dog's heads, coal black bodies, bat's wings, and blood-shot eyes. In their hands they carry brass-studded scourges, and their victims died in torment. Their task was to hear complaints brought by mortals for offences committed against the natural order and hierarchy—from insolence of the young to the aged, children to parents, hosts to guests, or homicide, and particularly matricide, patricide, fratricide or sororicide—and to punish such crimes by hounding the offenders relentlessly seeking vengeance and retribution.

So we have an archetypal pattern here, made bigger as archetypes do with big four-letter words like kill (aka ending, separation, or death whether it be physical, spiritual or psychological) and fuck (aka over-involvement, merging, lovemaking, or lust whether it be physical, spiritual or psychological). They leave us to fill in the actual human shadings like dislike, disengage, disrespect, obliterate, destroy, compete, hate; or idealise, depend on, klingon, adore, and loved-up. Where there is sex there is death, where there is death there is sex—le petit mort. Each contains the germ of the other. As Dylan wrote: "He who is not busy being born is busy dying." Both sex and death attend each other's births, weddings and funerals.

The Daedalus-possessed person demands absolute loyalty and is narcissistically paranoid about the intentions of others (think palace intrigue, food-taster for the King, Stalin, Pinochet, Putin, Trump, or Fake News) and cunningly plots to kill before being killed. Daedalus' murderous envy of Talos' creativity led him to murder his nephew. In turn, Daedalus loses his own son, not through Icarus' hubris, flying too high and being disobedient as the story is commonly read, but as a fated, and unconscious, punishment for the murder of Talos.

There has been a literary and historical denial of Daedalus' homicide, just as we are "in denial" of the murder of our planet. In the age of Trumpian bombast we could say that this may be the greatest denial we have ever seen in the history of the world. Daedalus remains the ingenious inventor whose technological nous can solve all problems. The myth has become institutionalised into a story about Icarus' arrogance and disobedience in which young hubris, arrogance and pride are inextricably and fatefully linked with death. We see this played out on the cultural stage when soldier-sons are sacrificed and idealised for the elusive father-ideal of "freedom," and on the planetary stage when the Daedalus growth culture will not let itself be bested by those climate change fanatics.[16]

Phaethon ("the shining one") was accused of being born of adultery and, anxious to prove his lineage by word and deed, he went to his father Helios' palace in the east. Helios recognised him and swore by the river Styx (an irrevocable oath) that he would grant whatever request the young man made of him. On that pledge, Phaethon asked to drive his father's sun-chariot for a day with which Helios led the sun across the heavens each day. Helios attempted to dissuade his son with warnings about the difficulty controlling the powerful horses that pulled the chariot. His father surrendered to his son's wishes and Phaethon set out across the sky. But, inexperienced with such powerful beasts, he soon lost control of the horses. As a result, he drove the chariot too close to the earth, scorching the plains of Africa, and too far from it, turning the land ice-cold. Eventually, after complaints from the stars in the sky and the earth itself, Zeus strikes Phaethon with a lightning bolt, killing him. His flaming body falls into the river Eridanus, and his sisters the Heliades, who harnessed the horses for him, are turned to black poplar trees as they mourn him.

On the face of it, this seems a similar story to that of Daedalus and Icarus. As before the problem is not with the son—impetuous with immature frontal lobes—but with the father. In our modern culture car insurance companies, who won't offer adult rates until age 25, are the father who says wait a bit, not so fast, think of the risk. Extreme sports are deaf to this, as they should be at that stage of life and limb. But if an extreme skier or mountaineer should kill themselves—tragic as it might

---

16. In February 2018 the White House withdrew the nomination of Kathleen Hartnett to head the Council on Environmental Quality. She had described the belief in "global warming" as a "kind of paganism" for "secular elites." She has called environmentalists "Marxists" and also said the goal of climate activists and the United Nations was an all-powerful, one-world government and "planetary management." www.cnn.com/2018/02/03/politics/nominee-withdraw-council-environmental-quality/index.html

be and tragic that everyone saw it coming—their death doesn't affect the whole planet. With Daedalus he involves his son in a risky, and eventually fatal venture, to save himself from imprisonment by King Minos. The telling difference with Helios is that he accommodates to and enables his son's wish for a risky venture. What could possibly go wrong? Daedalus is the murderous father who kills his son by commission. Helios is the absent father who kills his son by omission. One is the shadow of the other. Daedalus-like growth and development is ecocide, plain and simple. Helios-like denial and neglect are its shadow accomplices.

5

THE BOAR HUNT
GROINS AND GORING

OVID'S STORIES thus far are relatively short but the story of the Calydonian boar hunt is much longer and is divided into four parts: the cause; the boar is roused; the kill; and the spoils. It is like a dream within a dream and adheres to the same structure.

The land of Calydon had had a fruitful year and King Oeneus decreed that the first fruits of the crops be given in honour of the deities —corn to Demeter, wine to Dionysus, and the oil of olives to golden-haired Athena. All the Gods were praised from the lowest to the highest —except one. Only the altar of Artemis, the goddess of the hunt, wild animals, wilderness, childbirth, virginity and young girls, was neglected and left without incense. "Am I to suffer this indignity?" she cried, "Though I am thus dishonoured, I will not be unrevenged!" So an avenging wild boar was sent to ravage the fair land of Calydon.

Greek mythology is replete with stories of the gods being slighted, miffed, or cuckolded, and feeling angry, lustful, jealous and vengeful as well as merciful, compassionate, kind and generous. They embodied the full breadth, depth and height of human emotional and physical life including Artemis' rage at being forgotten. Contrast this with the pale, anorexic, sexless, bloodless, contracted, country vicar, turn-it-sideways-and-it-disappears body of some Christian lives. All milquetoast chastity and charity, not to mention temperance, diligence, patience, kindness, and humility, just for a start.

Almost all spiritual paths have physical practices such as the martial arts (aikido, hapkido, jiu-jitsu, yoga) or breathing practices such as pranayama, some developed as early as 2000 BCE. However, the denial and even debasement of the body is endemic within the Abrahamic religions.[1] The Christian equivalents of kung-fu, judo, or muay thai, are hard to find. A faintly fundamentalist community I was acquainted with had yoga classes three mornings a week. However, they were called stretch classes as the use of the word yoga was anti-Christian. The gifts of the People of the Book are of the mind and the intellect, nopt of the body. It may be that the Jewish people are the only people who have won more Nobel prizes than Olympic gold medals.

Artemis and Atalanta

Artemis, or Diana as she was known in Rome, was the elder twin of Apollo, the sun god. Being a moon goddess, she carried a silver bow, a quiver full of arrows and was often accompanied by a deer. Her name means "She Who Slays". She went to Pan, the god of nature, who gave her the hunting dogs who accompanied her. She was the Lady of the Beasts, who hunted with men in her company but was chaste, not beholden to men, and was easily offended by them.

Actaeon, a young hunter wandering in the forest, once chanced upon the moon-goddess, bathing naked. As punishment for seeing her nakedness, Artemis turned him into a stag. He was then torn apart by his own hunting dogs. Artemis also sent a scorpion to kill the young Orion after he accidentally touched her. Artemis symbolises the independent, wild, feminine spirit who is complete unto herself—that's present tense—she is still alive and moves among us.[2]

She wants no contact with the masculine, she has plenty of her own, thank you, maybe too much. She walks her own path and is life-giver

---

1. As in the oldie, "Why do [add your preferred fundamentalism here] prohibit sex? Because it might lead to dancing".
2. Sergeant Neagley of the Jack Reacher novels is a modern example.

and death-bringer. She values nature over human feelings and relationships. She is not the providing, nourishing, abundant Demeter of the farmer and olive tree grower. She is not the cool, logical and principled Athena of the academic. She is not the lanced and tranced, passionate Aphrodite of the lover. She is something more ancient and distant from human concerns that lives in wildness, wilderness and pristine nature. It can kill us or cure us. Artemis is the purity of nature itself, of unpolluted streams, unconquered peaks, the remote forest, the undiscovered Shangri-La, the unseen waterfall. But Artemis is also the death-bringer aspect of pure nature, with no concern for human feeling. The cliff does not weep for the falling climber, the surf does not heed the drowning swimmer.

People since time before time have gone to the forest and the mountains to find what is hidden in themselves. It is in nature that our own nature reveals itself. Artemis doesn't live in the city. Artemis is virginal. She is untouched by the trappings of culture. She is the psyche that has a mind of its own uncoloured by thoughts, attitudes and expectations of the world outside. She is the psyche that does not foist its psychology onto others and the world around it, forcing them to carry what the individual is unconscious of. Neither is she penetrated by the neediness of others. She is as far from co-dependence as you can get. Edward Edinger writes:

> The Artemis woman tends to be efficient, self-sufficient, and not amenable to personal intimacy. As an inner experience, the Artemis principle appears as an attitude that is coldly factual and impersonal and can be as aloof and indifferent as nature. It will be experienced as cruel because it is indifferent to personal human feelings and harsh toward weakness and regressive tendencies. The Artemis woman is devoid of sentimentality in contrast to Demeter, who tends to be sentimental and protective. One might say that Artemis believes in survival of the fittest, and in men we might call her the natural anima. She has no compunctions about being cruel to weakness, but is helpful to

strength, and so is growth-promoting to those for whom growth is possible; she will be hated by the regressive side of humanity.[3]

The growth-oriented, monotheistic global culture is like the young Actaeon. It has wandered into something that is too big for it. Narcissistically, it believes that dumb matter is only there for its exploitation. Like Actaeon in his innocence, it does not have the wisdom, experience, street-smarts, bush-lore, common sense, or respect needed to go walkies in the bush at night. Actaeon is unprepared for a confrontation with nature itself and pays with his life. His boyish innocence is in fact murderous. So is our consumptive culture. Artemis will have her revenge.

Artemis' vengeance in the form of the Calydonian boar destroys, as nature does, all the signs of agriculture and farming. The grapes, the corn, and the cattle are the first domestication and violation of nature's virginity. All cultures who live close to the Earth know we are stewards, only, with a long-term lease on which rent must be paid. The land itself and the spirits that live there should be talked to, fed, remembered, honoured and kept in good relation, just as we would do with our human neighbours. In KwaZulu (Land of the Zulu) my friend, when pointing out directions or the landscape, would never point directly to a mountain with his finger, he would always indicate, looking away as a mark of respect, with his elbow.

If the spirit of a place—not some remote spiritual value in heaven, removed from matter—but the mana, the essence, the wairua, the qi (and a thousand other names) of that particular hillside, that grove up the valley, this stream here, that mountain over there, are not honoured then matter will go wrong, the harvest will fail, the floods will come, the eyes of the cold will freeze the vines and the teeth of the sun will eat the corn. King Oeneus forgot about Artemis. And she does not like to be forgotten. Now, her wrath incurred, she sends the most masculine of animals, the wild boar, to seek retribution.

Ovid continues: The avenging boar was as large as the bulls of green Epirus, and larger than the bulls of Sicily. His burning, bloodshot eyes

---

3. Edinger, *The Eternal Drama*, Kindle 870.

seemed coals of living fire, and his rough neck was knotted and thick-set with bristles like sharp spikes. Hot foam flecked his broad shoulders, and his tusks were like the tusks of an elephant. Discordant roars came from his hideous jaws and lightning belched forth from his throat scorching the green fields.

He trampled the green corn, in vain the threshing-floor had been prepared, in vain the barns await the promised yield. The vines and heavy clusters of grapes were scattered in confusion, and the fruits and branches of the olive tree, whose leaves should never wither, are cast on the ground. He raged amongst the cattle, which neither dogs nor shepherd could protect; and the brave bulls could not defend their herds. The people fled in all directions from the fields, only safe behind the city walls. There seemed no remedy to save the land, till King Oenus called upon a band of men, united for the glory of great deeds.

Oeneus dispatched his heralds, inviting all the bravest fighters of Greece to hunt the boar, and promising that whoever killed it should have its pelt and tusks. Some of the great Hellenic warriors heard the call and came, ardent for some desperate glory: Theseus, the hero who slew the Minotaur, and his friend Perithous, son of Ixion; Castor and Pollux, the divine twins, sons of Zeus and Leda the swan, one famous for his skill in horsemanship, the other for his boxing; Jason of the Argonauts; Deucalion, son of Prometheus; Laertes, father of Odysseus; Lynkeus with his fleet-footed brother Idas; the Argonaut Acastus, swift of dart; Meleager, the son of Oenus; Nestor, the Argonaut who fought the Centaurs; Peleus, father of the great Achilles; Lelex, the storyteller of Metamorphoses, and many, many others. Like Genesis, when we hear of fathers and sons, blood-lines and lineages, begatting and begetting at the beginning, the masculine is about.

But wait... there was one woman. Her name was Atalanta. "The virgin of the groves of Mount Lycaeus, glory of her sex; a polished buckle fastened her attire; her lustrous hair was fashioned in a knot; her weapons rattled in an ivory case, swung from her white left shoulder, and she held a bow in her left hand. Her face appeared as maidenly for a boy, or boyish for a girl".

Her father, Iasus, had wished for a male heir and Atalanta's birth disappointed him so cruelly that he left her to die on the Parthenian Hill near Calydon, where she was suckled by a bear sent by Artemis. Atalanta grew to womanhood among a clan of hunters who found and reared her, but remained a virgin and always carried arms. She was sent to join the hunt by Artemis herself and, as the goddess knew, this would cause division amongst the men. Many of them refused to hunt alongside a woman. But Meleager, smitten by Atalanta, convinced them to allow her to join the hunt.

The boar

The hunt was bloody and dangerous but the first blood to be shed was human-ish. The company advanced in a half-moon, some paces apart. Atalanta posted herself at the extreme right some distance from her fellow-hunters, the Centaurs, Hylaeus and Rhaecus, who had joined the chase. They decided to ravish her but as soon as they turned towards her Atalanta shot them both down and went to hunt at Meleager's side. The warriors followed the boar's tracks into virgin forest. The dogs were unleashed and hunting nets were spread out upon the forest floor.

The boar was driven out from a marshy hollow crashing loudly against the trunks of the trees, pushing some of them over. The dogs were tossed aside by its tusks. Echion threw the first spear, but it missed. Jason's spear went wide of the mark, then Mopsus cried out a prayer to Apollo and hurled his spear. It hit the boar but failed to wound it. Artemis stole its iron tip as it flew through the air. But the boar was enraged and sparks flashed from its eyes. It breathed flames and charged the band of warriors. Eupalamus and Pelagon were felled, and their friends snatched them up from where they lay. Enaesimus turned to flee but the boar slashed the sinews behind his knees and he crumpled to the ground. Nestor used his spear to vault into the branches of a tree, and looked down at the boar from a safe height. The boar then sharpened his tusks on the bark of an oak, before ripping open the thigh of Hippasus.[4]

The wild boar is the one of the most widespread of mammals and its natural range stretches from South East Asia, where it originated,

---

4. Adapted from www.writer2001.com/boars.htm

through to Europe. It has been introduced into Australia, New Zealand and North America. It lives in matriarchal groups of related females and their young, both male and female. Mature males are usually solitary. The earliest evidence of domestication dates to about 13,000 BCE and it is the ancestor of all modern pigs. It can weigh up to 300 kgs (but usually 100-150 kgs), run at 40 kph (the fastest human reaches 45 kph), overturn boulders of up to 50 kgs, and jump to a height of 1.5 metres. The boar is known for its ferocity and courage, its refusal to yield, and is even more dangerous when cornered. One of the favourite sports of young men in New Zealand's rural areas (which is most of the country) is "pig hunting" in the dense bush. Their other hobbies are killing themselves driving home after a Saturday night on the piss, or going deer hunting and shooting a mate by mistake.

The boar is a mythological figure in cultures world-wide. To the Anglo-Saxons, the fierce wild boar was a symbol of strength and fertility; its image adorned their helmets and it was ceremonially eaten along with apples at the mid-winter feast. In Welsh myth the quest of Culhwch involved the pursuit of the huge man-boar Twrch Trwyth, a king who had been turned into a boar for his wickedness.[5] The boar with its crescent-shaped tusks was seen as symbolic of the Great Goddess, reflecting her three faces as battle goddess, mother goddess and finally, as the Great Sow, the devourer. Depictions of the Medusa show her with tusks emerging from her mouth and Polynesian female demon masks often have tusks. Most of the Greek heroes had to kill a boar at one time or another. As the fourth of his twelve labours Hercules had to capture the Erymanthian boar. The Norse god Freyr possessed a great boar Gullibursti (Golden Bristles) on which he rode. Vishnu, in the form of the boar Varaha, rescued the earth when, overburdened, it sank below the cosmic waters.

For an adolescent the boar may be the school bully or the unattainable girl; for a young adult, the boar may be the Marine Corps, a university degree, or overcoming an addiction. For Western culture, the boar is unlimited growth—a beast yet to be confronted.

---

5. Layard, *Celtic Quest: Sexuality and Soul in Individuation*.

The kill

In the chaos of the charging boar, several of the men were wounded, castrated, disembowelled, or killed either by boar or by the javelins of their fellow hunters. Castor and Pollux, the twins, sent their javelins towards the boar but it retreated into dense undergrowth. Then Atalanta fired an arrow that lodged below its ear, staining the bristles with a trickle of blood. Meleager, pleased at her success, pointed this out to his friends and told her that she would be honoured for her prowess. The men, shamed by this, let fly with their weapons but their spears hit each other and fell to the ground. Then Ancaeus, boasting that his double axe was better than a woman's weapon, rushed for the boar and, standing poised on tiptoe, prepared to let the blade down on the beast's neck.

The boar, anticipating his blow, struck him in the upper groin with his twin tusks and Ancaeus' organs slipped and trailed from his body onto the earth. Pirithous rushed toward the brute, but was stopped by a warning from Theseus, who launched his spear. The spear missed and lodged in an oak tree. Jason threw his javelin, but his aim was poor, and it killed one of the hounds. Meleager let fly two spears at the boar; the first missed and stuck in the ground, but the second lodged in the middle of the beast's back. The boar, writhing in fury and agony, could only wait for the fatal thrust. It slavered foam and blood and Meleager buried his spear in its shoulder.

Groins and goring

Ancaeus' derring-do gets him gored and disembowelled. Charging at a human, the tusks of a full-grown boar will wound at the level of the upper groin, the genitals, and the lower abdomen. In myth and legend a wound to the groin symbolises injury to the masculine generative power by the feminine forces of nature. Sometimes the wound is fatal, but sometimes the hero grows stronger in overcoming the boar and overcoming death. We see this, for example, in the stories of the Fisher King, wounded in the thigh, in whose kingdom nothing will grow and it becomes a wasteland. In the story of Venus and Adonis, Adonis is gored in the groin by a boar and dies from the injury. But Odysseus, wise hero, wore the scar of the boar's tusk on his thigh and it was by this wound that he was recognised by his wife Penelope on his eventual home-coming to Ithaca.

Groins, goring and horns. Yes, it's all sexual. Where there is death there is sex. The rush of killing and the rush of dying are one and the same. Killing, blood-lust or pain brings an erection. Ask any sadist—or masochist for that matter. And listen to Shakespeare in his poem Venus and Adonis, "And, nuzzling in his flank the loving swine / Sheathed unaware the tusk in his soft groin".[6]

Matriotic war

Boys will be boys. With no time for reflection in the heat of battle and the fog of war, the Calydonian heroes press on not pausing to think. Actually, when you're facing a boar who is about to charge any questioning of this direct-erect-action is taken as irritatingly stupid. But in fairy tales it is the old man of the forest or the talking animal who poses the right question just at the moment when the hero is about to rush into action. He has to stop and think—not something heroes are renowned for, requiring, as it does, a level of introspection, wisdom and self-knowledge that the hero has yet to come by. If he did he might ask, "What might all this mean, that my buddies have been killed, that the boar is goring everyone, and that woman over there has drawn first blood?"

But he doesn't think at all and just acts blindly. And that's the whole point. Introspection would get in the way of having the experience, whether painful or pleasurable. Insight only comes much later—in life, in the VA hospital, or at the funeral. Thankfully, there are heroes who do go to war when needed and they deserve our admiration, thanks, and care for having put themselves in harm's way. Patriotism and death get their valour duly honoured.

What about matriotism? What about women who carry a child for nine months? The word matriotism barely exists. More women have

---

6. Shakespeare, *Venus and Adonis*, 1115.

died giving birth than men have died giving war. Mussolini was right when he said, "War is to man what maternity is to woman". But, I think, not in the way that he meant it.

War is always a done deal, a fait accompli, already backed into a corner with no choice. That simple, tiny corner is no place to consider and reflect on the forces that brought us there. The military psyche is well suited for the conduct of war but is useless at preventing it. But then, once out of the tight spot, the battle done, amnesia sets in: "We need to move on" or "We can't think about it now". A generation later, reflection might come, but the immediacy is gone and current agendas sweep insight aside. Masculine consciousness has no present and no past. It lives in a fantasy world shorn of present-ness and past-ness where future goals, plans and achievements are everything, but nothing has happened yet. In later years this disowned memory returns as nostalgia, sentiment and PTSD.

A wider view is needed—9/11 was thousands of years in the making. It was not the Reagan-dim, Bush-simple battle of the forces of good against the forces of evil. Nor is it the Trumpety-trump boasting of strength over weakness. The hero archetype has saturated Western culture with disastrous consequences for the others who share this planetary home. It's done its dash and needs to be put out to pasture and given a job more suited to its limited nature.

Notice that Atalanta has not killed the boar, she has only drawn blood. Her victory is a symbolic death, she has counted coup. Any shaman, magician, conjurer, sorcerer, alchemist, sangoma, curandera, clever woman, or medicine man worth his or her salt knows that if something dies in this world it comes alive in the other world and we feed the other world through our constant dying. But, if death is needed, the gods and goddesses will accept either a physical death or a spiritual death. The two are different forms of the same thing. Death and change is what matters, not their form or location but our flat earth, hyper-rational, concrete culture doesn't know the difference. So physical death it must be.

War and the spilling of blood is often the only way that consciousness can be changed. If a cultural psyche is thin-skinned, hot-headed, narcissistic, and vulnerable to insult, then nature has to resort to drastic measures. There is a time for heroism, but its proper shelf-life is short. In our global culture heroism is revered and its life expectancy is extended past its prime even into old age, and it intrudes into areas that are none of its business. So we hear of fighting cancer and the battle against [name your disease]. With the heroic taken for granted we are not listening to the obvious or asking the right questions. The hero, simpleton that he is, wants actions and answers. Now.

The spoils

Meleager delivered the final lance to the boar and so he received the spoils. But he had fallen in love with Atalanta and, in honour of her drawing first blood, he awarded the skin and head, with its magnificent tusks, to her. The men were outraged. Meleager's two uncles considered it disgraceful that a woman should get the trophy, saying it was theirs by birthright and succession if Meleager did not to take it. "Come, girl, set them down. Do not steal our trophies of honour, and do not let too much faith in your beauty deceive you, lest your love-sick friend turns out to be no help to you". They took the gifts away from her, and denied Meleager the right to give them. Angered by their challenge, Meleager ran his sword through the heart of the first, swiftly killed the second, and again gave the skin to Atalanta.

Meleager's mother, Althaea, had been told of her son's victory and she was on her way to the temple with offerings when she saw the bodies of her two brothers being carried back. The sound of her grief sounded throughout the city, but when she discovered that it was Meleager that had killed them, her sorrow turned to rage and she plotted her revenge.

When Meleager was born, the Three Fates, daughters of Erebus (Darkness) and Styx (Night), appeared to Althaea. Such was their power their decrees could be revealed to Zeus but even he could not change the outcome. Clotho, who spun the thread of life, and decided when a person was born and when gods or mortals were to be saved or put to death said that Meleager would have a noble spirit. Lachesis, the goddess of chance, drew out the thread and declared that he would be a hero. Atropos, the inescapable destiny of the individual, was the one who cut the thread with her shears. Her decree was that Meleager would live as long as the log that was burning in the fire before Althaea should last. Althaea quickly threw water over the log and hid it away.[7]

Now she brought out the log and ordered a fire to be built. Four times she tried to throw the log on the fire, but each time she stopped herself. Her mood changed from fury to compassion and back again. Finally, her feelings for her brothers became greater than those for her son and, after a long prayer to the Furies, she cast the log into the flames. Far away, Meleager felt the heat and began to burn from within dying an agonising death. The house of Meleager was laid waste by the grief wrought by Artemis. Althaea killed herself and Meleager's sisters threw themselves into his tomb, sobbing. At last, satiated by the destruction, Artemis transformed them all into guinea hens, the Meleagrides.

---

7. Adapted from *The Metamorphoses of Ovid*, translated by Mary M. Innes, Harmondsworth, 1955.

6

THE LOVER SURVIVES

AFFECTION AND CONTRITION

LET me recap the story up to now in Book VIII of Metamorphoses. We have the downfall of King Nisus brought about by his daughter Scylla who then drowns herself. Minos refuses to sacrifice what is precious to him (the white bull) and as a result the feminine suffers and Pasiphae gives birth to the Minotaur. The young Ariadne, Minos and Pasiphae's daughter, falls in love with Theseus and helps to slay the Minotaur on the promise of marriage, elopes with Theseus on his return to Athens, but is abandoned by him on the island of Naxos. Then Daedalus, idealised as inventor and craftsman, consciously murders his nephew, Talos, and unconsciously murders his son, Icarus. In short, the feminine in female form drowns, births monsters, and is abandoned. The feminine in male form, as Talos and Icarus, is murdered.[1]

This dream-story about the disastrous relationship with the feminine continues when King Oeneus of Calydon neglects to honour Artemis after a successful harvest. Angered by this slight, she sends an avenging wild boar, which kills several of the heroes called to the hunt. But with the awarding of the spoils to Atalanta, protegé of Artemis, the

---

1.   Robert Graves translates Talos as "sufferer" and Icarus as "iocarios" meaning "dedicated to the Moon-goddess Car".

tide in the stories turns. With the re-emergence of the feminine (albeit in quite a masculine guise) the boys fight amongst themselves and Meleager kills both his uncles. Althaea, his mother, then suffers the impossible decision of whose side to take—her son or her brothers? She sides with the dominant, regressive masculine forces, throws the brand into the fire, and her son burns from within. In her remorse, Althaea kills herself, and her daughters, Meleager's sisters, are consumed with grief. They cry incessantly until Artemis changes them into guinea fowl, the Meleagrides. Guinea fowl, like the partridge, know how to stay close to the earth and camouflage themselves. The grief of women has been hidden for millennia.

Now we come to a decisive turn in the dream story of Metamorphoses where the emphasis shifts from the contents of the narrative to the authority of the narrator, as the stories are now told by the river-god Achelous and the old and wise Lelex, a companion of Theseus. Rather than the mostly human deeds of Minos, Theseus and Daedalus, the gods and goddesses now play a part, indicating a shift from matter toward spirit, from ego to unconscious. What follows are the stories of Achelous, Baucis and Philemon, and Erysichthon.[2]

River-god

Theseus, having done great deeds in Crete, was returning to Athens but Achelous, swollen with great rains, opposed his journey and delayed his steps.

> "O famous son of Athens, come to me, beneath my roof, and leave my
> rapid floods; for they are wont to bear enormous beams, and hurl up
> heavy stones to bar the way—mighty with roaring, down the steep
> ravines. And I have seen the sheep-folds on my banks swept down the
> flood, together with the sheep; and in the current neither strength
> availed the ox for safety, nor swift speed the horse. When rushed the

---

2. I quote Brookes Moore's translation of Metamorphoses at length in this chapter as it retains the mythic tone of these central stories more so than a modern précis. See also A J Kline, *Ovid: The Metamorphoses*, 547-610.

melting snows from mountain peaks how many bodies of unwary men this flood has overwhelmed in whirling waves! Rest safely then, until my river runs within its usual bounds—till it contains its flowing waters in its proper banks." And gladly answered Theseus, "I will make good use of both your dwelling and advice." And waiting not he entered a rude hut, of porous pumice and of rough stone built. The floor was damp and soft with springy moss, and rows of shells and murex arched the roof.

So the human hero who has overcome the fearsome Minotaur is halted by a force of nature. But nature is welcoming. The river god offers hospitality to Theseus just as in the next story Philemon and Baucis offer hospitality to the gods. In this way matter and spirit remain friends.

After finishing the wine and food, Theseus, looking out over the waters, asked, "Tell me what name the island has, though it seems more than an island!" The river-god replied:

What you see is not one island but five pieces of land that lie together. This will make you less astonished at what Artemis did when she was slighted at Calydon. Those islands were once nymphs. The people had slaughtered ten bullocks and invited the rural gods to the festival, but forgot me as they led the festal dance. I swelled with rage, as fierce as when my flood is at its fullest. I tore forest from forest and field from field, and swept the nymphs into the sea. Then, at last, they remembered me. At the place they walked, the ocean and my waters separated the land and split it into the islands, the Echinades, out there in the waves. But one island is far, far off. The sailors call her Perimele. I loved her and stole her virginity. Her father, unable to accept the loss of her maidenhood, threw his daughter from the cliffs into the sea. I caught her and held her as she swam, I cried: 'O Poseidon, you who rule over the restless waves, and lie closest to the earth, grant a place to one drowning by her father's anger, or allow her to be that place herself!' As I spoke, fresh earth enfolded her body and a solid island rose.

The spirit-in-matter (Achelous) that is neglected and forgotten turns into its destructive form. Matter is *mater*, the mother of us all. Grandmother Earth speaks, not as spirit does through dreams and the unconscious, but through rough matter—weather, seasons, the birds, the four-leggeds, the six-leggeds. All cultures have a history of divinatory practices, the opening of discussions between the visible and non-visible worlds.[3] These relied on the skilled observation of changes in matter to divine the future: the cracks in a heated tortoise shell that became the I Ching; the bones of the Xhosa sangoma; the haruspication of entrails by the Roman augurer; the coffee grounds of the Turkish fortune-teller; or the ceiba seeds of the Maya daykeeper.

Matter—such a neutral word, neutered and without life or emotion, like our attitude. Does the physicist love her electrons, does the chemist have wet dreams about organic compounds, does the economist swoon over his statistics?[4] As William Blake said, "Eternity is in love with the productions of time" so Achelous is in love with, not all the islands in the wine-dark Aegean, but just one. Spirit is in love with matter. The gauzy, diaphanous, saccharin-sweet "love of humanity" or the testos-terone-saturated, patriotic "love of freedom" don't cut it in the rough and tumble world of matter. Love only survives in the affection for the particulars of this person, this curve, this morning sound, this place, this face, this moment. But, but... the love-making between spirit and matter, between Achelous and Perimele, offends her father who throws her off a cliff to her death, just as indigenous cultures have been thrown off the cliff by the father of progress.

This archetypal scene of the enraged father, who imagines he owns matter and the feminine, is alive and well. Some years ago, a police officer in Dubai recounted being called to a tragedy that unfolded during one family's day at the beach. The children were swimming when suddenly, the 20-year-old daughter began to scream for help. Two

---

3. See Marie-Louise von Franz, *On Divination and Synchronicity: The Psychology of Meaningful Chance.*

4. Last year, for instance, four mathematicians proved a new, more accurate upper bound on Ramsey numbers — the first advance of its kind since 1935. "I was floored" on hearing the news, one mathematician said. "I was literally shaking for half an hour to an hour." https://www.quantamagazine.org/why-complete-disorder-is-mathematically-impossible

male life guards rushed to help the young woman. However, the father stopped them. He believed that if these men touched her, she would be dishonoured. He told them that he preferred his daughter to die before being touched by a strange man. He was tall and strong, became violent with the lifeguards, and prevented them from rescuing his daughter. She drowned.[5]

Jung and Philemon

Before we walk down the path towards the final stories in Book VIII of Metamorphoses—those of Baucis and Philemon, and Erysichthon—let's take a jakkalspad past Jung's lifelong relationship with an inner guide and teacher he called Philemon. The name means "loving, affectionate one" from the Greek *philein* "to love." Philos is a "friend" and philo- means "loving, fond of, tending to" as in philanderer, homophilia, philanthropy, philharmonic, Philip, philosophy, Philadelphia and so on. In the Bible, Paul wrote a letter from prison to his friend Philemon.

In his Collected Works Jung, not surprisingly, mentions the name Philemon only twice, in both instances referring to Goethe's Faust. Likewise, in his published letters, he mentions Philemon only twice. He does go into some detail in his autobiographical *Memories, Dreams, Reflections*, which was published not long before he died. His relationship with this inner figure was not publicly articulated in works published during his lifetime.

Privately though, it was a different matter. In 1920, Jung purchased some land on the upper shores of Lake Zurich and in 1923 he began building Bollingen, his country retreat, which he often described as the home of Philemon. In a letter of January 2, 1928 to Count Hermann Keyserling he wrote, "I built a little house way out in the country near the mountains and carved an inscription on the wall: *Philemonis sacrum —Fausti poenitentia*."[6] The inscription was carved over the entrance to

---

5. The father was later arrested and prosecuted. www.emirates247.com/news/emirates/2015-08-09-1.599613
6. *Letters 1*, p. 49, January 2, 1928.

the original Tower at Bollingen. It was covered over when an annex was built in 1927, but Jung carved the inscription again in 1934 above the inner door to his retiring room.

Jung's words are commonly translated as "Shrine of Philemon, Repentance of Faust." The translation of sacrum as shrine, temple, or holy place is clear enough. However, poenitentia has several meanings including regret for what has been done or not done; or the pain, grief or distress associated with contrition, the first of the three acts of penance—contrition, confession and reparation.

The word *poine* in ancient Greek meant "penalty or punishment." In Roman mythology, Poena was the spirit (daimona) of retribution, vengeance, recompense, punishment and penalty for the crime of murder. She attended Nemesis, the goddess of divine retribution. The Latin word *poena* gave rise to English words such as subpoena and penitentiary (*tentia* means power or ability).

So we have a mixture of regret, pain, grief, punishment, and contrition that is associated with repentance. As one of the stages on the way to salvation in the Christian church, repentance is described as a turning away from sin. Penance is one of the seven sacraments of the Catholic church whereby sins against God are absolved. The harsh rigours of early monasticism and the practices of the later Christian church such as abstinence from meat on Fridays as penance, tell us something about the strength of coercion needed to keep the eyes of the faithful turned toward heaven and not straying elsewhere. Psychologically, repentance is the dawning awareness of how we have betrayed others, ourselves and the world by not living our full potential. Ecologically, it is the darkening awareness of how we have sold the only home we have for a mess of pottage.

But penance is not a Twitter apology. It is a long, hard road to living a different life. The early Church knew this and was tough on sinners. First it demanded contrition (Latin, meaning to grind into pieces, crushed, bruised, worn down) with a heart that is humbled, broken and contrite. It is a "sorrow of the soul." Saint Gregory the Great[7] wrote:

---

7. Pope Saint Gregory I (c. 540–604 CE) was Pope from 590 to 604 CE. He instigated the first recorded mission from Rome, the Gregorian Mission, to convert the pagan

"We who have departed from him delighted by pleasures, may return to him embittered by tears... and that the heart which a demented joy had flooded may be burnt clean by wholesome sadness, that what the elation of pride had wounded might be cured by the dejection of a humble heart... Hence it is said 'a bruised and humbled heart God does not despise.'"[8] The dissing of pleasure, joy and pride aside, we know that spirit and the unconscious responds positively to the ego's growing signs of readiness, as Gregory describes. For Christianity the grinding agent was usually guilt and religious coercion. For the psyche, it is the crumbling of long-held attitudes of the ego and submission to the realisation that the old way doesn't work any more.

Next comes confession. For Christians this was a public statement of the ways in which the penitent had offended God—who seems to be easily offended. On the inside, it is a conscious awareness of the collapse of old ways and an attempt to pour the new understanding into the vessels of words or images. Then, and only then, comes the third stage of reparation where the penitent makes amends through prayer, devotions, or sacrifice.

But let's turn all this on its head, because this is where Jung's repentance of Faust leads us. Let's say it's not the Father but the Mother—this planet we live on—whom we have offended and sinned against. Do we have the emotional intelligence, the capacity of heart, the humbleness, to feel sorrow, regret, and contrition for the damage we have wrought? Can we as a collective confess to one another and to the Earth? Will she still listen to the beauty of our praise-songs? Can we begin to make amends and reparation? Or is it too late?

In Memories, Dreams, Reflections and in The Red Book, Jung goes into some detail about his experience of Philemon as an autonomous figure of wisdom, what today might be called a spirit guide.[9] There are those who work with the collective by their presence in this material world—such as the Dalai Lama—and there are those who work with

---

Anglo-Saxons in England to Christianity—an instance of colonisation a thousand years before Columbus.

8. Jeffrey, *A Dictionary of Biblical Tradition in English Literature*, 157.

9. For further details see C G Jung, *Memories, Dreams, Reflections*; *The Red Book*, 200 et seq.; and Owen, *Jung and the Moon Cycles*, 109–114.

individuals by their presence in the other world. As this notion gets no respect in most of Western culture there is no suitable word other than spirit guide which is often associated with flakiness. In some traditions they are called the Dream Teachers.

After he and Freud parted ways in 1912, Jung began his "descent into the unconscious" he experimented with what he later called "active imagination," allowing himself to sink into the dreams or fantasies that his unconscious presented to him. He encountered, in one of his descents into the depths, an old man with a white beard, who explained he was Elijah, and a blind, beautiful young girl who astonished Jung by telling him that her name was Salome.[10] The figure of Elijah soon evolved into Philemon, an old man who was lame and who had the horns of a bull and wings the colour of a kingfisher, and four keys in his right hand. While painting this image, Jung found a dead kingfisher—a rarity in that area—in his garden.

The phenomenological experiences associated with these figures of his inner world brought home to him that there were things in the psyche that had their own life. He then made the discovery that he could talk to the figures he encountered and find out what they wanted of him, and he made it a rule never to let a figure leave until it told him why it had appeared.[11] He began to write down his fantasies in what he called the Black Book and elaborated on them, in the form of paintings (including one of Philemon), in The Red Book. In May 2000 the heirs of Jung's estate decided to permit publication of The Red Book and the Philemon Foundation was established in the early 2000s to bring out his other unpublished works. In Memories he describes his first dream of Philemon:

> There was a blue sky; like the sea, covered not by clouds but by flat
> brown clods of earth. It looked as if the clods were breaking apart and
> the blue water of the sea were becoming visible between them. But the
> water was the blue sky. Suddenly there appeared from the right a
> winged being sailing across the sky. I saw that it was an old man with

10. MDR, 181.
11. Hannah, *Jung: His Life and Work*, 115.

the horns of a bull. He held a bunch of four keys, one of which he clutched as if he were about to open a lock. He had the wings of the kingfisher with its characteristic colours. Since I did not understand this dream image, I painted it in order to impress it upon my memory.[12]

He mentions him in his Zurich lectures in 1925 and in The Red Book:

[Philemon] said I treated thoughts as if I generated them myself, but, according to his views, thoughts were like animals in a forest, or people in a room, or birds in the air. He said, "If you should see people in a room, you would not say that you made those people, or that you were responsible for them." Only then I learned psychological objectivity. Only then could I say to a patient, "Be quiet, something is happening." There are such things as mice in a house.... For the understanding of the unconscious we must see our thoughts as events, as phenomena.[13]

Oh Philemon? Truly you are the lover who once took in the Gods as they wandered the earth when everyone else refused them lodging. You are the one who unsuspectingly gave hospitality to the Gods; they thanked you by transforming your house into a golden temple, while the flood swallowed everyone else. You remained alive when chaos erupted. You it was who served in the sanctuary when the peoples called out in vain to the Gods. Truly, it is the lover who survives. Why did we not see that? And just when did the Gods manifest? Precisely when Baucis wished to serve the esteemed guests her only goose, that blessed stupidity: the animal fled to the Gods who then revealed themselves to their poor hosts, who had given their last. Thus I saw that the lover survives, and that he is the one who unwittingly grants hospitality to the Gods.[14]

---

12. MDR, 207.
13. C G Jung, *Introduction to Jungian Psychology: Notes of the Seminar on Analytical Psychology Given in 1925*, 103.
14. *The Red Book*, 315.

So it is the lover who survives. Not the fittest, not the strongest, not the boldest, not the faith-ful, not the elect, not the martyrs. I set Jung's words alongside those from another tradition.

> "The life of a warrior cannot possibly be cold and lonely and without feelings," Don Genaro [Carlos Castaneda's nagual benefactor] said, "because it is based on his affection, his devotion, his dedication to his beloved. And who, you may ask, is his beloved? I will show you now." [he spins above the ground]... "This is the predilection of two warriors," [Don Juan] said. "This earth, this world. For a warrior there can be no greater love.... Only if one loves this earth with unbending passion can one release one's sadness," don Juan said. "A warrior is always joyful because his love is unalterable and his beloved, the earth, embraces him and bestows upon him inconceivable gifts. The sadness belongs only to those who hate the very thing that gives shelter to their beings." Don Juan again caressed the ground with tenderness. "This lovely being, which is alive to the last recesses and understands every feeling, soothed me, it cured me of my pains, and finally when I had fully understood my love for it, it taught me freedom".[15]

Baucis and Philemon

During the gradual emergence of the shoots of this book from the late 1980s onward I was puzzled by the fact that little had been written by Jungians about the Baucis and Philemon myth in Ovid's Metamorphoses, even after the publication by the Philemon Foundation in 2009 of Jung's Red Book, which contained his paintings of Philemon. What was this curious caesura in the Jungian literature— an elision, a blind spot, an omission? And why? Jung, privately anyway, was a thinking-intuitive seer who was prophetic—and by that I mean able to see outside his time and culture—and an easy target for cheap scepticism. Were Jungians gun-shy about showing this face of Jung more boldly? But it doesn't matter really. Jung has already done the work in the dream and it will bear fruit in its own time.

---

15. Castaneda, *Tales of Power*, 292–293.

The story of Baucis and Philemon appears nowhere else in Greek or Roman mythology other than in Metamorphoses. I originally intended to write only about the Baucis and Philemon story. But I went back to Book VIII of Metamorphoses and found, to my surprise, that the stories that come before (Minos and Scylla and onwards) and after (Erysichthon and Mestra) were part of a larger arc. I had not intended to write about these myths but they pointed to wider themes—spirit, the unconscious, and the feminine—that concerned Jung throughout his life. Metamorphoses was written at the beginning of the Age of Pisces and Jung wrote at length in Aion about the changes during and at the end of the Piscean Age and the future of humankind. Both Ovid and Jung are prophetic. As a result, I have included all the stories in Book VIII.

Briefly, the story tells of an older couple who offer *xenia* or hospitality to Zeus and Hermes who are travelling in disguise and had been turned away at many a door on their travels. One who does not welcome the stranger is a xenophobe. After receiving food and drink from Baucis and Philemon the gods reveal themselves and Zeus' punishment for the xenophobia of the other inhabitants of the land was to bring a great flood. Baucis and Philemon were saved and their humble home was turned into a temple to the gods where they served until they died together, transformed into an oak and a linden tree.

But first let's go back to Achelous' story of Perimele. After telling the story the river-god fell silent. The story had gripped them all but one. Ixion's haughty son Pirithous—a known despiser of the living Gods—scorned it as an idle tale. He laughed at those who heard, and said, "A foolish fiction, Achelous! How can such a tale be true? Do you believe there is a god in heaven so powerful, a god to transform created shapes?"

Scepticism is good. It is a questioning attitude toward any body of knowledge or belief. Its modern version, regrettably, is scientific scepticism that takes suspicious pleasure in hunting down pseudoscience and irrationality, and bringing light into the ignorance and darkness of superstition and folk-belief. However, modern scepticism only has one gear and one direction. It is unable to be sceptical about itself. Scepticism is an issue of the father-line and is the conjoined twin of religious faith via their shared certainty. So in order to understand it, we might first look to Perithous' father, Ixion.

Ixion murdered his father-in-law and was driven mad with guilt by what he had done. The neighbouring rulers were so offended by his act of treachery and violation of xenia (hospitality, guest-friendship) that they refused to perform the rituals that would cleanse him of his guilt. In Greek mythology, he was the first man guilty of slaying his own kin-folk. He was shunned by those around him. However, Zeus took pity on Ixion and brought him to Olympus. But instead of being grateful for Zeus' hospitality, he grew lustful for Hera, Zeus's wife, and tried to rape her, a further violation of xenia. Zeus found out about this and wanted to determine if the report was true so he made a cloud-nymph (Nephele) in the shape of Hera and tricked Ixion into coupling with it. (From the union of Ixion and Nephele came the Centaurs— chimeras like the Minotaur, born of an improper union). When Ixion bragged that he had slept with Hera, Zeus ordered Hermes to bind him to a fiery winged wheel that was set spinning across the heavens for eternity.

This Greek version of the Christian hell or the karmic wheel shows how seriously hubris and the violation of xenia was regarded. Philostratus said, "If you only would bear in mind the fate of Ixion, you would never have dreamed of falling in love with beings so much above you. For he, you remember, is bent and stretched across the heaven like a wheel." So even before the story of Baucis and Philemon is told we have a hint of a lineage getting above itself, of inhospitable conduct and its punishment.

Wise Lelex then rebuts Perithous with his own experience of seeing the two sacred trees of Baucis and Philemon and describes a watery realm where transformation can take place.

> Such impious words by Pirithous found no response in those who
> heard him speak. Amazed he could so doubt the truth before them all,
> Lelex, wise in length of days, stood to vindicate the Gods. The glory of
> the living Gods, he said, knows no limit and whatsoever they decree
> comes to pass. And I have this to tell, for all must know the falsehood
> of such words. Upon the hills of Phrygia I have seen two sacred trees, a
> lime-tree and an oak, so closely grown their branches interlace. A low

stone wall is built around to guard them from all harm. And so you may not doubt it, I have seen the place, for Pittheus had sent me there to attend his father's court. Nearby are stagnant pools and fens, once habitable land, now the haunt of coots and cormorants. But it was not so always.

So there we have it—the opposites are struck—Lelex versus Pirithous. Science versus religion, personal experience versus personal opinion, wisdom versus knowledge, faith versus reason, spirit versus matter. Perithous' scoffing at tradition and not-yet-seen things is reserved for the young, chronologically or culturally, and science is young, let's say 500 years old at most. It is Lelex, the one of age, wisdom and words, who takes him to task. He says he has seen something with his own eyes near a place full of life—a swamp.

Swamps, and other wet, dark muddy places, are not much valued by our culture. Not high enough for a good view, can't build there, can't swim there, can't surf there, who knows what lurks underneath, breeds malaria and disease, not deep enough to sail on, propellers and weeds don't get along, and they're generally unfit for human habitation. James Hollis, Jungian analyst, titles his book *Swamplands of the soul: new life in dismal places*. Tolkien describes the Dead Marshes, near the Gates of Mordor: "Cold, clammy winter still held sway in this forsaken country. The only green was the scum of livid weed on the dark, greasy, milky surfaces of the sullen waters. Dead grasses and rotting reeds loomed up in the mists like ragged shadows of long forgotten summers."

But life arose from Carboniferous swamps. Marshes, swamps, bogs, muskeg, quagmires, wetlands, bayous, sloughs and fens are found worldwide—the Amazon floodplain, the wetlands of the Tigris-Euphrates river system (the Fertile Crescent and so-called cradle of civilisation according to Western history books), the Okavango Delta in Botswana, the Brazilian Pantanal (the largest wetland in the world), the Okefenokee swamp in Georgia, the Great Dismal Swamp in Virginia, the Florida Everglades, and the Hudson Bay muskeg in Ontario.

Unproductive and with little "property value," low lying areas and swamps have been "reclaimed" for agriculture and habitation by humans for thousands of years. Europe has lost almost half its wetlands.

New Zealand has lost 90% of its wetlands in only 150 years.[16] The world may have lost over 80% of its wetlands since 1700 CE.[17] We are reminded here of Goethe's story of Faust. Faust meets his end in the midst of great plans to extend the land granted to him by the Emperor by draining the marshes and pushing back the sea. On the reclaimed land, he plans to establish a paradise on Earth where he believes humankind, having vanquished the forces of nature, will become free. We may not like our liver or kidneys but our body cannot live without them. Mangrove swamps are essential for water filtration and purification. Other swamp-gifts are flood control, fish production, carbon storage, and wildlife habitat. All for free!

> Long ago, Lelex continued, this place was visited by mighty Zeus, together with his nimble-witted son, Hermes, who first had set aside his rod and wings. They wandered as weary travellers over all the land, begging for their food and bed. And at a thousand houses, all the doors were bolted and no word of kindness given—so wicked were the people of that land. At last, by chance, they stopped at a small house, whose humble roof was thatched with reeds and straw—and here a kind old couple greeted them. The good dame, Baucis, and Philemon, her devoted man, seemed of the same age. They had been wedded in their early youth, in that very cottage and had lived in it, and grown together to a good old age. They were contented with their lot because they knew their poverty, and felt no shame of it. They had no need of servants; the good pair were masters of their home and served themselves; each the other's commands were easily obeyed.

The tradition of xenia—hospitality to the stranger—has existed in all cultures throughout history. The stranger, unknown as yet, is neither friend nor foe. Psychologically, we might think of it as welcoming,

---

16. New Zealand Department of Conservation, "New Zealand's Wetlands at Risk: 2 February 2018." www.doc.govt.nz/news/2018/new-zealands-wetlands-at-risk
17. The reported long-term loss of natural wetlands since 1700 CE averages between 54–57% but the loss may be as high as 87%. There has been a much (3.7 times) faster rate of wetland loss during the 20th and early 21st centuries, with a loss of 64–71% of wetlands since 1900 CE. Davidson, "How Much Wetland Has the World Lost?"

having curiosity toward what life brings us, without pre-judgement until it reveals its true nature, good or ill, to us. But the rational ego is xenophobic towards what is not familiar. Psychological hospitality welcomes what life offers us, inner or outer. It provides sanctuary for the divine. Marie-Louise von Franz said this about the unknown visitor:

> This tale of Ovid's [Baucis and Philemon] was extremely timely: as happens periodically in the course of history, all religious life in his time had become calcified into purely external state ceremonies and had thus lost its psychic influence on humanity. In the Roman ruling class, power prevailed rather than interpersonal Eros, form rather than inner experience. Jupiter was no longer a living archetypal figure of order in the human psyche, but rather the guarantor of power to the Roman Empire. As for Mercury, it was primarily his mercantile side that had developed, his deceitful and thievish character. He was no longer the purveyor of hidden messages from the beyond and also no longer the god of love and fertility who had once come from Mount Cyllene. Patriarchal order overshadowed the maternal domain of outer and inner nature. Although the poets of that period compensatorily sang the praises of return to the bucolic life, this remained a sentimental, aesthetic game hovering above the abyss of melancholy that smoldered in the depths of the psyche.
>
> This motif of a god or gods who come to men [like Khidr, or Elijah at the seder] in a disguised form is an archetypal theme that crops up in many areas of culture, but as it seems to me, always as a compensation for a similar need. That is to say, it crops up at a time when personal encounter with and individual relationship to the divine has become a necessity, outside the institutionalised forms and views of religious life…. In the Ukraine today, people still say, "Guest in the house, God in the house"; and in my opinion the ubiquitous belief in the sacredness and inviolability of the right of the guest to hospitality belongs to the same archetypal motif as the god who comes down to humanity as an unknown visitor.[18]

---

18. Von Franz, 'The unknown visitor in fairy tales and dreams'. In *Archetypal Dimensions of the Psyche*, 59.

Entering the humble home, Hermes sets aside his wings and his caduceus, the staff with intertwined snakes surmounted by wings. Now he has become earthbound and predictable but is still the god of boundaries, transitions, and the crack-between-the-worlds, the mercurial trickster around whom miracles happen. He is accompanied into the cottage by his father, the mighty Zeus. So the lowest of the low provides shelter for the highest of the high. As well, their arrival is secret, veiled and disguised. The humans don't know that gods walk among them. This is not lightning bolts, wheels of fire, or the heavens opening like a God who goes to great lengths to impress with his power. No, they are just ordinary travellers until the wine, the blood of life, the offering to the gods, the sacrament, the draught of spirit, the gift of communion between humans and gods, is miraculously replenished.

With bending necks Zeus and Hermes entered the low door. The old man bade them rest their wearied limbs, and set a bench, on which his good wife, Baucis, threw a cloth. Then with kindly bustle she stirred up the glowing embers on the hearth, and then laid tinder, leaves and bark. Bending down she breathed on them with her ancient breath until they kindled into flame. Then from the house she brought a store of faggots, small twigs, and broken branches, and above them swung a kettle, not too large for simple folk. And all this done, she stripped some cabbage leaves, which her good husband gathered for the meal. With a two-pronged fork he let down a chine of bacon, which had been carefully saved, from aloft, cut a little portion and put it to seethe in boiling water.

All the while they tried with cheerful conversation to beguile, so none might notice a brief loss of time. Swung on a peg they had a beechwood trough, which quickly with warm water filled, was used for comfortable washing. And they fixed, upon a willow couch, a cushion soft of springy sedge, on which they neatly spread a well-worn cloth preserved so many years; 'twas only used on rare and festive days; and even it was coarse and very old, though not unfit to match a willow couch!

Now as the Gods reclined, the good old dame, whose skirts were tucked up, moving carefully, for so she tottered with her many years, fetched a clean table for the ready meal—but one leg of the table was too short, and so she wedged it with a potsherd—so made firm, she cleanly scoured it with fresh mint. And here is set the double-tinted fruit of chaste Minerva, and the tasty dish of cornels, autumn-picked and pickled; these were served for relish; and the endive-green, and radishes surrounding a large pot of curdled milk; and eggs not over-done but gently turned in glowing embers—all served up in earthen dishes. Then sweet wine served up in clay, so costly! all embossed, and cups of beechwood smoothed with yellow wax. So now they had short respite, till the fire might yield the heated course. Again they served new wine, but mellow; and a second course: sweet nuts, dried figs and wrin-kled dates and plums, and apples fragrant, in wide baskets heaped; and, in a wreath of grapes from purple vines, concealed almost, a glistening honeycomb; and all these orchard dainties were enhanced by willing service and congenial smiles.

Our story now tarries over simple but sumptuous taste, smell, sound and colour. The unsteady table, eggs not overdone, springy sedge, the chine seething in the pot. Two kinds of experience remain memorable over many years. One, when we are outside of ourselves—ex-stasis or ecstasy. The other, its opposite—for which we have no ready word for because it hides in plain sight and falls unnoticed beneath eyes that look upward—is the texture of detail, the small things, the smell, the sound, the wind, the sky, the look, the touch that leaves its impression on our skin and its memory in our body. So the gods come down to Earth and they are met with the earthiness of the shared meal and the hospitality of Baucis and Philemon. As much as those in physical bodies wish to ascend to spirit, to leave, to see diaphanous forms, to progress to higher planes, so the spirits are queueing up to get into this world to touch and be touched by its beauty known nowhere else in all of Creation.

But while they served, the wine-bowl often drained, as often was replenished, though unfilled, and Baucis and Philemon, full of fear, as they observed the wine spontaneously increasing when it should dimin-ish, raised their hands in supplication, and implored indulgence for their simple home and fare. And now, persuaded by this strange event

such visitors were deities unknown, this aged couple, anxious to bestow
their most esteemed possession, hastily began to chase the only goose
they had—the faithful guardian of their little home—which they
would kill and offer to the Gods. But swift of wing, at last it wearied
them, and fled for refuge to the smiling Gods. At once the deities
forbade their zeal, and said, "A righteous punishment shall fall severe
upon this wicked neighbourhood; but by the might of our divinity, no
evil shall befall this humble home; but you must come, and follow as we
climb the summit of this mountain!"

When Zeus and Hermes revealed their presence, Baucis and Philemon
were willing to sacrifice their goose, to bestow their most esteemed
possession and their provider of food and protection. But the goose
took shelter in the lap of the gods. As with all sacrifices, it is the motivation that matters not the form. Zeus and Hermes did not want the
goose sacrificed but wanted to know if the humans were willing to make
a sacrifice. A material symbol of the event will do if it is infused with
immaterial heart and spirit. As soon as the goose spoke to them by
taking shelter in the lap the gods, the old couple stopped their wild
goose chase.

The goose is a waterbird and flies between earth and sky. It is found
around bodies of fresh water. Water dissolves, baptises, mixes, cleanses,
invigorates, it invites change, solution and dissolution. Brahma, the first
creator, was often shown mounted on a goose. Nemesis tried to escape
Zeus's attentions by changing into a goose. Aphrodite rode a goose. In
the fifty-third hexagram of the I-Ching (Development/Gradual
Progress) the individual lines symbolise the gradual but unerring flight
of the wild goose. Around the Great Lakes of Ontario thousands of
geese flying noisily above herald the coming of winter or, on their
return, spring. They take us to other places and other times, they tell us
that another season has passed in the turning of the circle of life. Mary
Oliver writes, beautifully, about "Wild Geese":

> You do not have to be good.
> You do not have to walk on your knees
> for a hundred miles through the desert repenting.

You only have to let the soft animal of your body
love what it loves....
Meanwhile the wild geese, high in the clean blue air,
are heading home again.
Whoever you are, no matter how lonely,
the world offers itself to your imagination,
calls to you like the wild geese, harsh and exciting -
over and over announcing your place
in the family of things.

The wild goose is a symbol of conjugal fidelity because it is believed that the surviving bird never takes another mate after the death of the first. Domestic geese have been used for centuries as watch animals and guardians. They are aggressive, protective of their flock, and will make noise if intruded upon. But the goose also has connotations of fatefulness as well as faithfulness. If someone's "goose is cooked" it means that their fate is set and misfortune will befall them. "A wild goose chase" is a futile waste of time and effort. In Aesop's fables we read of "killing the goose that lays the golden egg," warning about the inevitable perils of greed, compulsively wanting more, and the act of killing the very thing that provides what is of highest value.

Now comes the archetypal story of the apocalypse, the flood, Ragnarok, or the great conflagration, after which only a few survive.

> Both obeyed [Zeus' command] and, leaning on their staves, toiled up the steep hill. Not farther from the summit than the flight of one swift arrow from a hunter's bow, they paused to view their little home once more; and as they turned their eyes, they saw the fields around their own engulfed in a morass, although their own remained—and while they wept bewailing the sad fate of many friends, and wondered at the change, they saw their home, so old and little for their simple need— put on new splendour, and as it increased it changed into a temple of the gods. Where first the frame was fashioned of rude stakes columns of marble glistened, and the thatch gleamed golden in the sun, and legends carved, adorned the doors. And all the ground shone white with marble rich, and after this was done, the Son of Saturn said with gentle voice,

"Now tell us, good old man and you his wife, worthy and faithful, what is your desire?"

Philemon counselled with old Baucis first; and then discovered to the listening Gods their hearts' desire, "We pray you let us have the care of your new temple; and since we have passed so many years in harmony, let us depart this life together—let the same hour take us both—I would not see the tomb of my dear wife; and let me not be destined to be buried by her hands!

At once their wishes were fulfilled. So long as life was granted they were known to be the temple's trusted keepers, and when age had enervated them with many years, as they were standing, by some chance, before the sacred steps, and were relating all these things as they had happened, Baucis saw Philemon, her old husband, and he, too, saw Baucis, as their bodies put forth leaves; and while the tops of trees grew over them, above their faces—they spoke each to each; as long as they could speak they said, "Farewell, farewell, my own"—and while they said farewell; new leaves and branches covered both at once.

The people of Thynia still point out two trees which grew there from a double trunk, two forms made into one. Old truthful men, who have no reason to deceive me, told me truly all that I have told to you, and I have seen the votive wreaths hung from the branches of the hallowed double-tree.[19] And one time, as I hung fresh garlands there, I said, "Those whom the Gods care for are Gods! And those who worshipped are now worshipped here."

The oak is known for its strength and endurance. The density of the wood means that it burns bright and long, and has great strength for building. It is the national tree of the USA and many other countries. It was sacred to Zeus and to Thor in Norse mythology. The linden (known as basswood in North America and the lime tree in the UK) is sacred in Slavic mythology and is the national tree of Slovenia. Its wood can be sanded to a smooth finish and is resistant to warping once seasoned. From the bast under the bark of the basswood strong cordage

---

19. In Thailand large trees often have offerings placed at their feet or sashes wrapped around their trunks.

and rope can be made and the honey gathered from basswood flowers has a distinctive taste and fragrance. The oak and the linden are both trees that throw up circles of suckers around themselves. Their circles of life overlap.

The dance is both one and two, each separate but intertwined. "Each the other's commands were easily obeyed." Gone are the necessary urgings and urgent necessities of the first half of life. Gone is the longing for oneness. The oak and the linden are symbols of the masculine and feminine in good relation. Providing a home for the gods and goddesses in the smallness of things, on this small Earth, is what survives the flood.

The man who ate himself

So we end the Baucis and Philemon story with the old couple, lovers of their place and each other, tending the shrine of the gods and then, at the moment of death, shape-shifting into the intertwined trees, forever in each other's embrace. Importantly for us, the story that comes immediately after that of Baucis and Philemon is the compensatory story of Erysichthon. His name means "earth tearer".

The first we hear of the story of Erysichthon is in the *Hymn to Demeter* by the Hellenic poet Callimachus (c. 305–240 BCE). Better known though is the story by Ovid. Both Callimachus and Ovid tell the first part of the story but Ovid adds, significantly I think, a second part involving Erysichthon's daughter, Mestra.

The story begins with mention of Proteus, the shape-shifting sea god who has the gift of prophecy. Now our story moves from the permanence of the trees, whose toes hold fast to the land, to the ever-changing sea and the possibility of foretelling the future.

> Lelex finished his story, and this miraculous event, and he who told it,
> had astonished them. But Theseus above all. The hero asked to hear of
> other wonders wrought by Gods. The Calydonian River-God replied,
> and leaning on one elbow, said to him: "There are, O valiant hero,
> other things whose forms once-changed as these, have so remained, but
> there are some who take on many shapes, as you have, Proteus, dweller

of the deep—the deep whose arms embrace the Earth. For some have
seen you as a youth, then as a lion, a furious boar one time, a serpent
next, so dreadful to the touch—and sometimes horns have made you
seem a bull—or now a stone, or now a tree, or now a slipping stream, or
even—the foe of water—next a fire".

Proteus was the eldest son of Poseidon, the sea god. He was the
herdsman of the sea-creatures belonging to his father. In Greek *protos*
means first, and in English the word protean means the first form,
capable of assuming many forms, continually changing in nature, and
showing great flexibility or versatility. Proteus had the gift of prophecy
but avoided those who questioned him about the future by changing
shape and form. He would only yield and answer to those who captured
him in the form he took.

Jung wrote at length about Mercurius, the elusive spirit sought by
the alchemists, who has much in common with Proteus. The physical
element of mercury is poisonous and slippery, it reacts and combines
with everything, and it gets away from us. It has to be chased and caught
and bottled. But, like capturing mercury, knowledge of the future, the
unknown, the unconscious, the way things are going, is only attained
with some effort. This effort is a marriage of introverted, feminine intuition and extraverted, masculine action.

In Homer's *Odyssey* (c. 8th century BCE) Menelaus became
becalmed on his journey home from Troy. He learned from Proteus'
daughter Eidothea ("the knowing goddess") that if he could capture her
father, he could force him to reveal which of the gods he had offended
and how he could propitiate them and return home. *Eido* in Greek
means to see, perceive, pay attention to, to know, to understand. *Thea*
means goddess. Euripides said that Eidothea had divine knowledge of all
things present and to come—a gift inherited from her grandfather
Nereus who was the eldest son of Pontus, the Sea, and Gaia, the Earth.
Thus all matter has memory of its past and its future.

For the early Greeks all of nature was a visible manifestation of the
divinities. Every spring, river, waterfall, swamp, cleft, cliff, hill and
mountain was inhabited by the spirit of the place. Nature was alive and
personified, no less real than gravity or mitochondria. The tides of

human affairs were governed by the unseen gods and goddesses who moved among people and took great interest their doings. Even our most human capacities for thought and emotion were an expression of their presence. Among the children of Aether (Air) and Gaia (Earth) were Dolor (Pain), Dolus (Deceit), Ira (Wrath), Penthos (Lamentation), Ultio (Vengeance), Intemperantia (Intemperance), Altercatio (Altercation), Oblivio (Forgetfulness), Timor (Fear), Superbia (Pride), Incestum (Incest), Pugna (Combat), and so on.

Western consciousness, disparagingly, calls this cosmology panpsychism or animism, and regards it as a characteristic of "primitive" societies. "Primitive" is a word peculiar to Judeo-Christian-Islamic consciousness, a consciousness that pities those peoples it characterises as backward and as having yet to achieve a moral or judicial code, who surrender themselves fatalistically to the forces of nature, who know nothing of free will, freedom, and the power to shape one's own life. But these same civilised cultures had their origins in their surrender of free will to a single God who ruled them all and who was tyrannical in his retribution and punishment and equally tyrannical in his love and forgiveness.

In the Odyssey, the goddess Eidothea came upon Menelaus when he was close to nature, by himself, and away from the collective. There was no extroverted action on his part, just a receptive opening. Since always, people have gone to the places that are far from people and close to nature—the desert, the mountaintop, the bush—to find their own nature. But this is not solitary navel-gazing. Watching what happens inside and outside, sitting with the four elements in the four directions, receiving the boost of the Earth, noticing the obvious, calling in the teachers, attending to dreams—allows inner and outer to draw closer. And it's hard work—not 9 to 5 hard work but work requiring focus, attention and not going to sleep in front of the TV.

As the worlds of spirit and matter draw closer, the lightning bolt of illumination, the flash of insight, the moment of conversion, of surrender, jumps the gap between them. But long before such exhibitions of light and fire, the soft darkness was there, rising up from the ground beneath our feet through our cells and blood and breath. Why do we need fireworks, displays of divinity and power that transform sinners into saints, bad guys into good guys—and all in the twinkling of an eye? These demonstrations are only needed if we're a bit thick and have refused the moist wisdom of the Earth.

Alone on the shore, Menelaus is visited by the goddess. Eidothea tells him that an ancient sea-god, Proteus of Aigyptos [Egypt], a vassal of Poseidon, often comes to this place:

> If you can ambush and capture him then he will tell you how to return home. At midday he lies down to sleep under the arching caves, and around him is a throng of seals. You must disguise yourself in seal skins. First Proteus will pass along all the seals and count them; then, having viewed them and made his reckoning, he will lie down among them all like a shepherd among his flock of sheep. As soon as you see him lying down, you must all summon up your strength and courage and hold him fast there despite his struggles and his endeavours to elude you. He will seek to foil you by taking the shape of every creature that moves on earth, and of water and of portentous fire; but you must hold him unflinchingly and you must press the harder. When at length he puts away all disguise and questions you in the shape he had when you saw him resting, then cease from your constraint.

Cunning, thieving and trickery were common amongst the Greek heroes—no compulsive, moral, upright honesty here; no don't ever tell a lie; no cunning that shades into cruelty; no one-dimensional courage and bravery when the occasion requires something different—and this occasion requires some trickery (albeit with the help of the goddess). Proteus will only tell us the future if we can recognise who he is and catch him in the form he has changed to. He is Mercurius. He is a trickster, In other words, we must be flexible and prepared to see what might show up disguised as something else, hidden in plain sight, and in plain form. Don Juan called it "catching the cubic centimetre of chance".

The future is not fixed, it too has will and intention. To strip it of personage, as if we can create and are fully in charge of our own future, is offensive. It will reveal itself only to those it thinks have half a chance of doing something with what is revealed. All things (most anyway) are double-layered, two-faced, duplex, manifest and latent, this world and the other world, matter and spirit. The great enterprise of science has been to take things at face value, only one side, just as they are, just the facts, ma'am. This was in reaction to centuries of superstition, false gods, folk beliefs, old wives tales, fairy tales, fallacies and myths that had been denuded of their symbolic and life-giving meaning. Only the desiccated husk of collective beliefs remained. It was time for a change and so the Age of Enlightenment was born.

But now the great pendulum of history has swung too far the other way. Instead of collective panic at some approaching apocalypse, or the fear of hell and damnation hectored from a Sunday morning pulpit, there is a collective numbness at the disenchantment of the world. We are left one-legged and one-dimensional, unable to catch Proteus in the form in which he appears. Mercury escapes us—it's all just a coincidence, a random event, not statistically significant, not above the base rate or, more often, we don't even see it. Achelous continues his story:

> Erysichthon's daughter, Mestra, had that power of Proteus. Her father
> scorned the majesty of all the Gods, and gave no honour to their altars.
> It is said he violated with an impious axe the sacred grove of Demeter,
> and he cut her trees with iron. Longstanding in her grove there grew an
> ancient oak tree, spread so wide, alone it seemed a standing forest; and
> its trunk and branches held memorials, fillets of wool, votive tablets,
> garlands of flowers, witnessing how many prayers the goddess Demeter
> granted. And underneath it laughing Dryads loved to whirl in festal
> dances, hand in hand, encircling its enormous trunk, that thrice five ells
> [about twenty metres] might measure; and to such a height it towered
> over all the trees around, as they were higher than the grass beneath.

Callimachus in his *Hymn to Demeter* (3rd century BCE) also describes the beauty of Demeter's grove:

> In holy Dotion dwelt the Pelasgians and unto thyself [Demeter/Ceres]
> they made a fair grove abounding in trees; hardly would an arrow have
> passed through them. Therein was pine, and therein were mighty elms,
> and therein were pear-trees, and therein were fair sweet-apples; and
> from the ditches gushes up water as it were of amber. And the goddess

loved the place to madness, even as Eleusis, as Triopion [in Karia], as Enna [in Sicily].

Erysichthon was the son of Triopas and when ill-fortune befell the house of Triopas, he resolved to build a banquet hall. He hastened to Demeter's grove with twenty attendants, all men-giants armed with hatchets and double axes. He shamelessly rushed into the grove saying to the priestess, "Vie back, lest I fix my great axe in thy flesh! These trees shall make my tight dwelling wherein evermore I shall hold pleasing banquets enough for my companions".[20]

In Callimachus' story Erysichthon's mother makes excuses for him to avoid the coming of age rituals like boar-hunting. The classical scholar Torresson makes the case for Erysichthon regressing to a child-like state with appetites that are out of control. He describes a boy-man who believes the world is his, and he can do what he wants with it. Globally, this is our economic culture and individually it is Donald Trump. So it seems that Erysichthon wants to cut down Demeter's sacred grove so he can build a cosy place to have a good feed with his mates. What could go wrong?

The oak, as we have seen, has heart, endurance, longevity and strength. Rocks, sands, soils, minerals, gems, and crystals hold the phys-ical memory of a place over the span of aeons. Trees marry earth and sky and hold the emotional memory of a place over human generations. So stones and trees both serve as memorials, as keepers of memory, the recollection of what is not here but is always present. But now does anyone ask the granite if it longs to become a headstone? Or the oak if it wishes to be spoken to? Our discourtesy is profound.

Trees and groves (most trees like to live in a community) are sacred in all cultures—banyan, oak, ash, kauri, totara, or ceiba trees. In the Bhagavad-Gita, there is a fig tree rooted in heaven with its branches reaching earthward, each of whose leaves is a song of the Vedas. Yggdrasil is the cosmic tree of Norse mythology that connects heaven and earth and has nine roots plunging into nine springs, and the nine branches reach toward the nine heavens. The name means "ash tree" or

---

20. www.theoi.com/Olympios/DemeterWrath.html#Erysikhthon

"Odin's horse". Odin hung from the World Tree for nine days and nine nights, pierced by a spear, without food or water, before he received the wisdom of the Runes. On the ninth night he regained memory of what he had forgotten and saw the reflection of the Runes in the water. The Sephiroth of the Cabala are pictured as an inverted tree—a symbol which is also found in alchemy. It has its roots in the air and its branches in the "glorified earth" of a future world.

Trees are always associated with growth and learning and becoming (think of Eve and the Tree of Knowledge, and just look at your Kindle app). For the Maya the giant ceiba tree and the Milky Way were both the World Tree. (I omit the verb "called" which implies a separation between subject and object. The ceiba tree was the Milky Way. The Milky Way was the ceiba tree.) The ceiba produces small white flowers that are the souls of humans just as the Milky Way produces stars. The flower-soul grows and participates in creation by being cooked—by gaining a face and a heart. The ceiba tree follows the cycle of the Milky Way. It blossoms in the month before the Maya creation day of February 5 and bears fruit in the dry season around the spring equinox, March 21, just before the planting of maize. Humans are the blossoms of the World Tree raised from the three hearthstones of creation in Orion. The tree symbolises the growth of the human personality and the flowering of the soul. The World Tree is rooted in the lower world of the heavens and it flowers in the upper world of humans. We might also say that its roots are in the human sky and its branches are in the heavenly earth. Like the soul, it grows upwards to the sky and downward into the earth.

Trees have a spirit. In ancient Greece the spirits of place and nature were the nymphs. In other traditions they were called the elementals, little people, or fairies. The Naiads inhabited springs and streams. The Oreads lived in the mountains. Nereids lived in open water. Dryads inhabited trees and groves. Now, into this grove, in this place full of life and spirit, comes Erysichthon who refuses to bow to the majesty of the gods. Let's see what happens.

> Erysichthon, heedless of all things, ordered his men to fell the sacred
> oak, and as they hesitated, in a rage the wretch snatched from the hand
> of one an axe, and said, "If this should be the only oak loved by the

goddess of this very grove, or even were the goddess in this tree, I'll level to the ground its leafy head." So boasted he, and while he swung on high his axe to strike a slanting blow, the oak beloved of Demeter uttered a deep groan and shuddered. Instantly its dark green leaves turned pale, and all its acorns lost their green, and even its long branches drooped their arms. But when his impious hand had struck the trunk, and cut its bark, red blood poured from the wound—as when a weighty sacrificial bull has fallen at the altar, streaming blood spouts from his stricken neck. All were amazed.

Blood poured out of the wound. Yes, this tree is alive. To slay a tree sacred to Demeter was the desecration of something holy. Not only the act of felling of the tree but more importantly the attitude that would impel, or allow, Erysichthon to do that. Hardly first-degree murder, you might say. But look at what happens next.

One of his attendants boldly tried to stay his axe and spare the tree further damage but Erysichthon, fixing his stern eyes upon him, said, "Let this, then, be the price of all your pious worship!" So he turned the poised axe from the tree, and sheared his head from his body, and again began to chop the hard oak.

Once our feeling of kinship with all things is lost then the ploughing, the digging, the mining, and the clear-cutting become gateway drugs to the murder of our human kin. The threshold is lowered, the inhibitions are lessened, and the grandiosity is fed.

As he hewed the great tree a voice was heard from its heart; "Covered by the bark of this oak tree I long have dwelt a Nymph, beloved of Demeter, and before my death it has been granted me to prophesy, that I may die contented. Punishment for this vile deed stands waiting at your side." But no warning could avert his wicked arm. Much weakened by his countless blows, the tree, pulled down by straining ropes, gave way at last and levelled with its weight uncounted trees that grew around it.

Ovid's version of Erysichthon's ravaging of Demeter's grove is not the only one. We hear a similar telling (c. 723 CE) but with a different moral tone in St Boniface's account of the Christianisation of the Germanic peoples.

> Now at that time many of the Hessians, brought under the Catholic faith and confirmed by the grace of the sevenfold spirit, received the laying on of hands; others indeed, not yet strengthened in soul, refused to accept the lessons of the inviolate faith. Moreover some were wont secretly to sacrifice to trees and springs; others openly practised inspections of victims and divinations, legerdemain and incantations; some turned their attention to auguries and auspices and various sacrificial rites; while others, with sounder minds, abandoned all the profanations of heathenism.
>
> With the advice and counsel of these last, the saint attempted, to fell a certain oak of extraordinary size, which is called, by an old name of the pagans, the Oak of Jupiter. And when in the strength of his steadfast heart he had cut the lower notch, there was present a great multitude of pagans, who in their souls were earnestly cursing the enemy of their gods. But when the fore side of the tree was notched only a little, suddenly the oak's vast bulk, driven by a blast from above, crashed to the ground, shivering its crown of branches as it fell; and, as if by the gracious compensation of the Most High, it was also burst into four parts.
>
> At this sight the pagans who before had cursed now, on the contrary, believed, and blessed the Lord, and put away their former reviling. Then moreover the most holy bishop, after taking counsel with the brethren, built from the timber of the tree a wooden oratory, and dedicated it in honour of Saint Peter the apostle.[21]

Ovid now tells of what comes for Erysichthon. When the great tree fell the dryads rushed to tell Demeter.

> Terrified and shocked, the sister-dryads, grieving for the grove and what

---

21. *Donar's Oak*, Wikipedia.

they lost, put on their sable robes and hastened unto her, whom they prayed, might rightly punish Erysichthon's crime—the lovely goddess granted their request, and by the gracious movement of her head she shook the fruitful, cultivated fields, then heavy with the harvest; and she planned an unexampled punishment deserved, and not beyond his miserable crimes—the grisly bane of famine.

But because it is not in the scope of Destiny, that two such deities should ever meet as Demeter and gaunt Famine, she called forth from mountain-wilds a rustic Oread, and the goddess Demeter said to her, "There is an ice-bound wilderness of barren soil in utmost Scythia, desolate and bare of trees and corn, where Torpid-Frost, White-Death and Palsy and Gaunt-Famine, hold their haunts. Go there now, and command that Famine flit from there; and let her gnawing-essence pierce the entrails of this sacrilegious wretch, and there be hidden. Let her vanquish me and overcome the utmost power of food. Heed not misgivings of the journey's length, for you will guide my dragon-bridled car through lofty ether."

The spirit or daimon of hunger, famine and starvation was Limos (Greek) or Fames (Roman). She was the opposite force to Demeter, goddess of plenty and fertility. Destiny decreed that two could never meet and so Demeter sent an Oread, one rustic and close to nature, to carry her commands to Fames. Demeter had two dragons that carried her chariot through the air. Dragons, serpents and chimeras abounded in Greek myth and were often the guardians of sacred places or great treasures.

The defining stories of the Christian colonisation of Ireland and England was that both their patron saints overcame serpents. Saint Patrick supposedly banished snakes from Ireland (but there were none there to begin with) and Saint George slew the dragon.

And she gave to her the reins; and so the swiftly carried Nymph arrived in Scythia. There, upon the top of steep Caucasus, when she had slipped their tight yoke from the dragons' harnessed necks, she searched for Famine in that granite land, and there she found her clutching at scant herbs, with nails and teeth. Beneath her shaggy hair her hollow eyes glared in her ghastly face, her lips were filthy and her throat was rough and blotched, and all her entrails could be seen, enclosed in nothing but her shrivelled skin; her crooked loins were dry uncovered bones, and where her belly should be was a void; her flabby breast was flat against her spine; her lean, emaciated body made her joints appear so large, her knobbled knees seemed large knots, and her swollen ankle-bones protruded.

When the Nymph, with keen sight, saw the Famine-monster, fearing to draw near she cried aloud the mandate she had brought from fruitful Demeter, and although the time had been but brief, and Famine far away, such hunger seized the Nymph, she had to turn her dragon-steeds, and flee through yielding air and the high clouds. At Thessaly she stopped.

Grim Famine hastened to obey the will of Demeter, though their deeds are opposite, and rapidly through ether heights was borne to Erysichthon's home. When she arrived at midnight, slumber was upon the wretch, and as she folded him in her two wings, she breathed her pestilential poison through his mouth and throat and breast, and spread the curse of utmost hunger in his aching veins. When all was done as Demeter had decreed, she left the fertile world for bleak abodes, and her accustomed caves.

In a dreamful feast he worked his jaws in vain, and ground his teeth, and swallowed air as his imagined food; till wearied with the effort he awoke to hunger scorching as a fire, which burned his entrails and compelled his raging jaws. He demanded all the foods of sea and earth and air and tables groaned before him. so he, demanding all the foods of sea and earth and air, raged of his hunger, while the tables groaned with heaps before him spread; he, banqueting, sought banquets for more food, and as he gorged he always wanted more. The food of cities and a nation failed to satisfy the cravings of one man. The more his stomach gets, the more it needs—even as the ocean takes the streams of earth, although it swallows up great rivers drawn from lands remote, it never can be filled nor satisfied. And as devouring fire its fuel refuses never, but consumes unnumbered beams of wood, and burns for more the more 'tis fed, and from abundance gains increasing famine, so the raving jaws of wretched Erysichthon, ever craved all food in him, was only the cause of food, and what he ate made only room for more.

The natural world eats and grows but it also dies so it can jump up and live again. This is the death-that-gives-life. Barbara Kingsolver describes her in the *Poisonwood Bible*:

> First, picture the forest. I want you to be its conscience, the eyes in the trees. The trees are columns of slick, brindled bark like muscular animals overgrown beyond all reason. Every space is filled with life: delicate, poisonous frogs war-painted like skeletons, clutched in copulation, secreting their precious eggs onto dripping leaves. Vines strangling their own kin in the everlasting wrestle for sunlight. The breathing of monkeys. A glide of snake belly on branch. A single-file army of ants biting a mammoth tree into uniform grains and hauling it down to the dark for their ravenous queen. And, in reply, a choir of seedlings arching their necks out of rotted tree stumps, sucking life out of death. This forest eats itself and lives forever.

The global economy is based on the fantasy of constant annual growth. It does not want to die. The only things that are growing but not dying are the GDP, the global population, and military spending. Our global culture has been eaten and swallowed by the archetype of growth and giantism and, like Erysichthon, it wants more.

In modern terms, Erysichthon has an addiction. If economic growth was a substance it would be diagnosed as an addiction. At base it is an addiction to matter and bigness. But nothing disappears—what was ignored or despised in spirit shows up in matter but in demonic, destructive form. Erysichthon was unable to honour the altar of Demeter the goddess of abundance and fruitfulness. Now she has returned with a vengeance. Now he is greedy for what she can provide but it does not satisfy him and, even more, it makes him want more of what is unfulfilling. He ends up being cursed with an insatiable appetite. Poor fella, in the end the only thing left is himself which (or is it whom?) he begins to devour. He is in a death spiral.

We have not honoured the world of matter and it returns in our addictions to substances—money, shopping malls, development, highway, cars, Coke and McDonald's—and our consumption knows no bounds. Donald Trump is the myopic poster child for this illness, and illness it is. He states that there is enough natural gas in the USA to last another 100 years and coal to last another 250 years and this will make America great again. No mention of what then? No mention of our children's children unto seven generations. Will they too be stricken like Erysichthon?

Mestra

Ovid, writing 250 years after Callimachus, adds a second and parallel part to the Erysichthon story and heralds what is to come over the next 2,000 years of the Piscean era.

Erysichthon's gluttony at last had wasted his ancestral wealth, his raging hunger suffered no decline, and his insatiate gluttony increased. When all his wealth at last was eaten up, his daughter [Mestra], worthy of a fate more kind, alone was left to him and her he sold.

His daughter was all he had left—and he sold her as a slave. Yes, in his desperation he sells his daughter into slavery. This is the psychological picture of a culture that has sold this planet for lithium and *lebensraum*.[22] This never happens under conditions of adversity or poverty. It is only in circumstances where the ego has never been humiliated, relativised or learnt its proper size, that this inflation and grandiosity comes sliding in on a shrimp sandwich, to use a Swedish metaphor.

Mestra went to Poseidon (Neptune to the Romans) and he gifted her with the ability to shape-shift. Each time Mestra was sold she turned herself into an animal. But each time she returns to her father. Her father, seeing her new-found ability to shape-shift, uses it for his own ends. He resells her over and over again to feed his addiction. But what did we expect? He's a risk-taker, an entrepreneur, ready to make a deal, grow the business, and capitalise on opportunities. Even the miraculous

---

22. Lebensraum (living space) was the ideology that led to the Nazi invasion of East and Central Europe.

ability to change form is not seen for what it is, the life-giving gift from the other world, but it is only another commodity to be used.

Mestra is a daughter bound to her father. He might be the economic father, the personal father, the academic father, the career father, or the legal father, and she has to play by the father's rules. But, like an abused partner who returns again and again to the abuser, she eventually refuses to be sold again and hastens to the sea shore.

> Descendant of a noble race, the girl refusing to be purchased as a slave,
> then hastened to the near shore of the sea, and as she stretched her arms
> above the waves, implored kind Neptune, her lover, with her tears,
> "Oh, you who have deprived me of virginity, deliver me from such a
> master's power!"

Matter is feminine. Women are earth-beings. Men are sky-beings. When violence is done to matter, violence to women follows. When violence is done to women, violence to matter follows. Matter–women, women–matter, both are different forms of the same thing.[23] Curiously, some might take that as a form of misogyny or as disempowering or disrespectful. If that is the case, I can't help you.

In Maoridom, however famous you are, however far away you are, however rich you are, when you come back to the marae you are just another cuzzie-bro. And when you speak your name it comes last. You come fifth in line—after your mountain, your river, your iwi, and your hapu. Abraham Lincoln said, "Nearly all men can stand adversity, but if you want to test a man's character, give him power." Nothing wrong with power, just takes some skill to handle it. Erysichthon failed the test.

Neptune (Poseidon to the Greeks) was the god of the sea. Mestra refused to be enslaved but who does she turn to in her search for freedom? She was a lover of Neptune. Her first lover (perhaps her only lover, we don't know) was a god. In her distress, Mestra goes not to her friends, nor her partner (if she has one), nor her community, nor her

---

23. For a recent version of this read Terry Tempest Williams' superb article https://www. theguardian.com/lifeandstyle/2022/feb/15/living-in-a-womans-body-like-earth-we-are-changing-quickly-through-the-violence-of-climate-collapse

culture. These are all land-animals. She returns to her first experience of being connected to, connected with, ravished by, loved by, spirit. Or, in psychological terms, the Self.

Two threads here. First, she refuses to be enslaved. To refuse she must see that she is enslaved, then give birth to the desire for freedom, then oppose her predicament. This may be a lifetime's work for an individual woman, or seven generations work for the family, or 2,000 years of work for a culture. The long game is important. Second, she returns to the sea of her deepest nature—and is changed (as we shall see) into a man. Whenever the journey goes deep enough or far enough we meet the opposite side of ourselves and become one-hearted. At the deepest layers of the psyche, under conditions of death and war, orgasm and ecstasy, and danger and distress, all things can turn into their opposite— a woman can be more aggressive than a man, and a man can be more tender than a woman.

> Although the slave master, seeking her, had seen her only at that moment, Poseidon changed her quickly from a woman to a man, by giving her the features of a man and garments proper to a fisher-man: and there she stood. He even looked at her and cried out, "Hey, there! Expert of the rod! While you are casting forth the bit of brass, concealed so deftly in its tiny bait— gods-willing! let the sea be smooth for you, and let the foolish fishes swimming up, never know danger till they snap the hook! Now tell me where is she, who only now, in tattered garment and wind-twisted hair, was standing on this shore— for I am sure I saw her standing on this shore, although no footstep shows her flight."
>
> By this she was assured that the favour of the god protected her; delighted to be questioned of herself, she said, "No matter who you are, excuse me. So busy have I been at catching fish, I have not had the time to move my eyes from this pool; and that you may be assured I only tell the truth, may Poseidon, God of ocean witness it, I have not seen a man where I am standing on this shore—myself excepted—not a woman has stood here."
>
> Her master could not doubt it, and deceived, retraced his footsteps from the sandy shore. As soon as he had disappeared, her form

unchanged, was given back to her. But when her father knew his
daughter could transform her body and escape, he often sold her first to
one and then another—all of whom she cheated—as a mare, bird, a
cow, or as a stag she got away; and so brought food, dishonestly, to ease
his greed. And so he lived until the growing strength of famine,
gnawing at his vitals, had consumed all he could get by selling her: his
anguish burned him with increasing heat. He gnawed his own flesh,
and he tore his limbs and fed his body all he took from it.

With nothing else to gorge Erysichthon eats himself. When Mestra is
freed from the power of her father, the father self-destructs. When
women come into their rightful power the patriarchy crumbles. This
cannot but happen but may take generations. There is hope for our
planet.

This story ends the eighth book of Metamorphoses.

Heracles

We will leave Metamorphoses at the end of Book VIII but before we
leave, I will mention briefly Book IX which describes, consistent with
our theme, the story of the fall of the masculine with the death of
Heracles at the hands of his wife Deianeira. Heracles, the most
renowned of all the Greek heroes, was known for his extraordinary
strength, courage, ingenuity, and sexual prowess. The twelve labours of
Hercules are well known. The first eight labours were the killing or
capture of animals like the Erymanthian Boar or the Stymphalian Birds.
A young man needs to overcome his animal nature and "prove him/her-
self" by completing a Herculean task like getting a job, overcoming an
addiction, finishing a degree, being selected for the All Blacks, or having
a relationship, as a rite of transition to adulthood. Sport often carries
this archetypal function in modern culture.

Hercules' ninth labour was different—and we have seen the significance of nine. It was to retrieve the magic girdle of Hippolyta. The
girdle was a symbol of her authority as Queen of the Amazons.
Hercules' usurpation of the power of the feminine in his ninth labour
shifted the nature of his subsequent labours. The tenth (rustling the

cattle of the giant, Geryon) and eleventh labours (stealing the sacred apples of the Hesperides) related to farming and agriculture which are steps toward civilisation. The twelfth labour (capturing Cerberus, the three-headed dog who guarded the Gates of Hades) was less about strength and killing and more about trickery and using the help of others such as Hermes.

The first story in Ovid's ninth book is about Heracles winning Deianeira's hand by wrestling with the river-god Achelous, god of all fresh water and son of Gaia and Oceanus. Achelous shape-shifts into a bull, one of his many forms, but Heracles eventually defeats him and tears off one of his horns. Later Heracles gives the horn to the Naiads, the nymphs of fountains, wells, springs and streams who transform it into the cornucopia, the horn of plenty and abundance. The second story in Book IX is about Hercules' agonising death after donning the shirt of Nessus, the centaur, soaked in the poison of the Lernean Hydra and given to him—unwittingly the stories say—by Deianira (Greek, meaning husband- or man-destroyer) on hearing rumours of his infidelity.

And so it will go. The heroic masculine overcomes Achelous, a force of Nature itself, and this brings a cornucopia of plenty and abundance. The advance of civilisation continues when Heracles slays Nessus, the centaur, who had lusted after his wife. Centaurs symbolise the union of instinct and spirit. Half-human and half-horse, they were known for their Dionysian nature, lechery, drunkenness and savagery—they tore people limb from limb. But they were also revered, like Chiron whose pupils included Achilles, Aeneas and Theseus, for their wisdom and teaching. When Heracles killed Nessus he slaughtered not only the savagery but also the wisdom. He slew the centaur with an arrow tipped with the poisonous blood of the Lernean Hydra that he had slain as one of his Twelve Labours. With revenge in mind, the dying Nessus told Deianeira to take his blood-stained cloak, infused with the hydra's poison, and save it for a time when she needed to strengthen the love of her husband.

Many years later, after Heracles deeds and labours had brought him fame, Deianeira heard that he was in love with another woman.

Distraught, and only seeking ways to keep his love, she gave him the poisoned cloak of Nessus. Wittingly or not, she took her revenge.

The poisoned garment, cleaving to him, ripped his skin, heat shrivelled, from his burning flesh. Or, tightening on him, as his great strength pulled, stripped with it the great muscles from his limbs, leaving his huge bones bare—as with Erysichthon. Even his blood audibly hissed, as red-hot blades when they are plunged in water, so the burning bane boiled in his veins. Great perspiration streamed from his dissolving body, as the heat consumed his entrails; and his sinews cracked, brittle when burnt. The marrow in his bones dissolved, as it absorbed the venom-heat. After he has killed his animal wisdom and fallen out of relationship with the feminine. So the greatest of heroes dies in agony

Heat-death by climate change, we could say.

Hubris and Nemesis

All men make mistakes, but a good man yields when he knows his course is wrong, and repairs the evil. The only crime is pride. —Sophocles, *Antigone*

Hubris calls for nemesis, and in one form or another it's going to get it, not as a punishment from outside but as the completion of a pattern already started. —Mary Midgley

Get down off the cross, we need the wood! —Anon.

Since the end of the World War II, the United States has fought three "small" wars... we lost all three of them and for the same reason—hubris. —Andrew Greeley

"We need some great failures—we ever-successful Americans—conscious, intelligent, illuminating failures." (Lincoln Steffens, 1866–1936). Easy for him to say. It's hard to be illuminated by failure in a country where success is a national religion. It's hard to say "no, we can't" in a country that spent its first century conquering a continent and its second conquering much of the world. The American character, wrote Arthur Schlesinger, Sr, "is bottomed upon the profound conviction that nothing in the world is beyond its power to accomplish." But that conviction is a lie. —Peter Beinart[24]

Pride goes before destruction, a haughty spirit before a fall. —Proverbs 16:18

Most people can bear adversity. But if you wish to know what a man really is, give him power. —attributed to Abraham Lincoln by Robert Ingersoll, 1884

The Greeks, who shaped the basis of western thinking, lived in mortal fear of humanity's hidden hunger for the infinite and referred to it as *hybris,* the one true sin in their moral code. Whoever desired or possessed too much was implacably punished by *nemesis.* Yet the Greeks themselves were to pioneer an unprecedented level of ambition that began to reverse that taboo. —Luigi Zoja[25]

This section had difficulty in finding a comfy place in this book. But the homeless epigraphs and abandoned quotes seemed to want to nest here. It was, I suppose, because hubris is the theme of the whole book and colours all its chapters.

Most of us live inconsequential lives (as far as the collective is concerned) feeding off the crumbs of comfort, family, belonging, success, and pleasure. We are but small, recyclable life-forms. The finitude of our horizons makes us long for infinitude beyond our insignificance, and to be larger and be seen as larger in our own eyes and the eyes of others.

Much has been written on hubris' cousin, narcissism, beginning with with Freud's essay "On Narcissism" in 1914 and continuing through Heinz Kohut's and Otto Kernberg's psychoanalytic contributions, to Christopher Lasch's sociological perspective, to the burgeoning

---

24. Beinart, *The Icarus Syndrome: A History of American Hubris.*
25. Luigi Zoja, *Growth and guilt,* 1.

of popular interest in the last 20 years. But less has been written on hubris which covers our territory perhaps better than narcissism.

As always, the Greek myths tell us about the difference. They lie at the fracture line between the older indigenous traditions and the newer rational discoveries of Aristotle, Euclid, or Socrates. They had a polytheistic liveliness combined with a sober questioning of all things. Not being too pagan they appealed to, and were the ancestors of, our Western consciousness. And, conveniently, they lived in the neighbourhood.

The story of Echo and Narcissus is told in Ovid's Metamorphoses and Robert Graves re-tells the myth. Narcissus was the beautiful son of the river-god Cephissus and the Naiad Liriope. Naiads are female spirits who inhabit fresh water fountains, wells, springs, streams, or brooks. The seer Teiresias told Leiriope, the first person ever to consult him: "Narcissus will live to a ripe old age, provided that he never knows himself."

By the time Narcissus reached the age of sixteen, his path was strewn with heartlessly rejected lovers, both men and women. One day Echo, an Oread or mountain nymph, came across Narcissus walking in the woods. She fell deeply in love and followed him. Echo had been cursed by Hera, Zeus's wife, because she distracted Hera from finding out about Zeus's affairs with her garrulous conversations. Thus cursed, she was only able to speak the last words spoken by another person. Narcissus sensed he was being followed and shouted "Who's there?". Echo repeated "Who's there?" She eventually rushed to embrace him but he said "Hands off! May I die before you enjoy my body." Echo whispered "Enjoy my body" and fled, humiliated. She was heartbroken and wandered the rest of her days until nothing but an echo of her voice remained.

Nemesis, the goddess of revenge, heard of this and decided to punish Narcissus. One day, thirsty after hunting, the goddess lured him to a pool. He leaned over the water and saw his beauty in the reflection. Narcissus, until now unapproachable and immune to love, did not realise it was his own image and fell deeply in love with it, as if it was somebody else. At first he tried to embrace and kiss the beautiful boy in front of him, but then recognised himself and lay gazing, enraptured, into the pool, hour after hour. How could he endure both to possess and yet not to possess? His grief was destroying him, yet he rejoiced in its torment; knowing at least that his other self would remain true to him, whatever happened. He realised that he could not have what he so ardently desired, and plunged a dagger into his breast. From the blood that soaked the earth, a gold and white narcissus flower sprang up. The name and fragrance of the narcissus (Greek, *narkao*, to benumb) is associated with the word narcotic.

The story of Narcissus is a more human, and more recent, story but Hybris was an ancient goddess, born in the company of the gods and goddesses, and expressing the full range of human vices and virtues. She was the goddess or spirit (daimona) of insolence, hubris, reckless pride, arrogance and outrageous behaviour in general. Her Roman name was Petulantia. She was the daughter of Erebos, the primordial god of darkness, and Nyx, the goddess of night. Amongst her many siblings were Senectus (Old Age), Mors (Death), Letum (Dissolution), Continentia (Moderation), Somnus (Sleep), Somnia (Dreams), Amor (Love), Epiphron (Prudence), Discordia (Discord), Miseria (Misery), Nemesis (Retribution), Euphrosyne (Good Cheer), Amicitia (Friendship), Misericordia (Compassion), Styx (Hatred), and the three Parcae (Fates).

Hesiod said she was the daughter of Night, who in turn was the daughter of Chaos. Night, without having lain with any other creature, also gave birth to hateful Doom, black Fate, Death, Sleep, Dreams, Blame, and Woe, as well as the Hesperides, the Moirae or Destinies, and the ruthless avenging Fates or Keres. Night, then, was a shapeless element, parthenogenetic, and preceded by the primal disorder of Chaos. Thus we have three absences: the absence of other, the absence of light, and the absence of order. This is the heritage that Hybris brings in her retribution.

Hubris is not associated with a clinical disorder like Narcissus and its branches spread wider than the foibles of an individual. Anciently, it wields more archetypal power and with it comes a greater lack of consciousness that accompanies such a state of archetypal possession. The Greek word hubris (Latin, superbia) means haughtiness, pride, vainglory, conceit, vanity, overconfidence or arrogance. It indicates a lack of social and emotional reality-testing and an overestimation of one's own competence or capabilities. As well as the benumbing self-love of narcissism it also encompasses a contempt towards the other—a desire to be more important, holding oneself above others, and adopting a superior manner. Dante's definition was "love of self perverted to hatred and contempt for one's neighbour." Even more than the daily commerce of relationships between humans, hubris was an arrogant violation of the limits set by the gods or by human society, and failing to observe the divine equilibrium among god, man, and nature. Trump is hubris on the hoof.

The Catholic church considered superbia to be the most serious of the seven deadly sins and the source of the other sins because it assumed oneself to be greater than God. Lucifer's superbia and his desire to compete with Dad and his younger brother Jesus, led to his fall from heaven. But nowadays, we think of superb as just another superlative.

Hubris was the antithesis of two Greek values: aidos (shame and humble reverence before the law) and sophrosyne (self-restraint, a sense of proper limits). Aidos was the shame felt before the eyes of their fellow citizens after committing an unjust act. One was divine justice, the other social justice. Acts of hubris angered the Olympian gods to restoring justice and equilibrium. Nemesis was sister to Hybris and daughter of Nyx. Her name almost certainly comes from *nemo*, "to distribute" and *nemesis* "dispenser of dues." Her Roman equivalent is Fortuna. Originally she was the goddess who dealt or distributed appropriate gifts to mortals. The word nemesis originally meant the apportionment of fortune, neither good nor bad, each according to their fate. Happiness and unhappiness were measured out by her, taking care that happiness was not too often or too much. Later, nemesis came to mean the disturbance of this right proportion and the sense of injustice that could not allow it to pass unpunished. She was the goddess of retribution for evil deeds and undeserved good fortune and those who showed hubris and arrogance before the gods. She was a personification of the indignation and resentment aroused by those who acted with apparent impunity, or who had undeserved good fortune.

In WWII the Japanese coined the term for another kind of hubris, "victory disease." After the initial successes of Pearl Harbour and other victories in the Pacific in 1941, the Japanese navy suffered a catastrophic defeat at the Battle of Midway in 1942. Victory disease refers to the complacency or arrogance brought on by a victory. The result is a disastrous defeat.

But victory disease was around well before WWII. In 1314, the overconfidence and lack of preparation by Edward II, known as The Hammer of the Scots, resulted in his disastrous defeat at the Battle of Bannockburn by the Scots led by Robert the Bruce. In 1415, at the Battle of Agincourt, the English were heavily outnumbered by five to one, but the arrogance of the French knights, and accuracy of the English longbows, led to the rout of the French. Disastrously, Napoleon invaded Russia in 1812 with a force of about 600,000 French soldiers, of which about 40,000 returned. In 1879, at the Battle of Isandlwana, Zulu warriors equipped mainly with spears and shields defeated British forces armed with modern firearms and artillery. In 1941 Hitler invaded the Soviet Union in Operation Barbarossa with almost four million troops, the largest invasion force in history, against almost three million on the Soviet side. He underestimated Soviet military resilience, counted on the success of old tactics, was confident of quick victory, but did not count on getting caught in the Russian winter or rasputitsa (mud season). Millions died on both sides.

7

THE HEART OF HEAVEN
ASSUMING AUTHORITY

WE MOVE NOW from the stories of Ovid's Metamorphoses to the calendars of the Maya of Central America.[1] Both are oracular and prophetic. They both give us, in different ways, a reading of the map of time outside of our cultural, scientific, political and parochial concerns. Time has no bias, and no emotional, political or cultural leanings. Purely objective we might say.

The deep currents in the dream, like great whales rising to the surface, break through into the world as historical events in time and space as well as corresponding cosmic events visible in the sky. It is the rise and fall, the birth and death, of particular archetypal powers that give rise to what we know of as culture. For many indigenous peoples, notably the Maya, time is holy. It is often represented by several gods or goddesses, each representing a different aspect of time. The Maya have year-lords and day-gods. In Greek mythology there is Oceanos or Cronos, the god of time as a river or ocean; Nike, the goddess of the moment of balance between victory and defeat; Kairos, the god of the opportune moment; and the Moirae, goddesses of fate.

The daily cycles of the sun, the monthly cycle of the moon, the

---

1. Adapted from Owen, *The Maya Book of Life*, 425–436 et passim.

annual cycle of the seasons, human pregnancy, birth to puberty, mid-life, the twenties, the forties, the sixties, the century, the millennium, the Platonic Year are all rhythms of nature and psyche. Many cultures have cyclical notions of time, for example, the Hindu yugas, the Aztec sun cycles, the Maya Long Count, or the astrological ages. More recent Eurocentric-ish examples of the cyclical nature of civilisations are Oswald Spengler's *Decline of the West* (1922), Arnold Toynbee's *A Study of History* (1936–1961), William McNeill's *Rise of the West* (1963), Felipe Fernandez-Armesto's *Civilizations: Culture, Ambition, and the Transformation of Nature* (2000), or Jared Diamond's *Collapse: How Societies Choose to Fail or Succeed* (2005).

Spengler believes that the lifespan of cultures followed the seasons. Spring is the time of the birth of the religion of that culture. All great cultures have behind them a great religion. Western culture is one of directedness and will. Spengler refers to it as Faustian. In its autumn phase the culture develops into a civilisation—and begins to break down. Mega-cities are characteristic. Spengler saw our culture as having finished its summer around 1800.

The orderedness of time as observed in the movements of the heavenly bodies over centuries gives an understanding of how energy moves between substance and spirit. The prophecies of various cultures are a seeing of how spirit will manifest in a particular way as matter moves through time. Time is a way of staying aligned with the rhythms and cycles of the Creator. Because every deviation from the Self, or the God-image within as Jung called it, is associated with a disturbed relationship with time, those who are closer to the tempo of the Self are more aligned with the rhythms of nature, and vice-versa. But in Western culture time has lost its numinosity and become a secular commodity. Time is saved or spent, wasted or bought.

The Heart of Heaven

Down the middle of the central bulge of the Milky Way runs a dark cleft which is not the absence of stars but the presence of interstellar dust and gas clouds that obscure the stars behind. The intersection of the ecliptic with the dark rift is what the Maya called the Heart of Heaven, the

Cosmic Womb of the Great Mother. The ecliptic is the path of the sun along which lie the constellations of the Zodiac. It is the place where the sun is reborn every 26,000 years. From their astronomical observations and their knowledge of time, the Maya priest-astronomers created something astonishing. It was a calendar, called the Long Count, that predicted the date of the next rebirth of the sun from the cosmic womb, on December 21, 2012. The oldest Long Count date yet found in the archaeological record corresponds to 32 BCE but the Maya scholar Munro Edmonson believes that the Long Count emerged around 355 BCE.[2]

The calendars of the Abrahamic religions are counted from an event that happened in the past. For example, the Jewish calendar dates from the day of creation (3761 BCE), the Christian calendar dates from the birth of Christ (0 BCE), and the Islamic calendar from the year of the hijrah when Mohammed moved from Mecca to Medina (622 CE). But with the Long Count the important date was not when the calendar started but when it ended, over 2,000 years into the future from its creation. This is quite the reverse of the Western Gregorian calendar based on the birth of an earth-child (Christ) in the past. The Maya calendar is based on the birth of a sun-child in the future.

The Great Year

To explore this further we need to briefly review the concepts of the solstice, the precession of the equinoxes, and Maya calendrics. The winter solstice is the time when life's energy is at its lowest. The word "solstice" means "the sun stands still" in Latin. This refers to the fact that the sun apparently rises and sets at the same time over the course of three days. The winter solstice is the day of least sunlight and the shortest day of the year, but marks the beginning of increasing daylight —the old year is ending and another will be born. This is seen in worldwide myths about the death and rebirth of a deity, or a great mother giving birth to a celestial boy child at this time of the year, as in the story of Christ. Over 2,000 years ago the dark rift of the Milky Way could be

---

2. Munro Edmonson, *The Book of the Year: Middle American Calendrical Systems.*

observed some thirty degrees above the horizon as the winter solstice sun dawned. However, early Maya sky-watchers noticed that every winter solstice the centre of the dark rift moved closer and closer to the horizon and the sun at its moment of dawning. This is called the "precession of the equinoxes."

The Earth is not a perfect sphere and this, combined with the gravitational pull of the sun and moon, causes its axis to inscribe a cone in space, like a spinning top whose spindle wobbles. To observers on Earth, it causes the position of a fixed point to move slowly "backwards" through the constellations over thousands of years. The easiest way to notice this slow movement of the stars is at any fixed time each year. By historical convention, the spring equinox in the northern hemisphere is taken as the reference point, and the movement is called the precession of the equinoxes.

Knowledge of precession goes back as far as the Neolithic period and over two hundred myths and over thirty cultures knew about precession, some going back to 10,000 BCE.[3] The Greek astronomer Hipparchus was the first in the West to write about precession in 128 BCE.

At this historical time the North Pole points to Polaris, the Pole Star. But this point moves slowly through the heavens and takes about 26,000 years to complete one revolution through the constellations. This is called a Platonic or Great Year. Thus the equinox point takes about 2,160 years to pass through each of the twelve constellations and at present it is passing from Pisces to Aquarius. Each Platonic Great Year represents a profound shift in human culture. The astrological ages are approximately as follows. (The dates of course are arbitrarily set by what Christianity chooses as the zero point—the birth of Christ). I have simplified the ages to make each one exactly 2,160 years, for the purpose of illustration.

Sagittarius 19,440–17,280 BCE
Scorpio 17,280–15,120 BCE

---

3. Suggested by Giorgio de Santillana, *Hamlet's Mill: An Essay on Myth and the Frame of Time.*

Libra 15,120–12,960 BCE
Virgo 12,960–10,800 BCE
Leo 10,800–8640 BCE
Cancer 8640–6480 BCE
Gemini 6480–4320 BCE
Taurus 4320–2160 BCE
Aries 2160–0 BCE
Pisces 0–2160 CE
Aquarius 2160–4320 CE
Capricorn 4320–6480 CE

The tincture of time

The Maya and the Aztec accorded time and number more texture, shape and sacredness than Western culture. For them, time was a living, conscious, holy entity. They used a number of calendars for different purposes but unlike our Gregorian calendar, which is based on the number ten and marks the passing of decades and centuries, the Maya used a vigesimal system based on the number 20. The calendrical cycles are the *haab* and the *tzolkin*, both in use today by Maya daykeepers. The tzolkin is the divinatory calendar, a continuously revolving round of thirteen numbers and twenty day names (13 x 20 = 260 days). It is based on the length of human pregnancy, 260 days being nine lunar cycles of slightly less than 29 days. The haab is the secular year of eighteen months of twenty days = 360 days with an extra five days to make up the solar year. When the tzolkin (13 x 20 days) was used in conjunction with the haab (18 x 20 days) the cycles synchronised every 260 x 365 days or 52 years. This was the time when the Aztec held their New Fire ceremonies.

The Maya units of time were days or k'ins, months or uinals of 20 days, years or tuns of 360 days, katuns of 20 years, baktuns of 400 years, pictuns of 8,000 years, and so on. To the historical Maya, the 20-year katun and the 400-year baktun were the most significant. Each year was called a tun or stone because the end of the year was marked by setting a stone or stela in the ground. Stela 1 at Coba shows the longest recorded time period known in the ancient world with glyphs up to 13×20^{21}

tuns or 13 times 20 years, to the power of 21. The place for the 22nd power glyph is left blank. In comparison, in Hindu cosmology the life span or Cycle of Brahma, a Mahakalpa, is 10^{22} seconds or 311 trillion years. The Maya set the beginning of the current Fifth Age at 0.0.0.0.0 which means 0 baktuns, 0 katuns, 0 tuns, 0 uinals, 0 kin. In the Gregorian calendar this date is August 11, 3114 BCE. Similarly, the current Hindu cycle of time or yuga began in 3102 BCE.

So why that date? Because after one Great Year, Five Ages, 13 baktuns, 5,125 years or 13 x 144,000 days, like the hands of the clock coming back to twelve again, the calendar would end and restart again at 0.0.0.0.0 on December 21, 2012. Note that the Maya calendar does not end in 2012 but the current 13-baktun cycle does and so does the Fifth Age. Why December 21, 2012? Because that day saw the triple rebirth of the sun: the daily rebirth of the sun from the darkness of the night, the solstice rebirth of the sun from the longest night of the year, and the galactic rebirth of the sun from the Heart of Heaven. In addition, the sun was almost exactly in the middle of four planets aligned on the arms of the sacred tree with Venus at their head.

According to the Maya, our Sun and all of its planets rotate in cycles in relation to the centre of the galaxy, or Hunab-Ku, the central light of the galaxy. This complete cycle of the Great Year was called a galactic day and each age was a portion of the galactic day. The first age is the galactic morning (23,000–18,000 BCE), when our solar system is just coming out of the darkness to enter the light. The second age (18,000–13,000 BCE) is the midday, when our solar system is closest to the central light. The third age (13,000– 8,000 BCE) is the afternoon, when our solar system begins to come out of the light. The fourth cycle (8,000–3,000 BCE) is the late evening and middle of the night, when our solar system has entered its furthest cycle from the central light. The fifth and last cycle (3114 BCE–2012 CE) is the deepest part of the night before dawn, when our solar system is in its last cycle of darkness before starting again.

So this current 13-baktun cycle is different from the others—it is the last of five ages in both Maya and Aztec cosmologies. The number five is the quintessence—the summing up at the centre of what has happened in each of the four directions around the wheel, and it catalyses the turning of the next wheel. The Aztec calendar stone indicates that each "sun" or "age" lasts 100 calendar rounds (5,196 years). The Maya Long Count of 13 baktuns is 5,125 years. So five ages make one full precessional cycle—five Aztec ages are 25,980 years, five Maya 13-baktun cycles are 25,625 years, and a precessional Great Year is 25,765 years. As this Great Year comes to a close, and the precessional point moves from the constellation of Pisces to Aquarius, it is accompanied by profound dangers and opportunities for the human species and all life on this planet.

2012

The year 2012 saw not only the rebirth of the sun but other astronomical phenomena as well. The Dresden Codex refers to the "The Birth of Venus" in 3114 BCE.[4] This was the rising of Venus on one horizon at the same time as the Pleiades were setting below the opposite horizon. In 2012 we witnessed "The Death of Venus" when Venus was setting while the Pleiades was rising. Then on May 20, 2012, something else occurred—the sun, the moon and the Pleiades passed through the zenith at the Maya site of Chichen Itza. This event occurs only during a 72-year time window, from 1976 to 2048. Right at the centre of this time window is the year 2012. Quetzalcoatl was a symbol for this sun-Pleiades-zenith conjunction.

Finally, Maya prophecy holds that the world of new consciousness would be born on the date of the second of the pair of Venus transits on June 8, 2012. The winter solstice in 2012 was a knot in the Loom of Time that held all these physical and spiritual events together in the dream—the World Tree, the crossroads of the Milky Way and the ecliptic, the rebirth of the sun from the darkness, the hope of resurrection, the hope that human love and the warmth of life will prevail against the coldness of the galactic night, the hope that the universe is on our side

---

4. The Dresden Codex is the oldest surviving book from the Americas. It came to light in the mid-1700s and is kept in the Saxony State Library in Dresden. It is composed of 78 accordion-style pages with Mayan hieroglyphics illustrating Maya history and astronomical knowledge.

and we are not just an accident lost amongst the stars, and the hope that life will jump-up and live again in a time beyond our own.

On the morning after the northern hemisphere's shortest night on December 21, 2012 an event occurred that has not happened for 26,000 years. The sun was in the centre of the Sacred Tree, the Heart of Heaven, and First Father, our sun, was reborn from this Cosmic Womb of the Milky Way, the Great Mother.

John Major Jenkins concludes: "The 260-day tzolkin calendar is based upon the 260-day period of human embryo-genesis, and, on a higher level, the 260-day tzolkin symbolises, or structures, the 26,000 year period of precession, what we might call human spiritual embryo-genesis. The Maya believed that the 26,000 Great Year of precession is a spiritual gestation period for humanity, and that the 2012 alignment will catalyse the birth of what has been growing on this planet for 26,000 years. For the Maya, Father Sun's movement into union with Cosmic Mother's heart also signified the insemination, or seeding of what will come to fruition in 26,000 years".[5]

"But," I hear the measurers say, "2012 has come and gone and we are still here. Nothing big has happened!" Wait a while, I say.[6]

End of days

The day of December 21, 2012 dawned just like any other day, no different from the millions of days before or the millions of days after. It does not matter whether the astronomical events happen on a specific day or not. It does not matter what people do on that day. Life will go on. The archetype of the rebirth of the sun, which gives light, life and joy to the People, is happening in the dream all the time. In star time, a day, a year, or a decade does not make much difference—it is the process not the data point.

However, this archetypal and spiritual potential can only come into being and know itself if there are human hands to touch it, human consciousness to give it witness, human longing for its presence, human

---

5. John Major Jenkins, *Maya Cosmogenesis 2012*, 77.
6. I wrote this chapter in early 2013.

joy to celebrate it, and human grief to mourn its passing. So indeed, the day and the year does matter. Not because anything apocalyptic will happen on that day—that's just good copy for The Skeptical Inquirer or New Age magazines—but because the event attracts human attention, interest, fear, and fascination. All of which are a landing beacon for spirit. They call down power and feed the other world.

The moment, which is just like any other, is like the alchemical earth which is common and is found everywhere, but can be transformed into gold. The past has gone, future is yet to come, only the present moment is real. It is a point in time and space where the two worlds of spirit and matter can touch through the actions and choices of humans. We can align ourselves with the greater rhythms of the cosmos and both spirit and matter can be changed. Our ceremonies are magnified by the fact that this major ending and beginning resonates with all other endings and beginnings past and future. This why Maya rulers conjured and ceremonialised at the katun and baktun endings to plant seeds for a time beyond their own.

There is great hope in this Fifth Age, the fifth Movement of humanity's Book of Life, the age of Assuming Authority at the end of this Great Year. It may be the first time in history where sufficient human consciousness has accrued for the Personal History of previous ages to be erased and to make the passage from one Great Year to the next possible without destruction.[7]

But there is also great despair and we must not turn away from the sight of our destructiveness. The stakes are much higher than ever before. We are so estranged from matter that we suffer the opposite problem to those humans who lived at the beginning of this Great Year 26,000 years ago, or at the beginning of this Age 5,200 years ago. Then, humans needed civilising by their own hand. We needed civilisation not to protect us against the ravages of nature but to protect nature against the ravages of civilisation.

The rise of monotheism was marked by great doctrines of mercy, love and justice between humans. Now half the world's population is

---

7. For a further discussion of the Movements of the Book of Life see Owen, *The Maya Book of Life*, Chapter 6.

monotheistic. For 2,000 years the focus has been on love between humans—less murder, less cruelty, less savagery, more mercy, more justice, more equality, more love. All this is good. But it has been at the expense of the same ideals in our relationship with the natural world. As we have become more thoughtful of our fellow humans we have become more forgetful of All Our Relations. Monotheism has been the prime instigator in this great forgetting. Now consciousness has become linear and vertical. We are crucified between above and below. D H Lawrence wrote:

> We ought to dance with rapture that we should be alive and in the flesh, and part of the living, incarnate cosmos. I am part of the sun as my eye is part of me. That I am part of the earth my feet know perfectly, and my blood is part of that sea. My soul knows that I am part of the human race, my soul is an organic part of the great human soul, as my spirit is part of my nation. In my own very self, I am part of my family. There is nothing of me that is alone and absolute except my mind, and we shall find that the mind has no existence by itself, it is only the glitter of the sun on the surface of the waters. So my individualism is really an illusion. I am a part of the great whole, and I can never escape. But I can deny my connections, break them, and become a fragment. Then I am wretched.[8]

Apocalypse anytime

A synchronicity is a resonance, a similarity, an agreement, between two events that occur together in time but apart in space. They seem to have no observable, causal connection. One event is an inner event (a thought, an image, a feeling, a sense, a dream) and the other is an outer event. One in spirit, one in substance. They are a sign that spirit and matter have touched, approached, or at least shown an interest in each other. Ceremonies are planned synchronicities, so to speak, like the annual Lakota Sun Dance, the Maya 20-year and 400-year ceremonies, the Anishinabe winter sweat lodges, the Catholic Mass, Easter services,

---

8.   D. H. Lawrence, *Apocalypse*, 1930.

or Matariki.[9] The use of ceremony at those times, and in those places where spirit and matter are in proximity, enables the two to come closer so that something happens.

The shadow aspect of this ceremonial observance of cosmic timing emerges in paranoid, apocalyptic, prophetic, end-of-the-world movements or naive beginning-of-the-new-age predictions. Here the true nature of the event is either demonised or idealised. In non-monotheistic traditions the end of the world has been called Ragnarok (Norse) or Kali Yuga (Hindu). In monotheistic religions it is the End of Days (Judaism), the Qiyamah (Islam), or Judgement Day, the Great Purification, the Quickening, and the Rapture in Christianity.

Eschatological (Greek, *eschatos*, last) writings about the end of time or the end of an epoch exist in all the major religions but few indigenous cultures have prophecies writ so large and dramatically as in monotheism. There are, for example, the Hopi prophecies or the Anishinabe Seven Fires. But "Hopi warnings are not a prophecy, but predictions based on knowledge of human nature and the history of previous worlds destroyed by hubris. It's an intuition based on centuries of careful observation of nature and people." In other words it is scientific and based on painstaking observations.[10] Religions or cultures that hold apocalyptic beliefs tend to be those where the seeds of the collapse have already been planted, for example, big cities, writing, and centralised power, both religious and secular. All of which are regarded as hallmarks of "civilisation" (and inflation). Indigenous predictions are uncomplicated statements but what are we to make of the Biblical seven plagues, the Great Whore of Babylon, the golden cup of filth, and the rapture in the Book of Revelation? Why all the drama?

All religious prophecies describe dramatic movements and changes in the realm of spirit brought about by an omnipotent god or gods which will bring catastrophic changes. But let's notice the bigging-up.

---

9. Matariki is the Maori name for the Pleiades. They rise in midwinter (June) and herald the start of a new year. Traditionally, it was a time for remembering the dead, celebrating new life, and preparing the ground for the coming year.

10. "A Hopi Messenger—Prophecy or Prediction?", *Sacred Land*, October 12, 2017, www.sacredland.org/hopi-messenger-prophecy-or-prediction. See also Vine Deloria, *C.G. Jung and the Sioux Traditions*.

Did John of Patmos' revelations, which he attributed to his Yahweh, a local deity at the end of the Mediterranean, really speak for the fate of the Ainu of Japan or the Tehuelche of Patagonia? Will the Day of Judgement by Allah really apply to the Sami of Norway, the !Kung of Botswana, or the Chao Leh of the Andaman Sea? But this time it's different. Looking ever upward, monotheistic religions have taken their eye off the ball, so to speak, and now the apocalypse will happen from below not from above.

The word apocalypse (Greek, *apokalupsis*) means the uncovering of what has been hidden, or revelation. The last book of the bible, Revelation describes the visions of the future given to Saint John the Divine on the island of Patmos. Later, the word apocalypse came to mean the coming of a deity to judge, punish or reward humanity and bring about a new order. The word used in the sense of a catastrophic event, such as the end of the world, is a recently derived meaning.

Psychologically, writes Edward Edinger, the archetype of the apocalypse is the earth-shattering advent of the Self into full, conscious realisation. From the ego's point of view this is the end of its world. The many themes and images include: a final judgement, tribulation, reward or punishment; destruction (earthquakes, plague, famine); the separation of opposites (the good from the bad, the just from the unjust, the righteous from the sinners); the bestowal of grace, paradise and eternal life; earthly bodies ascending to heaven (the rapture); and heavenly bodies come to earth (the coming of the saviour).[11]

But, as Ovid, Goethe and Jung have described, the tidal earthquake of change has been imprisoned in the heavens of religion for so long it is now forced to express itself in matter in the form of destructive events. Apocalyptic movements have waxed and waned over the course of history and at the beginning of the twenty-first century, fundamentalist, apocalyptic beliefs are increasingly sweep through the collective.[12] As evidenced, for example, by the appeal of the Left Behind series.[13] All such movements seem incapable of learning from the past and ignore

---

11. Edinger, *Archetype of the Apocalypse*, 4.
12. Stephen Hunt, *Christian Millenarianism*.
13. https://en.wikipedia.org/wiki/Left_Behind

the obvious—that we are still here. So we must assume that a powerful archetype is at work which overrides simple reality-testing.

We can approach apocalyptic writings in four ways. First, dismiss them as religious rubbish. Second, accept them as religious gospel. Third, view them as a physical sign of a spiritual event. Fourth, view them as a spiritual sign of a physical event. The first two views do not concern us here. With regard to the third and fourth possibilities, suffice to say here that all cultures throughout history have had their dreamers, prophets and visionaries who have predicted the end of the world but it is only in the last two thousand years that such apocalyptic visions have gone global, so to speak. The many Western eschatological writings (Islamic, Judaic and Christian) may have only half the story. They leave out the subjective (and unconscious) meaning of their prophecies—the end of *their* religious world-view and *their* mode of consciousness. The Book of Revelation is a highly symbolic but also highly literal description of the end of the Christian aeon, and how Yahweh and Christianity will treat the Earth as a result of Yahweh's pathological behaviour. But, on the other hand, it might just be about the end of our physical world. Period.

Global terrorism, global conspiracies, global climate change, global fundamentalism and the global economy all spring from the same source. The state of infantile and grandiose denial that is the global economy says the earthly mother will continue to supply us with all our needs and our standard of living will improve forever. "Mummy (that's Mommy for North Americans) Earth will always be there for us and look after us," says Baby Trump, turning again to suckle on the oily, petroleum breast. "Drill, baby, brill".[14] Fear of the power of the earthly mother has led to a flight upwards to the throne-world of the heavenly father far removed from the Earth. This masculine world has spawned sterile brother-religions, the colonisation of matter, the hatred of women, the survival of the fittest and, because it has cast itself out from the rest of Creation, a suicidal civilisation.

This denial is the physical twin to the spiritual belief that the heavenly father will rapture us upward—if we have behaved properly—into a

---

14. Probably taken from "Burn, baby, burn" in the 1965 Watts riots in Los Angeles.

paradise with a spiritually better standard of living. The fundamentalist belief in the global economy and the fundamentalist belief in jihad have the same quantum of religious fervour attached to them. One believes in lethal and unrestricted materiality, the other in lethal and constricted spirituality. Now it has come about that the most fanatically material, the West, is at war with the most fanatically spiritual, Isis. The worst, as Yeats wrote, are full of passionate intensity, driven by an archetype that is beyond their control. What is the result? A global economy, which ostensibly values prudent financial management, that has been on a manic spending spree for the last five hundred years without checking the bank account. Only five countries in the world have no debt. The national debt of the USA, the richest country in the world, now stands at $20 trillion. Please make sense of this for me.

Seemingly, no one has considered the obvious, and done the sums, despite the warnings. We will run out of oil, of steel, of fish, of forests, of water, of food, of room. Profits? Stock markets? Money supply? All based on growth. Can we imagine an economic model that does not include annual growth? Our inability to do so is a measure of our denial. As the Club of Rome pointed out in 1972 there are limits to growth. It's like watching the apocalyptic train crash in slow motion. And crash it will.

8

ORACLES MODERN: FAUST, TITANIC AND 9/11

JUST WATCHING WHAT HAPPENS

WE LEAVE BEHIND the ancient oracles of Ovid and the Maya and turn to more recent literature and events which, perhaps not oracular in the ancient sense, were harbingers of what is to come and what is already here.

Goethe

Johann Wolfgang von Goethe (1749–1832) was a poet, novelist, playwright, natural philosopher, and diplomat. Of broad talent, his work includes epic and lyric poetry; prose and verse dramas; memoirs; an autobiography; literary criticism; scientific treatises on botany, anatomy, and colour; and four novels. And he was a painter and illustrator.

He was a literary celebrity by the age of 25, following the success of his first novel, *The Sorrows of Young Werther*. A member of the Duke of Weimar's privy council, he sat on the war and highway commissions, and implemented administrative reforms at the University of Jena. His first major scientific work, *The Metamorphosis of Plants*, was published in 1788. In 1791, he was made managing director of the theatre at Weimar. Ralph Waldo Emerson named Goethe as one of six "representative men" alongside Plato, Napoleon, Swedenborg, Montaigne, and

Shakespeare. There are frequent references to Goethe's writings throughout the works of Hegel, Schopenhauer, Kierkegaard, Nietzsche, Spengler, Hesse, Mann, Freud, and Jung. His poems were set to music throughout the eighteenth and nineteenth centuries by a number of composers, including Mozart, Beethoven, Schubert, Brahms, Mendelssohn, and Massenet.

Faust was Goethe's magnum opus and considered by many to be the greatest work of German literature. He first set out a rough outline in the winter of 1771–1772 when he was 22–23 years old. He did not pursue the project further until his return from Italy in 1790, aged 40, when he converted the play from prose to poetry.[1] He published Part One in 1808 and Part Two, which concerns us here, was published posthumously in 1832.

Faust

The historical Johann Georg Faust (c. 1480–1540) was an itinerant alchemist, astrologer, and magician. He became a folk legend and inspired many literary works such as Christopher Marlowe's play *The Tragical History of Doctor Faustus* (c. 1587), and *The Devil and Daniel Webster* (1937) by Stephen Benet, as well as operas by Gounod and Berlioz, and works by Wagner, Schumann, Liszt, and Mahler.

The Protestant Reformation of Martin Luther in Germany and Henry VIII in England in the early 1500s loosened the hold of the Roman Catholic church and set the stage for the emergence of the Enlightenment during the 1700s. The latter encompassed ideas, now unquestioned in Western culture, which centred on reason as the primary source of authority and legitimacy, and ideals such as liberté, égalité, fraternité (freedom, equality and fraternity), progress, tolerance, constitutional government, and the separation of church and state.

Voltaire (1694–1778) and Jean-Jacques Rousseau (1712–1778) argued for a society based upon reason rather than faith and religious doctrine, for a new civil order based on natural law, and for knowledge

---

1. For the psychological significance of age 40 see Owen, *Jung and the Moon Cycles*, 116–128.

based on scientific experiments and observation rather than superstition and ignorance. The political philosopher Montesquieu (1689–1755) introduced the idea of the separation of government powers, a concept which was adopted by the authors of the United States Constitution. The United States declared its independence from British rule in 1776, and the storming of the Bastille and the fall of the monarchy took place in 1789.

Goethe wrote Faust—prophetic, as we shall see—against the background of these upheavals in collective consciousness which erupted from a long incubation in the collective unconscious. An archetypal energy will only emerge out of the endless potentials in the collective unconscious as a new idea or discovery or movement when either it is needed as a compensation to collective consciousness, or if the time is right—for the archetype, that is, not for humans. We must assume that archetypal forces have their own life and timing that is outside of our ken. Monotheists might call this "the will of God".

The common theme in writings about Faust is that he is a successful academic but is dissatisfied with his life. He makes a deal with the devil, selling his soul for worldly knowledge, pleasure and power. A "Faustian pact" refers to a situation where an ambitious person surrenders their integrity in order to achieve power and success.[2]

Philemon and Baucis (reprise)

The strands of our story—this historical aeon, apocalypse, Earth, Jung, Philemon, and Goethe—are all woven together in Faust. The second part of Faust tells the story of Ovid's Philemon and Baucis and we shall wander through Goethe's reweaving of the story. However, Goethe disavowed any relationship with Ovid's story. "My Philemon and Baucis... have nothing to do with that renowned ancient couple or the tradition connected with them. I gave this couple the names merely to elevate the characters. The persons and relations are similar, and hence

---

2. The legendary Delta blues guitarist Robert Johnson (1911–1938) reputedly made a deal with the devil, at a Mississippi crossroads, in exchange for his genius with the guitar. His song "Crossroads" was recorded by Eric Clapton and Cream in 1968.

the use of the names has a good effect".[3] If we take this at face value—
which Jung did not, saying Goethe was "trying to conceal his vestiges"
—it suggests that Goethe was unaware of the meaning of his drama and
was "inside" the archetype, with no external objectivity towards it.

Faust struck a deep chord in Jung. His first major work, *Psychology
of the Unconscious*, was littered with references to, and discussions of,
Faust.[4] In a letter of February 28, 1932 to Max Rychner he wrote:
"Faust is the most recent pillar in that bridge of the spirit which spans
the morass of world history.... It seems to me that we cannot meditate
enough about Faust, for many of the mysteries of the second part are
still unfathomed. Faust is not of this world and therefore it transports
you; it is as much the future as the past and therefore the most living
present".[5]

Jung explicitly linked his Philemon with the figure of that name in
the second part of Faust. In a letter to Paul Schmitt, dated January 5,
1942, he wrote:

> You have hit the mark absolutely: all of a sudden and with terror it
> became clear to me that I have taken over Faust as my heritage, and
> moreover as the advocate and avenger of Philemon and Baucis, who,
> unlike Faust the superman, are the hosts of the gods in a ruthless and
> godforsaken age.... I would give the earth to know whether Goethe
> himself knew why he called the two old people 'Philemon' and 'Baucis.'
> Faust sinned from the beginning against these first parents. One must
> have one foot in the grave, though, before one understands this secret
> properly.[6]

In a letter of June 7, 1955 to Alice Raphael, he added,

> Ad Philemon and Baucis: a typical Goethean answer to Eckermann!
> trying to conceal his vestiges. Philemon (= kiss), the loving one, the

---

3. June 6, 1831, cited in Goethe, *Faust*, tr. W. Arndt, New York: Norton, 1976, p. 428.
4. First published in German in 1912, it was extensively revised by Jung in 1952 and is Volume 5 of the Collected Works.
5. *Letters* 1, 88–89.
6. *Letters* 1, 308.

simple old loving couple, close to the earth and aware of the Gods, the complete opposite to the Superman Faust, the product of the devil.... The risk is, that the artifex becomes identical with the goal of his opus. He becomes inflated and crazy.... There is a 'demon' in the prima materia, that drives people crazy. That's what happened to Faust [and Erysichthon] and incidentally to the German nation. The end was the great conflagration of German cities, where all the simple people burned to death.[7] .... Faust II is a great prophecy of the future anticipated in alchemical symbolism. The archetype is always past, present and future.... Faust's own future will be destroyed through the fire of concupiscentia and its madness.[8]

Around 1958 he wrote: "When Faust, in his hubris and self-inflation, caused the murder of Philemon and Baucis, I felt guilty, quite as if I myself in the past had helped commit the murder of these the two old people. This strange idea alarmed me, and I regarded it as my responsibility to atone for this crime, or to prevent its repetition.... Later I consciously linked my work to what Faust had passed over: respect for the eternal rights of man, recognition of 'the ancient,' and the continuity of culture and intellectual history".[9]

Finally, Edward Edinger said, "Goethe's Faust is a 'document of the soul' of major importance for the psychological understanding of modern man. It is perhaps the central 'collective dream' of the Western psyche during the final quarter of the Christian aeon."[10]

Mephistopheles

Faust, Part One is personal and Faust, Part Two is archetypal. The central themes of Faust are searching, longing, desire, power, and love.[11] In Part One the story opens with God and Mephistopheles (the Devil)

---

7. Jung refers here to the bombing of Dresden and Hamburg.
8. Sonu Shamdasani, Who is Jung's Philemon?, *Jung History*, 2007, www.philemon-foundation.org/resources/newsletter-jung-history
9. MDR, 235, 249.
10. Edinger, *Goethe's Faust*, 9.
11. Ibid., 25.

bargaining for the soul of Faust, an academic who has long searched for enlightenment through scholarly knowledge.

The psyche is aristocratic, that is, it has a hierarchy and structure. (It is also democratic but that is not the point here). When one drive exceeds its allotted place then it becomes "devilish." Mephistopheles is the diabolical psychic function that has broken loose from the hierarchy of the psyche and enjoys independence and absolute power.[12]

Mephistopheles tricks Faust into leaving his academic pursuits and he plunges into life. In his adventures he encounters Gretchen, a young virgin, and goes on to magically conjure up Helen of Troy. Eventually the Emperor, in gratitude for Faust's help in gaining victory in war, grants him rights to the coastline of the Emperor's domain. His great plan is to extend the land by draining the marshes and pushing back the sea. There he plans to establish a paradise on earth, won from the ocean bed, where he believes humankind, winning the struggle over the forces of nature, will become free.

Marie-Louise von Franz comments:

If Faust had not met him he would have killed himself, or else withered away as a bookworm. But Faust could not stand up to Mephistopheles. He fell victim to an inflation and, at the end of the tragedy, to the lust for power. *That* is how Mephistopheles became his destroyer. Jung was disgusted, therefore, when Mephistopheles was disposed of at the end and relegated to hell, through the angel's cheap trick.

Faust's fate shows what happens when the constellated archetypal image of Mercurius meets a weak and morally childish consciousness which cannot defend its ethical integrity;[13] he seduces it into betrayal and murder. For Faust, in order to wrest more land from the sea, disposed of that old couple, Philemon and Baucis, who, according to legend, were the only ones still worshipping the gods Jupiter and Mercury in a time of general decay and immorality. The arrogant,

---

12. CW 12, par. 88.

13. Mercury was, amongst other things, the god of boundaries, transitions, money, thievery, and shape-shifting. Faust was seduced by money and power. Money, like Mercury, is the only thing that can be changed into any other thing. Where there is money there is Mercury. For Donald Trump a relationship is a Mercurial, transactional event.

hybris-filled way in which we are today destroying the natural environment and whose evil consequences we are just beginning to recognize, corresponds to this Faustian inflation.[14]

Faust begins to drain his lands and builds a palace and a port for trading riches with foreign countries. However, his plans are frustrated because an old couple, Philemon and Baucis, live on the land and refuse to sell their cottage. Act V opens with a Wanderer who was shipwrecked many years before and saved by Philemon and Baucis. He returns to visit them and thank them for their kindness. They tell the Wanderer how "Right and left, the land is teeming, offering men a new existence." This scene ends with them going to the temple and praying to "an ancient God."

Faust plans to remove them from where they are and offer them "a new estate." He sends Mephistopheles and three "mighty men" to remove them from the house. Mephistopheles returns later and tells Faust that they knocked on the door but heard no reply. Then they banged down the door. "But we did not make much ado, / And quickly cleared them out for you. / The couple did not suffer much, / Fright stopped their hearts with scarce a touch."[15] Faust replies, "Did you not hear me that I bade, / Not robbery but simply trade? ... Commanded fast, too fast obeyed. / What hovers toward me like a shade?"

Faust denies any responsibility for the deaths, blaming Mephistopheles. After all he made his instructions clear and he cannot be responsible if they are not carried out. There is no sign of introspection and curiosity about how this should all come about on his watch. Just collateral damage.

Faust then feels "a shade" approach and four grey women appear—Want (or Lack), Debt-Guilt, Care and Need. Grey is the colour of no-colour. It is not the complete absence of colour like black or the mixing of colours as in white but it is halfway between black and white. It is the colour that is drained of colour and life. When someone is not well we say they look "a bit grey." Grey is the colour of Famine sent by Demeter,

---

14. Von Franz, *C G Jung: His Myth in Our Time*, 212-213.

15. A modern version is from Saudi Arabia: "Saudi forces 'told to kill' to clear land for eco-city". https://www.bbc.com/news/world-middle-east-68945445

from the cold northern regions, to punish Erysichthon. Faust has shut out want, guilt, need and care from his life. Now they're back.

Care

Want, Debt, Need and Care are all conditions of deficiency. The German word for debt (Schuld) also means guilt. Both imply a deficit—one a lack of money or lack of acknowledgement of debt, the other a lack of remorse for harm done. The Maya say that we are in debt to the other world for this gift of life and the spirits must be fed through the beauty of life and death—prayers, food, tears, art, dance and death—which does not have to be physical death, they will accept the beauty of symbolic death. So Faust does not acknowledge his debt to the land, or the spirits of the land, or the people of the land that he is taken for his own. He is deficient and does not know his deficiency.

But is Care a condition of scarcity and absence? The word has very different roots from what we would expect from its modern-day usage, where the histrionic wails, "You don't care about me anymore!" or the photo headline of a US state governor lying on the beach, after the state budget has fallen through, with the headline "Chris Christie has stopped caring." It is the ultimate slight, the deepest accusation of our lack of basic humanity. Everyone is supposed to care.

The root of the word care is the Old English *caru* meaning to sorrow, grieve, wail or lament. Careful means to be full of woe, anxious, full of concern. We wail for what we have lost. We cannot grieve for what we did not love. There is no care without grief and there is no grief without loss and absence of what we have cared for. Our "Western values" suffer from a surfeit of care, sweetened, dollied up and religiously sentimentalised. And all this care is reserved for our fellow humans. But what of care's companions—worry and grief for what has been and will be lost? There is none. Until the last 50 years or so human hubris and excess was a fairly local affair, confined to industrialised countries. Now they are global and there is no Planet B.

Faust is a rich man and the grey women will not go into his house. Want says, "I am turned a shadow." Guilt says, "I am out of place." Need says, "From me he would turn his pampered face." Care says that her sisters cannot and should not go into the house and forthwith slips in through the keyhole. But why Care and why through the keyhole? Want, need and guilt would leave no impression. Locks and keys symbolise opening and closing, entry and exit, freedom and imprisonment. The key to something is a solution to a problem. Care's entry through the keyhole suggests that the lament, loss and anticipatory worry that she embodies are the key to Faust's problems. She says to Faust: "Is Care a force you never faced?"

Faust replies:
Through all the world I only raced
Whatever I might crave, I laid my hand on
What would not do, I would abandon
And what escaped, I would let go
I only would desire and attain...

Care responds:
He whom I have conquered could
Own the world and not feel good
Gloom surrounds him without end
Sun shall not rise nor descend
Though his senses all abide Darknesses now dwell inside
And though he owned every treasure
None should give him any pleasure.

The last two lines remind us of Erysichthon. As far as we know Goethe did not draw on Ovid's story but the similarities are clear. Faust tells Care that he does not recognise her power and she should leave. He does not want to hear her "wretched litany" and "thousand miseries." (No doubt all the optimists who might read this book would applaud). Like Demeter's famine, Care leaves him with a curse—she breathes on Faust and makes him blind. He is rendered psychologically unconscious, unable to see, or to have any insight. This has profound implications if we read these stories as an outline of things to come. Faust does not let Care, the possibility of loss, into his heart. The prospect of any conscious guilt, remorse, regret or even ruefulness has gone. He was spiritually blind, now he is physically blind. He goes to his death with the damage buried deep.

When this comes to the surface, as it will, the force is multiplied like a beach ball pressed down under water and suddenly released. Then our children many times removed will fall into the deep crevasse of grief carved by our neglect.

Faust, blinded, hears the sounds of digging outside and thinks that ditches are being dug to complete the work of draining the marshes. Actually, the workmen are digging his grave. He gives voice to his final grand fantasy:

> A swamp still skirts the mountain chain,
> And poisons all the land retrieved;
> This marshland I hope yet to drain,
> And thus surpass what we achieved.
> For many millions I shall open regions
> To dwell, not safe, in free and active legions.
> Green are the meadows, fertile; and in mirth
> Both men and herds live on this newest earth,
> Settled along the edges of a hill
> That has been raised by bold men's zealous will.

With that Faust sinks to the ground and dies. In his final speech we can hear the familiar ghosts of development, colonisation, westward expansion, and the taming of nature. Mephistopheles waits by the grave to capture Faust's soul as soon as it leaves his body. The dangers encountered by the soul on its journey from the moment of death to its arrival on the Beach of Stars is known to many cultures, as witness *The Tibetan Book of the Dead* or the movie *Ghost* where dark shades try to capture Sam's soul after he is killed by a mugger. But angels come singing of roses and bliss-scented flowers. Mephistopheles begins to feel horny. "You hover there, come down: I feel a passion. Please move your lovely limbs in a more worldly fashion." While he is so distracted the angels make off with Faust's "immortal part." In other words, his soul.

The last scene returns to nature. It is set in "mountain gorges, forest, rock and desert with holy anchorites scattered up the mountainsides, encamped between clefts." Anchorites withdrew from the world into seclusion in nature or to an anchoritic cell, often a small room attached to a church which they never left, where they spent most of their time in prayer and contemplation. The ritual of consecration and enclosure in their cell was similar to a funeral rite—a dying to this world.[16]

So already we are drawn upward to heavenly contemplation and away from the Earth. Four heavenly fathers with ascending degrees of divine knowledge appear: Pater Profundus (the lowest), Pater Seraphicus (the middle), Pater Ecstaticus (higher) and Doctor Marianus (in the "highest, cleanest cell"). "Blessed Boys" (infants who died at birth and did not suffer any earthly travails) sing, "Strip off the lowly, earthly cocoon" and the "More Perfected Angels" intone, "To carry earth's remains still has distressed us. All earthly things have stains." And so on. Then a quaternity of four women appear. Magna Peccatrix (the Great Sinneress), the Samaritan woman, Mary of Egypt, and the Penitent One. Finally, the Virgin Mary (Mater Gloriosa) grants their wishes and ushers Faust into Heaven.

If we look under the heavy and heavenly Christian robes we discover that Faust's story has a somewhat forced and discordant ending. After his earthly dealings with Mephistopheles, the Emperor, Gretchen, Helen and his "development" of the swamp land with grandiose plans, comes a violent compensation after his death. We are pulled upward into the highest reaches of heaven where earth and matter are a stain and treated with disdain, like poor cousins who don't know better or earthly contaminants that are best removed. In other words, the supplicants will someday receive the grace of heaven and come to a much happier place but until then we'll maybe accept them if they scrub up properly before they come upstairs.

The saving grace is that after we have ascended into higher, purified realms and have heard from the heavenly fathers, the blessed boys (no girls), and the neutered angels, we then see biblical women who have more earth and gravitas to them. But to Goethe these women each had

---

16. Probably the best-known is the anchoress Julian of Norwich (1342–1416), author of *Revelations of Divine Love*, which was the first book in the English language known to have been written by a woman.

something to be ashamed of (great sins, being a Samaritan, adultery, and insatiable passion) except for the Mater Gloriosa, the Virgin Mary, who in contrast stands above all, clean and pure. Goethe ends Faust, with the following:

> O contrite hearts, seek with your eyes
> The visage of salvation;
> Blissful in that gaze, arise,
> Through glad regeneration.
> Now may every pulse of good
> Seek to serve before thy face,
> Virgin, Queen of Motherhood,
> Keep us, Goddess, in thy grace.
> All things corruptible
> Are but a parable;
> Earth's insufficiency
> Here finds fulfilment;
> Here the ineffable
> Wins life through love;
> Eternal Womanhood
> Leads us above.

So Goethe ends with the same Christian distaste for matter. But at least the triple-bodied goddess is alive in the other world, idealised but not completely obliterated or sanitised. There is hope yet for normal service to be resumed at some time in future. Goethe's view of heaven betrays its shadow. It cannot tolerate the transitory—eternity is all; it does not suffer insufficiency and urges fulfilment; it cannot leave the indescribable as such and must have completion; and it idealises purity. It is addicted to perfection.

Jung said, "What makes Goethe's Faust so profoundly significant is that it formulates a problem that had been brewing for centuries, just as Oedipus did for the Greek sphere of culture: how to extricate ourselves from between the Scylla of world-renunciation and the Charybdis of its acceptance."[17] Faust was unsatisfactory to Jung in many ways. He thought Faust was one-sided and he could not forgive Goethe for having dismissed Mephistopheles by trickery and portraying evil as innocuous.[18] Jung saw himself as someone who could carry on from where Goethe had lost his nerve. Life had set Jung a question, or he himself was a question posed to life. He felt he must give his own answer or else rely on the collective answer.[19] In his carving "Repentance of Faust" Jung acknowledged the question that he was an answer to. This had to do with the rewriting and reparation, so to speak, of the cheap ending of Faust. He did this in *Answer to Job*, written in the spring of 1951, seeing the monotheistic God in its wholeness both light and dark.

17. CW 5, par. 121.
18. MDR, 60–61.
19. Ibid., 318.

9

———

JUNG AND THE AEON

LAST VISIONS

JUNG OFTEN WROTE about archetypal changes throughout history but he did so most clearly in his work *Aion*. He left behind incalculable gifts, many yet to come into collective consciousness. Edward Edinger said that Jung was the new Aion, and that he could not have perceived the events of the aeon of Pisces unless he was already outside it and viewing it from the next aeon. He added, "The numinous reality of the psyche will no longer be carried by religious communities—the church, the synagogue, or the mosque—but instead it will be carried by conscious individuals."[1] Yes, the church, the mosque and the synagogue have had their day for some but Edinger's viewpoint is overly individual, I think, and ignores the original community. If recovery and renaissance is to come it will not only be within individuals but within a renewed, more conscious relationship with the largest community we have—this planet Earth.

Kairos

In ancient Greece there were three words for time, kronos, kairos and

———

1. Edinger, *The Aion Lectures*, 192–193.

aeon. Kronos is quantitative, tick-tock, profane, temporal time. Kronos is birthdays, getting older, biological clocks, diaries, deadlines and appointments. We must adapt, time and tide will not wait. We have to immerse ourselves in life in order to get one. We adapt to our collective reality and allow life to make its mark on us. Then, like the children of Kronos, we are eventually eaten by time.

Kairos is sacred, eternal time. It is the right time, the moment of opportunity, the perfect time, the qualitative time, the "now." In the New Testament kairos means "the appointed time in the purpose of God." It is the time when God acts. It cannot be measured, only experienced. In these moments everything "flows" timelessly and without effort. Time stands still, an hour passes in a second, a second stretches to eternity. These moments occur when we draw close to the other world, often in archetypal situations of intense creativity, danger, ecstasy, love-making, or death. They transcend kronos and stir emotions and realisations that result in decisive action. Carpe diem! Seize the day! Then we leave our mark on time itself. Kairos alters destiny and destiny alters kairos. To miss kronos is inconvenient. To miss kairos is tragedy.

The word monk comes from the Greek *monachos*, meaning single, solitary, or unique, which in turn derives from *monos* meaning alone and *monas* meaning one. In the monk's separation from the human world he draws closer to his own nature and nature itself. In so doing, he is able to notice what is his kairos and what is merely kronos. The culture of productivity does not know the difference.

Kairos moments (and now the dates become important) are those upon which personal or collective destiny turn. For example, Lincoln's two-minute Gettysburg address in November 1863 where he declared that "government of the people, by the people, for the people, shall not perish from the earth." Churchill's speech to the House of Commons in June 1940 when he said, "This was their finest hour." Kennedy's assassination on November 22, 1963. And 9/11.

Kairos is when our free will choice acts on what life offers us and diverts the stream of collective history or an individual life in unimaginable directions. Kairos is to align ourselves with the greater flow of life both in our history, our whakapapa, stretching back to the creation of the worlds both material and spiritual, and forwards to be the ancestors who are the kaitiaki, the custodians of the world that our great-great-grandchildren will inherit.

We have to be slow enough to be fast enough to catch kairos. When our relationship to the natural world is severed we lose our connection to kairos. The seasonal changes lose their meaning. Forests, streams, oceans and snow are less able to turn their robe. Time becomes linear and divisible. Moon time, sun time and star time are no longer visible. We take the jagged little pill and the web is torn.

Time connects us to experience. We talk of time as a commodity, being in time, on time, losing time, having too much time, not having enough time. All that is left of being outside of time are lazy summer afternoons in the deck chair. Time is no longer sacred so now we have disorders of time, where time is dismembered: dissociative disorder, attention deficit disorder, obsessive-compulsive disorder.

An aeon is an age or a long period of time, time without beginning or end. Aion, the god of eternal or cyclical time, is its personification. Both chronos and kairos are human time but an aeon is a totality that stands outside of time. Psychologically the ego is within the aeon. It cannot be objective about its own time and culture. However Jung was able to stand outside his time and view it objectively.

> The theme of this work is the idea of the Aeon (Greek, Aion). My investigation seeks, with the help of Christian, Gnostic, and alchemical symbols of the self, to throw light on the change of psychic situation within the "Christian aeon." The Christian tradition... is filled with intimations of a kind of enantiodromian reversal of dominants.[2] I mean by this the dilemma of Christ and Antichrist. Probably most of the historical speculations about time and the limitation of time were influenced, as the Apocalypse shows, by astrological ideas.... [T]he symbol of the Fishes for the Pisces aeon is the synchronistic concomitant of two thousand years of Christian development.... Because these texts relegate the appearance of Antichrist to the end of time, we are

---

2. Jung used the term enantiodromia to describe the emergence of the unconscious opposite over the course of time, from the Greek philosopher Heraclitus, *enantio-*, opposite or counter to, and *dromas*, running.

justified in speaking of a "Christian aeon," which, it was presupposed, would find its end with the Second Coming. It seems as if this expectation coincides with the astrological conception of the "Platonic month" of the Fishes.[3] If, as seems probable, the aeon of the fishes is ruled by the archetypal motif of the hostile brothers, then the approach of the next Platonic month, namely Aquarius, will constellate the problem of the union of opposites.[4]

During the summer of 1936, Jung found a dead snake with a fish in its mouth and was so struck by this synchronistic event that he carved it on the wall of the courtyard at Bollingen, his country retreat. The image, of the pagan spirit eating up the Christian spirit, and the reconciling symbol that would be born from these two opposites, was the major theme of Aion.[5] It was Jung who came across the snake and the fish and made meaning of it. In fact, it was Jung and his work who were the reconciling symbol.

In February 1944, Jung fell while on his daily walk and broke his leg. Whilst in hospital he suffered a thrombosis and was critically ill for three weeks. As a result of his experiences during this time when he was close to death, his work changed. Over the years, he had been urged to say something about the transference in psychotherapy, so in 1945 he took a part of *Mysterium Coniunctionis*, which he had written before his illness, and submitted it for publication as *The Psychology of the Transference*, which was published in 1946. These two works, together with Aion and Answer to Job, form a quaternity that came out of his illness. Jung probably began writing Aion in late 1947, when he was 72, and it was published in 1950.

The subtitle of Aion is *Researches into the Phenomenology of the Self*.

---

3. CW 9ii, ix.
4. CW 9ii, para 142. For a further discussion see Owen, *The Maya Book of Life*, Chapter 24, Temperate Man.
5. In editing the final draft of this chapter I walked out onto the verandah and a metre from me on the floor was a snake—about a metre long and pencil thin—with a gecko, wider than the snake and about a quarter its length, half swallowed. We watched, entranced and motionless, for a full five minutes until one of us moved involuntarily and the snake wriggled away in a flash sans lunch and the gecko so in the opposite direction.

As an intuitive in a dominant sensation culture, trying to keep his head down and not prejudice his scientific reputation, Jung was at great pains to describe his work as scientific. His writing is packed with numerous comparative literary, mythological and symbolic references, as if the sheer weight of scholarship would deter any criticism denouncing it as being unscientific or lacking in proof.

He said, in conversation with Margaret Ostrowski-Sachs: "Before my illness [in 1944] I had often asked myself if I were permitted to publish or even speak of my secret knowledge. I later set it all down in Aion. I realised it was my duty to communicate these thoughts, yet I doubted whether I was allowed to give expression to them. During my illness I received confirmation and I now knew that everything had meaning and that everything was perfect."[6]

His vast sweep of the two thousand-year period of the Piscean age ranges from succinct summaries of ego, shadow, anima and animus, through Christ as a symbol of the Self, the symbol of the fish, Gnosticism and alchemy, to a model of the structure and dynamics of the Self. Aion is about the archetypal significance of the Age of Pisces and the coming of the Age of Aquarius, and how the workings of archetypal processes during the Piscean era resulted in the Christ image (frequently associated with the fish) becoming one-sidedly spiritual and lacking in substance and instinct. The transition from one astrological Age to another comes about as the spring equinox moves, or precesses, out of one constellation into another. The lion-headed Aion was a Mithraic god and Jung was intensely involved in the study of Mithraism. Since Jung's death, it has come to light that the mystery of the precession of the equinoxes was at the centre of Mithraic initiatory ceremonies.

Trinity

In his essay "A Psychological Approach to the Dogma of the Trinity," Jung discussed how the Christian Father, Son and the Holy Ghost are

---

6. Ostrowski-Sachs, *From Conversations with C G Jung*, 68.

three stages of a developmental process.[7] He said that the world of the Father symbolises a childhood state, a pristine oneness with nature without critical judgement or moral conflict. The world of the Son is filled with longing for redemption and for the oneness when humankind was one with the Father. Now humans had free will but freedom from the law of the heavenly father or the instincts of the earthly mother (nature) brings about a sharpening distinction between the opposites and inevitable conflict. This two-ness oscillates between the opposites and eventually a third is triangulated in to resolve the conflict.

The progression to the third stage of three-ness is, psychologically, a subordination to the will of the unconscious (the Self). Theologically, it is obedience to the will of God. Just as the movement from the first stage to the second requires the sacrifice of childish dependence so the movement to the third stage requires that civilised independence has to be sacrificed. In Christianity the agency that brings together the seemingly irreconcilable opposites is called the Holy Ghost. Psychologically, Jung called this agency the Self.

At the third stage, because they are two forms of the same thing, I would substitute the Earth for the unconscious or the Self. With the Self, if we are fortunate, we eventually find our limits psychologically. Similarly, with the Earth, we will find our limits materially. But the global economy remains at stage one—a childish dependence, a kindergarten, or rather a nursery, with no adults in the room. It is a measure of our superficiality and parallels our "No worries, we can technology our way out of this" attitude to our earthly home.

This has its parallel in clinical psychology.[8] We think we can change ourselves by facile fiddling with our "cognitions." CBT (cognitive behavioural therapy) is a popular and "evidence-based" psychological treatment.[9] It is sufficient, mostly, is useful, and I use it in my practice.

---

7. CW 11, *Psychology and Religion: West and East*, par. 199–205.
8. In New Zealand clinical psychology training and practice is monocultural. CBT, DBT, ACT, ABA, PET and that's about it. Acronyms find a comfortable home here. Other jurisdictions such as North America or the UK have a broader base.
9. For an alternative view see the work of Jonathan Shedler. Shedler, J. (2018). Where Is the Evidence for "Evidence-Based" Therapy? Psychiatric Clinics of North America, 41(2),

But our extroverted culture is psychologically naive and has yet to develop much discrimination with regard to levels of psychological change. CBT is like giving McDonald's to someone who has never had food. It'll keep them from starving but it's not a real meal.

Aquarius

On the basis of Ptolemy's Almagest and the precessional calculations available in the 1940s, Jung said that the Age of Aquarius would begin between 2000–2200 CE. If the aeon of the fishes is ruled by the archetype of the hostile brothers then Aquarius, he said, would constellate the problem of the union of the opposites.[10]

He divided the Christian aeon into four quarters with a nodal point at each 500 year period. Beginning with the Desert Fathers around 300 CE monasticism, with vows of poverty, chastity and obedience, spread throughout the Near East and to Europe in later centuries. Benedict of Nursia (c. 480–550 CE) so abhorred the immorality of Roman society that, at the age of fourteen, he chose the life of a monk and lived as a hermit in a cave. He eventually founded the order of Benedictine monks at Montecassino and wrote the Rule of Saint Benedict. Monasticism was a mass collective effort to withdraw from the world, tame the instincts and the body, and subject them to the rule of God.

Halfway through the aeon, around 1000 CE, saw the rise of heretical sects like the Cathars and the split between matter and spirit became even wider. For example, the Cathars believed that all visible matter, including the human body, was created by Satan, and matter was therefore tainted with sin; they also believed that Christ did not incarnate in physical form in a material body so they refused the Eucharist; and they avoided anything that was a by-product of sexual reproduction. They were persecuted for their heresies by the Catholic

---

319–329. https://doi.org/10.1016/j.psc.2018.02.001; Shedler, J. (2010). The efficacy of psychodynamic psychotherapy. *American Psychologist, 65*(2), 98–109. https://doi.org/10.1037/a0018378

10. CW 9ii, par. 142.

Church, who held that there was only one God who created all things visible and invisible.

By the time Christ was born the turn had been well and truly made —upwards to spirit and away from the Earth. So the People of the Book (the Bible, the Torah and the Q'uran) were born, all things had been decided, nothing more needed to be done in the perfection of the single God's world. Contrast this with an indigenous view that the seeming stability and lawfulness of matter is but a reflection of the current habits of the Great Spirit. Indigenous laws, ceremonies and the decisions there from are not canonised or written down because they are unfinished. Just as the Creator is in a constant state of creation so the supposedly immutable, Newtonian "laws" of physics and chemistry are also evolving. Similarly, hear the religiosity of the Second Amendment. The right to bear arms is fixed, immutable and sacred within the holiness of the Constitution. The worshippers at that particular altar are mostly pale, male and stale.

I do not imply that indigenous cultures are inherently superior. As with Western culture, the "masses" are just as easily captured by religious fervour or mass movements. But there are also highly individuated women and men—war chiefs, medicine chiefs, shamans, clever women, men of high degree, curanderas—who are holders, keepers and teachers of profound bodies of knowledge at least the equal of, but different from, our Western knowledge. Collectively and most importantly, they are the holders and keepers of something that no longer exists in Western culture—an eros, a relationship, with the Earth.

God-image without

At the end of his life Jung said that, because the numinosity of the natural world had been stripped away by rationalism and science, the rediscovery of that withdrawn energy as the unconscious was inevitable.[11] In other words, when the world outside us died and became mere matter then the Self, the God-image within, had to be created internally. However, I would suggest that the Self—a psychological

---

11. C G Jung, *Man and His Symbols*, 85.

construct of wholeness—was in fact not primary but a secondary by-product of the separation from the wholeness of creation. The Earth itself was the primordial God-image without.

Our biases lead us to believe that spirit came first and was always the prime mover. But what if all things including spirit, the ineffable, or the unknowable, were born of matter? This suggests that the natural world embodies all the paradoxes and opposites that Jung attributed to the Self. The prime mover is matter in all its glory—moist and dark in its beauty robe, and resplendent as the stars in the night sky. In Spirit, her first born, this beauty is made hidden and invisible. But the first born, as is ever the case, kills the father just as Cronus (Saturn) killed his father Ouranos (the Sky) and ate his own children. The history of spirit has been a holocaust for the Earth.

Vertical ascensionism (a severe and untreatable terraphobia masquerading as godliness) and the strictures of monasticism in the first thousand years of the Fishes, combined with empiricism and empire in the second thousand years, left beauty and wholeness with no place to hide. This was the final phase in the gradual tearing of the web of relationship with All Our Relations that had begun after the end of the last ice age and the beginning of farming. But hide they did, in a place no-one, not even humans, would find them—within the human psyche.

The ability to take an objective attitude toward our own psyche is what we call consciousness. In order to have what Jung called ruthless self-knowledge one has to perceive our own psychological experience as an object rather than as a subject.[12] In other words to be outside it rather than inside it as the ego is. The psyche is not made by the ego, only discovered by it. We are not responsible for what we find in our psyche but are responsible for what we do with it in external reality. That is our fate.

Just as the individual ego is contained within the psyche and there is no capacity to view itself objectively, so the collective is unable to view itself and the planet we live on objectively. It is contained within the mother and has no objective relationship with what gives it life and beauty. Like Erysichthon, it will keep on eating itself until the end.

---

12. CW 9ii, par, 255.

This is evident in the tangle psychology has found itself in. Western hard science, which psychology longs to cosy up to, sees the body and the mind as separate. They don't have much to do with each other—though this bizarre belief is decaying slowly. If a connection between mind and body is found then it is a "scientific discovery" rather than a dissolving of the molasses of ignorance and stumbling on something that was there all along. When something goes wrong with the body the patient (the sufferer) is not held responsible but if something goes wrong with the psyche then "it's all in your mind." So there is a double standard. If we get physical problems it's not our fault but if we have emotional or mental problems it's all our fault. (Even now mental difficulties are more acceptable than emotional difficulties). There is little middle ground, its either one or t'other, as witness the flip-flop between "depression is just a chemical imbalance" versus "depression is just negative thinking." But either way, chemicals or cognitions will surely get you sorted.

When we lose contact with our roots, our relationship with the natural world, then we become "wretched" as D H Lawrence said. Jung put it this way: "When a living organism is cut off from its roots, it loses the connections with the foundations of its existence and must necessarily perish. When that happens, anamnesis of the origins is a matter of life and death."[13] Depth psychotherapy often begins with an anamnesis —a recollection of one's personal history. An- or a- means without, not, or having no. A-mnesia means lack of mind, having no mind, memory or forgetfulness. A simpler way of putting it would have been "remembering" but anamnesis implies "remembering not to forget." On Yom Hashoah, the Holocaust Remembrance Day, we remember not to forget. The double negative underscores the more nuanced meaning and the additional psychological work involved. In Christian liturgy the anamnesis is the prayer in reminiscence of Christ's sacrifice. In the midst of the great forgetting of our age we must remember not to forget. Not to forget our democratic relationship with all things that share our home.

---

13. CW 9ii, par. 279.

Primitive Jung

In Aion Jung captures the trajectory of the last 2,000 years that bring us to where we are now. But he wrote, I think, within the limitations of a Western world view—by this I mean the Hellenic-Judaic-Islamic-Christian tradition that is confined by that geography. He was interested in other non-indigenous cultures such as China or India but offers little about indigenous cultures. Although he had more experience of non-European cultures than most others of his time, his view was more typical of his time than not. He offers a mistaken and linear view of cultures that are closer to nature suggesting they are in an unconscious symbiosis with the Great Mother and thus lacking in consciousness.

Jung and others referred to surviving Greek, Roman and Egyptian written sources. The global wealth of oral knowledge does not appear in his writing. It has no existence. It has been forgotten—by the dominant culture, at least. So the sources that Jung uses, from the alchemists, to the Gnostics, to the early Christians, to Plato, to Homer, to early Judaism, to the Egyptians, takes us back all of 4,000 years maybe. Compare this to the 50,000-year living history of the Aboriginal peoples of Australia. Jung was beholden to what was available him—the Graeco-Roman tradition that came from a small part of the world now known as Europe and the "Near East". An area roughly 6–10% of the Earth's land surface.

Jung's span generously embraced many traditions but at times was dismissive of, or misunderstood, other traditions, for example, yoga. Of his generation there were few with his breadth of knowledge to gainsay him. On January 17, 1942 he wrote to Pater X. "Yoga, to me, is no more than a subject for research. It neither impresses nor deceives me. During my stay in India I saw for myself that yoga is not at all what we think. There Hatha yoga is often no more than acrobatics, or simply gymnastics; or else it is a physiological aid to concentration, an aid which these highly emotional people need very much in order to master themselves. In the course of these concentration exercises the individual gets into a dream state, or auto-hypnotic condition, which removes him from the world and its illusions. Since the goal of yoga is the void of deep sleep, yoga can never be a final truth for the occidental world."[14]

All Our Relations

Jung saw individuation as an *opus contra naturam*—a work against nature as symbolised in the Bible by the expulsion from the Garden of Eden. We might also consider individuation to be an *opus per naturam* —a work through nature—in that all things in Creation individuate and that it is not exclusive to humans, or to a human psychological process. Why would we think that it is an exclusively human attribute? Individuation is part of our biological and psychological heritage and is itself an archetype.

Jung said that individuation is always accompanied by guilt, or original sin. "Life itself is guilt,"[15] and "We know of course that without sin there is no repentance and without repentance no redeeming grace, also that without original sin the redemption of the world could never have come about...."[16] The process of individuation demands free will choice, which is a theft, an act of disobedience in stealing some of the monotheistic God's omnipotence. Prometheus stole the divine fire, the creative flame, from the Gods and was chained to a rock as punishment. Eve ate of the Tree of Knowledge and was expelled from the Garden of Eden. This theft brings on it the burden of consciousness—responsibility, awareness, and judgement.[17]

This individualistic guilt we can take to be true in Western culture but not necessarily in indigenous cultures. This introverted, personal guilt that Jung refers to results from escaping the gravitational pull of the monotheistic god, the unconscious, and the compulsions of the instincts and matter. It is the compensatory opposite of the extroverted social guilt in indigenous cultures which results from disloyalty to the

---

14. *Letters* 1, 310–311.
15. CW 14, par. 206.
16. CW 12, par. 36.
17. Wickes, *The Inner World of Choice*, p. 8.

group and All Our Relations. A Maori equivalent to Western guilt would be wakamā or shame in the eyes of one's whanau or hapu.

Mitakuye Oyasin is a Lakota phrase meaning "we are all related" or "all my relations" which includes all forms of life including what Western culture regards as inorganic matter—soil, rocks, stones, hills and mountains. In Maoridom, a *mihimihi* is an introduction of yourself on the marae. It tells people where you are from and who you are, linking yourself first to the land, your mountain, your river and sea, and then, in order, your whakapapa (your ancestry), your iwi (tribe), hapu (sub-tribe), and your marae (meeting place).

Western culture has defiled, denigrated and despiritualised matter and as a result has been forced to discover the obvious—that the unseen (the unconscious) exists. Because the unseen is denied and is farther from consciousness, it exerts a greater psychic influence in the process of individuation. Indigenous cultures live closer to the unconscious through a world of matter in which spirit is alive, so Western introverted guilt does not loom as large in the indigenous psyche.

Most importantly, indigenous cultures have not murdered Philemon and Baucis, those who offered a home to the gods. So the expulsion from the Garden of Eden is a quite literal story of the severance of Western culture from the land that supports it. That Western culture has taken this story either as theological dogma or as psychological symbolism is an indication of a blind spot—taken-for-granted and unexamined.

In his last major work *Mysterium Coniunctionis* and at the end of *Answer to Job,* Jung deals with the Assumption of the Virgin Mary. On November 1, 1950, Pius XII, in his papal bull *Assumptio Mariae,* proclaimed the dogma of the bodily assumption of the Virgin Mary into heaven. In Mysterium Coniunctionis Jung refers to an alchemical drawing in which—underneath the upper spiritual quaternary of Mary, God, Christ, and the Holy Ghost—a haloed man with wings, the body of a fish, and snakes for arms is being pulled out of a lump of matter.[18] "This is without doubt the anima mundi [the soul of the world] who has been freed from the shackles of matter, the filius macrocosmi of

---

18. CW 12, fig. 232.

Mercurius-Anthropos, who, because of his double nature, is not only spiritual and physical but unites in himself the morally highest and lowest.[19]"

Jung goes on to say, "The dogmatisation of the Assumptio Mariae... implies... the future birth of the divine child, who, in accordance with the divine trend towards incarnation, will choose as his birthplace the empirical man. This metaphysical process is known to the psychology of the unconscious as the individuation process".[20]

Here Jung perhaps has only half the story. He was heir to the Faustian legacy both as a man of his historical time, and as an introvert who was perhaps more identified with the spiritual end of the instinct/spirit polarity. (Although to be fair, Jung compensated for his intuitive gifts with the building of Bollingen, carving in stone, painting, and his love of cooking). In the figure of the extracted spirit, Jung sees only the introverted aspect of the coming archetypal changes, that is, how the God-image will incarnate, not through a collective saviour, but within each individual. However, Jung leaves out the extroverted aspect. A similar but more differentiated—and significantly twin-headed— image is seen in other alchemical pictures. For example, "The Rebis" appears as the tenth picture in the Rosarium Philosophorum on which Jung based *The Psychology of the Transference*.[21] As the feminine is restored to its rightful place, it will conceive a divine birth in matter, but this birth will be of twins, as in the twin-headed Rebis. One twin will be the inner relationship to spirit, the other twin will be the outer relation- ship to matter, the renewed and reclaimed relationship with the Earth and the honouring of All Our Relations.[22]

Jung and the End

Jung was able to sense movements in the collective psyche and from October 1913 to June 1914 he had several dreams and fantasies which

---

19. CW 14, par. 238.
20. CW 11, par. 755.
21. CW 16, Fig. 10. "The Rosary of the Philosophers" is a series of 20 woodcuts from the alchemical text *De Alchimia opuscula complura veterum philosophorum*, Frankfurt, 1550.
22. This chapter was written in 2000.

he later recognised as precognitions of the coming World War I. Toward the autumn of 1913 he felt a pressure that seemed to be inside him more and more as a concrete outer reality. In October 1913 he had a vision, which was repeated even more vividly two weeks later, in which he saw an enormous flood covering all the land between the North Sea and the Alps, but around Switzerland the mountains grew higher to protect the country. He saw mighty yellow waves, the flotsam of civilisation, thousands of drowned bodies, and then the sea changed into blood.[23] On January 22, 1914 he had another dream, which he painted in 1920, of a "ring of flames floating above a world of war and technology."[24] At that time the idea of war did not occur to Jung at all; it was, however, what war looked like from the point of view of the unconscious. The vision of the flood occurred nine months before the outbreak of WWI on August 1, 1914. War had been conceived in spirit and Jung had seen it.[25]

In order to understand his dreams and visions, Jung knew that he must go down into them. On December 12, 1913, during Advent as he was sitting in his study he let himself "drop" and plunged downward into a dark cave. He waded through icy water to the other end of the cave where he saw a glowing red crystal. Grasping it, he discovered a hollow underneath, where there was flowing water. The corpse of a youth, with blond hair and a wound to the head, floated by, followed by a gigantic scarab beetle, and then by a red, newborn sun rising out of the depths of the water. He tried to replace the crystal but a jet of blood leapt up and continued to spurt for an unendurably long time.

This was a vision of death and rebirth. On the collective level, the corpse represented the naïve rationalism of the 20th century that was bereft of life. In Egyptian mythology, the scarab beetle creates the new Sun god, the coming dominant consciousness, and pushes him up over the horizon. But these deep collective transformations are never possible without great blood sacrifice on another level, as Jung had dreamed.

The personal dimension of this vision emerged six days later when

---

23. MDR, 175–180, and Laurens van der Post, *Jung and the Story of Our Time*, 155.
24. Jaffé, *C. G. Jung: Word and Image*, 68.
25. Shamdasani lists twelve separate images, dreams or fantasies that Jung may have regarded as precognitive. The Red Book, 202.

he dreamed he was with a brown-skinned man on a deserted, mountain landscape. He heard Siegfried's horn sounding over the mountains and he knew they had to kill Siegfried with their rifles. When the hero appeared, they shot him. Jung was filled with disgust and remorse for having destroyed somebody so great and beautiful, and feared the murder might be discovered, but a downpour of rain obliterated all traces of his deed.

Jung awoke with a tremendous feeling of guilt and tried to go back to sleep, but a voice said to him that he must understand the dream immediately, and if he didn't, then he must shoot himself. In his bedside drawer lay a loaded revolver. (At age 19 Jung had begun his annual army service as is usual for Swiss citizens and so owned a gun). But Jung realised that the Siegfried problem—the heroic imposition of the will—was being played out within himself and in the world by the German nation. The dream showed him that the Siegfried attitude no longer suited him and therefore had to be killed.

This is a typical mid-life dream, when all the goals of achievement have been met and the Sun hero must die to allow life to flow onward.[26] So he began to cut away those things that kept him tied to the surface. He had already resigned from his position as editor of the Jahrbuch in October 1913; on April 20, 1914 he resigned as President of the International Psycho-Analytical Association, and on April 30, 1914 he gave up his post as Privatdozent at the university.

Jung's description of this time in late 1914 and early 1915 is typical of the unpredictable energy of the Chaotic Journey, particularly into the West.[27] He said it was a time during which a torrent of fantasies was released and he was in a continual state of tension, but he found himself calmed as he was able to transform his turbulent emotions into images.

On his Chaotic Journey, he had more dreams of a coming catastrophe (symbolising both WWI and Jung's inner conflict), which were repeated three times in April, May, and June 1914. In the dreams, a wave of cold descended from the Arctic in the middle of the summer

---

26. Von Franz, *C G Jung: His Myth in Our Time*, 109.
27. A Chaotic Journey is the unpredictable nine-month period when one travels from one structured three-year cycle to the next in the life span.

and everything turned to ice. In the third dream, however, in June, there was a resolution. At the end of the dream there was a leaf-bearing tree, without fruit, but the leaves had been transformed by the cold into sweet grapes laden with healing juice. Jung plucked them and gave them to a waiting crowd.

That month, on June 28, 1914, Archduke Franz Ferdinand, the successor to the Austrian throne, was murdered in Sarajevo, and on August 1, 1914 WWI began. Jung had begun his Chaotic Journey into the Little Moon of double Death and Change, on July 26, 1914, at age 39.[28] In 1913, Jung had dreamed of WWI. Soon after WWI ended in 1918 he had what he called a "visionary dream" of the coming of WWII. In a letter to Peter Baynes in August 1940, he said that in the dream he was returning from a trip to Germany and his clothes and skin were burnt. He had seen "fire falling like rain from heaven and consuming the cities of Germany. I had an intimation that the crucial year would be 1940." Jung went on to add something important about where the fire would come from. "Since 1918 I knew that a terrible fire would spread over Europe beginning in the North East."[29]

Indeed, 1940 was the crucial year of WWII. By the summer of 1940, Hitler dominated Europe from Norway to the Pyrenees, and the Nazi tide was turned back only by the Battle of Britain in September 1940. The decision that led to the consumption of Germany by fire was made in January 1943. In that month, at the Casablanca Conference, Churchill and Roosevelt decided to launch an around-the-clock strategic bombing offensive against Germany that resulted in the fire-bombing of Hamburg in July 1943 and July 1944, and more controversially, Dresden, in February 1945. Both cities were destroyed by firestorms. In Dresden 25,000 people were killed in one bombing. Compare that to the 50,000 British civilians killed by the Luftwaffe during the whole of WWII, and the 70,000 killed by the atomic bomb dropped on Hiroshima. Jung dreamed that the fire would come from the Northeast. Hamburg is in the north of Germany and Dresden is in the east. The Dresden bombing occurred 27 years after Jung's dream.

---

28. MDR, 234-235. Also CW 10, par. 371-487.
29. *Letters 1*, 285.

Jung began to write his fantasies in what he called The Black Book and elaborated on them, in the form of paintings, in The Red Book. In May 2000 the heirs of Jung's estate decided to permit publication of The Red Book. The announcement was made 39.0 years after Jung died in June 1961, as his death was entering the Moon of double Death and Change. Jung probably began painting in The Red Book around late 1914 and continued until the mid- to late-1920s. So three Big Moon Cycles later, at about 81 years of age, the introverted Red Book has come into elderhood and out into the world.

Jung had many prophetic dreams (no better word than prophetic but it's flypaper for sceptics) during his life. But one must ask, "Why these prophetic dreams by/for/to Jung in particular?" He disavowed, publicly anyway, any non-scientific leanings. But if we assume that the collective unconscious or spirit has agency, autonomy and intent then something appears. Narrative therapists, for example, and others have no difficulty in assigning intent and agency to the problem. This is the so-called "externalising" of the problem ("Anorexia has one job—it wants to kill you") but it removes the agency of the person who is experiencing the problem. They are now a victim of something. So we hear current snowflake-friendly (but responsibility-avoidant) descriptions like, "I am living with depression" (like it's a room-mate), "I am suffering from depression"; or "I am battling depression" rather than "I have depression" or, more personally, "I am depressed," or even "When I got to forty, I threw a depression."

But the line seems drawn when we come to experiencing spirit or the unconscious as having agency and intent. If it has intent who better to select than a famous psychiatrist such as Jung, not religious in the conventional sense, who is receptive and can articulate such matters.

Spirit and its archetypes speak in myth and symbol with its accompanying numinosity and emotional power, not sober, straight-line, step-by-step, evidence-based argument. The archetype of prophecy knows it's easy to have a revelation and start a religion. But it wants something better than mass movements and shouty preachers. For its growth and development spirit wants the material experience of its free will through the agency of humans.

Last visions

On May 30, 1961, eight days before he died, Jung dictated to his daughter his last visions, with instructions that the notes were to be given to Marie-Louise von Franz. The images were sobering. Jung made a drawing, with a caption under it that said, "The last 50 years of humanity." He died on June 6, 1961. Forty years later 9/11 happened. What we know of Jung's final vision is taken from the film *A Matter of Heart*.[30] Von Franz said to the interviewer:

> I don't want to speak much about it. One of his daughters took notes and after his death gave it to me, and there is a drawing with a line going up and down, and underneath is the last 50 years of humanity. And some remarks about a final catastrophe being ahead. But I have only those notes.... Well, one's whole feeling revolts against this idea but since I have those notes in a drawer, I don't allow myself to be too optimistic. I think, well, we have always had wars and enormous catastrophes, and I have no more personal fear much about that.... But the beauty of all the life—to think that the billions and billions and billions of years of evolution to build up the plants and the animals and the whole beauty of nature—and that man would go out of sheer shadow foolishness and destroy it all. I mean that all life might go from the planet.... I try to pray that it may not—a miracle happens.
>
> You know, when you study science fiction, you see there's always the fantasy of escaping to some other planet and begin anew again, which means give up the battle on this earth, consider it hopeless and give up.... Jung never thought that we might do better than just possibly sneak round the corner with not too big a catastrophe. When I saw him last, he had also a vision while I was with him, but there he said, "I see enormous stretches devastated, enormous stretches of the earth. But, thank God it's not the whole planet."

---

30. www.gnosis.org/gnostic-jung/Film-Transcript-Matter-of-Heart, Wagner 1986. www.youtube.com/watch?v=lxXyTrdgJKg

10

TITANIC
SISTER OF GIGANTIC

Christianity was mainly interested in repressing the chthonic gods and the emotions they constellate. In the realm of images, the repression was concentrated on the great god Pan, who came to personify the Christian devil. This meant that the Titans—who for the Greeks, personified evil, so to say—went unchecked, and thus what they represent in human nature was no longer reflected upon and, in the course of Western culture, got out of hand. [1]

IT'S NOT the fault of the plants, the animals had nothing to do with it, and the bacteria, no way. Two-leggeds and our excesses are to blame if this planet should falter and die. Two of our themes here graze side-by-side in the same paddock. One is bigness, giantism, expansion, inflation, and growth. The other is guilt, shame, responsibility, humiliation, and down-sizing. The English word excess comes from the Latin excedere (ex–out of, cedere–go out, go beyond) in other words to depart from the ordinary or the proper limits. Siddhartha Gautama, known later as the Buddha, not only rejected the extremes of asceticism but also the extremes of action. His abiding mistrust was for every form of excess.

---

1. Lopez-Pedraza, *Cultural anxiety*, 8.

The Buddha never spoke in the name of a god and never as divine revelation.[2]

This is in contrast to the monotheisms where Yahweh chose his own people, Mohammed was the prophet of Allah, and God sacrificed his only son. Protestantism, that later marriage of economic frugality and religious excess, began its work—always smugly described as hard—of creating a stock exchange that would exchange things that don't actually exist, the notion of the company as an insulator of individual responsibility, and missionising. Activity, aka creating wealth, was then unlinked from personal responsibility and individual needs. Growth and expansion, aka business and capital endeavour, was given free rein without limit. But nature is self-regulatory. Trees don't want to kiss the sky. Animals don't want to colonise the earth, nor birds the air. There is a natural instinct against excess that knows when enough is enough.

Myth

A myth is a story that is always present but never true. Local conditions —the who, what, where, when and how—fill in the details but the pattern is the same. It fades into the background when unneeded but comes to the fore when cultural or personal circumstances require. Myth is not culture-bound—the great emotions of anger, jealousy, sadness, love, and fear are shrivelled, hollowed-out, and disrespected when submitted to the modern psychology-lite of "emotion regulation skills" and "cognitive errors."

> Myth, is society's first medication" said Luigi Zoja, "arresting time and restoring us by sending us back to the roots of things. One can know a myth by heart and yet tirelessly return to hearing it told, year after year, always the same.... Myth was always true, even if certainly not in ways that our own morality and rationality find it easy to accept. It pronounced no well-honed ethical principles such as one finds in monotheism or in philosophical reflection; and it paid no allegiance to

2. Zoja, *Growth and Guilt*, 32

the forms of rational cognition that have since become typical of science".[3]

But those who are unconsciously living out a myth become puffed-up by something that is not them, and then they are enthusiastic (en-*theos*, possessed by the god). They believe they are unique, unaware that their pattern is a common as potatoes, repeated over and over since always with the same choice of endings. Falling in love is a good example.

Titans

In Greek mythology, the Titans were the pre-Olympian gods. According to Hesiod's Theogony (c. 700 BCE) they were the twelve children of the first parents Uranus (Sky) and Gaia (Earth). There were six male and six female Titans. Cronus mated with his older sister Rhea, who bore the Olympians: Zeus, Hades, Poseidon, Hestia, Demeter, and Hera. Cronus castrated his father Uranus with a sickle given to him by Gaia. He in turn was defeated by Zeus and the Olympians after a ten-year war. The vanquished Titans were banished from the upper world and forever imprisoned in Tartarus deep in the earth.[4] Tartarus is surrounded by an iron wall and the wall is surrounded three times by Night. Hesiod says that a bronze anvil falling from heaven would fall nine days before it reached the earth. The anvil would then take a further nine days to fall from earth and on the tenth day it would reach Tartarus.

The first task of the gods was to defeat the Titans. They were inhuman, too big, too lawless, too chaotic for ordered society. As Hillman points out, hubris is human grandiosity but titanism is excess on an archetypal scale. Zeus knew that the civilised order of the Olympian gods and goddesses could not come about unless the Titans were restrained. Now the Titans have returned to Earth. Let us recall, with Hillman, some of the titanic enormities: the two Great Wars; Hiroshima, Nagasaki and Bikini atoll; the World Trade Centres; millions of refugees; superpowers, supertankers, supermarkets, super-

---

3. Zoja, *Growth and guilt*, 9, 14
4. https://en.wikipedia.org/wiki/Titans#Hesiod

superfoods, and supersize; Olympic higher, further, faster; the Great
Depression; countries of 400 million and cities of 40 million; population explosions and suburban sprawl; corporate multi-nationals, corporate agriculture, and forever plastics.[5]

AI

The data sets are so big that we must invent a third blanket that insulates
from direct experience—artificial intelligence. The first line of defence
against direct experience is our personal "beliefs" or scientific "models".
The map is never the territory. "A mind that generalises rapidly" W B
Yeats said, "continually prevents the experience that would have made it
feel and see deeply" and describes the territory of J M Synge's writing.[6]
"He loves all that has edge, all that is salt in the mouth, all that is rough
to the hand, all that heightens the emotions by contest, all that stings
into life the sense of tragedy".[7]

The selfies and instagram are the second line, leading us to believe
that we are participating in life. The third line is artificial intelligence
which insulates us from the uncertainty of not knowing and thinking
that chatGPT—mental McDonald's—will enhance our learning.

But the vastnesses are so big, beyond human-size, that we cannot
comprehend. The arms of our mind and heart cannot encompass their
enormity, so we must turn away. But no! We are held, hypnotised by its
incomprehensibility and try to grasp what cannot be grasped.
Benumbed, the fingers of our understanding will not work in this kind
of cold, on this kind of scale. The result? We become numb—what the
psychiatrist Robert J Lifton called psychic numbing. It is the thousand-
yard stare, a clinically dissociative state. Culturally, the numbing is
attended by its compensatory inevitabilities—cruelty to self and others
(often via social media), random aggression (brought to you by the
Second Amendment), and berserker road rage.

---

5.   Hillman, *Huge is ugly*.
6.   John Millington Synge (1871-1909) was an Irish playwright and poet.
7.   W B Yeats, *The Cutting of an Agate*.

The Titanic

Finally, we come to the Titanic, the quintessence of bigness. At the height of Victorian superbia it was a singular emblem of titanism. The disaster has been taken as just that but it is one in a procession of oracular red flags.

The RMS (Royal Mail Ship) Titanic was operated by the White Star Line. Built in Belfast, its sister ships were the Olympic and Britannic. The latter was originally to be called the Gigantic. At 300 metres long it was planned to be longer than the Titanic's 270 metres but was modified after the Titanic's sinking. The White Star Line was funded by the Wall Street financier J P Morgan who was one of the five men, with Cornelius Vanderbilt, John D. Rockefeller, Andrew Carnegie and Henry Ford, who built the industrial titanism of the USA during the so-called Gilded Age in the last quarter of the 19th century.

The Titanic was the largest ocean liner of the time. The first-class accommodations were the height of luxury with a gymnasium, swimming pool, high-class restaurants, and hundreds of palatial cabins. She was reputedly "unsinkable" with watertight compartments and remotely activated watertight doors. So unsinkable that the lifeboats had only capacity for half of the 2,000-odd passengers. She was four days out on her maiden voyage from Southampton to New York and about 600 kms southeast of Newfoundland. It was a clear moonless night, the sea was like glass and reflected the stars. This absence of breaking waves made it more difficult for the lookouts to spot icebergs. She had entered what is now known as "Iceberg Alley" where, in late winter and early spring, the cold Labrador Current coming down between Greenland and Baffin Island brings melting icebergs to meet the warm Gulf Stream. That year it had been a particularly warm spring.

Just before midnight of April 14, 1912 the Titanic hit an iceberg a glancing blow on her starboard side. The rivets popped and six narrow slits—that covered a total area of only just over one square metre—were opened over a length of 100 metres about three metres above the keel. Five of her sixteen compartments were flooded. Two and a half hours later, in the early morning hours of April 15, she sank.

Of the estimated 2,224 passengers and crew aboard, more than

1,500 died, making it the deadliest sinking of a single ship up to that time. It remains the deadliest peacetime sinking of an ocean liner or cruise ship. Tragically, the disaster had excess, at a cost, all the way from her bolts (the No. 3 Best wrought-iron rivets held the prow and stern plates rather than the No. 4 Best-Best rivets, or even steel rivets) to her expansive promenades whose faces were unobstructed by lifeboat davits —and so fewer lifeboats—so as to afford a better view of the ocean. Disaster and excess are always attended by "economic necessity" and the cutting-of-corners to increase the profit margin. Boeing is the modern version.

The tragedy of the Titanic resonates with the archetypal power and fascination that big things exert on popular culture. It is the subject of innumerable movies and documentaries; the wreck was discovered by Robert Ballard in 1985; James Cameron's 1997 film Titanic became the first ever movie to take $1 billion at the box office; and the soundtrack became the best-selling soundtrack of all time.

11

GROWTH

ONE POINT SEVEN EARTHS

Aurea mediocritas: the golden middle way or golden mean. —Horace, *Odes* 2.10

All things in moderation, including moderation. —attributed to Oscar Wilde, G B Shaw and many others

Meden agan, nothing too much. —The second maxim, at the Temple of Apollo, Delphi

No city should be too large for a man to walk out of in a morning. — Cyril Connolly, *The Unquiet Grave*, 1944, p. 35.

FOR MANY YEARS I lived in a medium-size town where I could get to work in less than ten minutes by car. Now it's half-an-hour at least. The beach a block away was one of the most beautiful and longest in the world with great surfing and swimming. Right at one end of the beach was a grotty, one-storey, hotel-cum-bar that had character in its limbs and its patrons. The pace of the town was 1950s-slow. But it had an inferiority complex. It wanted growth, to biggy-up, it wanted development, and to be like Florida. Eww.

Now the hotel has been replaced by multi-storey apartments, cafés and shops (stores for North Americans). Lots of suburbs, not enough roads. And many of the suburban roads are cul-de-sacs making tsunami evacuation next to impossible. The beach is still beautiful but it looks like Miami and you can't get there easily through the summer traffic. The doggy-poo of development has left its stain.

The Latin *civitas* is the root of the English words, city and civilisation. Regrettably, our everyday language beguiles us into thinking that civilisation only comes from life in cities. Cities are not good for the planet. More destruction has been birthed from cities than was ever born from the countryside. Zoja concurs:

> The culture that lies at the basis of western civilization... makes a remarkable departure from the cultures of nearly all other civilizations:... the idea of productive technology as an agent of positive expansion. This culture, in short, is consciously committed to that "myth of growth".... But this culture is also characterized by an accompanying unconscious fantasy in which it continues to nourish taboos and fears of punishment that in the past were associated with arrogance and excessive fortune. It therefore continues to live in fear of catastrophe, the forgotten denouement of its myth. Unlimited growth is tantamount to the theft and unwarranted exercise of activities that belong to the gods.[1]

A "litany" is a series of sung or spoken prayers asking for the blessing of God and comes from the Latin for entreating or supplication. It also means a long and repetitious list of complaints. The litany of ecological disasters and climate change warnings can be found on thousands of sites on the internet, the data is valid and is available for all to see. Yet this is ignored by those who most need to hear it. For the moment, I ask the reader to bear with me while I complain... and supplicate.

Jung says of inflation, "In general we are not directly conscious of this condition at all, but can at best infer its existence indirectly from the symptoms. These include the reactions of our immediate environ-

---

1. Zoja, *Growth and guilt*. 17.

2 We are getting feedback about our inflation by way of climate change and a thousand other things. This process of inflation has taken about 4,000 years. And now global culture has popped the balloon and made a mess.

In the last fifty years more resources have been consumed by humans than in the whole of history of the human race. A second World War happening twenty-one years after the "war to end all wars" should have been our first clue. And "World" is a quaint example of Eurocentric grandiosity. What would the San people of the Kalahari, the Wajarri people of Western Australia, or the Hadza in Tanzania have made of the Holocaust? Did the uncontacted (at that time) Yanomami of Brazil know or care if the ones with long white faces killed each other? WWII was just the final salvo in the thousand-year war that has been waged against the planet that supports us.

Footprint

Around 10,000 BCE the global human population was about 4 million. In 5,000 BCE it was about 19 million. In 0 BCE it was about 230 million. In 1,000 CE it was about 320 million. In 1500 CE it was about 500 million. Around 1700 it started to go up the cliff, reached a billion around 1830, rose to 7 billion in 2010 and in 2023 is 8 billion.[3] Like any good business this means that we need to cut back, trim, make redundant, and let go of least 3.3 billion people to survive. Where are the Human Resources people when you really need them? Three billion is roughly the combined population of the two most populous countries in the world, India and China. Are social policies likely to slow population increase (15–20 million a year in 2018 in China)? I don't think so. In fact the opposite. China's one child policy (1980–2015) did not go well and in 2015 it was raised to two children then in 2021 to three. In 2019 Viktor Orban, the Hungarian prime minister, stated that Hungarian women with four children or more will be exempt for life from paying income tax. In 2022 Russian president Vladimir Putin,

---

2. CW 9ii, par. 44.
3. https://ourworldindata.org/population-growth#all-charts

adapting Stalin's Mother Heroine award, offered Russian mothers a cash bonus if they have 10 or more children. Mothers will get a one-off payment of 1 million rubles after their 10th child's first birthday (more than the average Russian salary of roughly 750,000 rubles). But only if all other nine children have survived.

At least 2 billion people—about 30% of the world's population who are Christian—would nod their heads to the words of Genesis: "And God blessed them. And God said to them, 'Be fruitful and multiply and fill the earth and subdue it, and have dominion over the fish of the sea and over the birds of the heavens and over every living thing that moves on the earth'".[4] So now we have 1.7 planet's worth of fruitfulness. Humanity's demand on the planet is now almost twice what nature can renew.

In 1960 humanity's ecological footprint—a measure of how much of the Earth's resources humanity uses—was about 0.7 Earths. Since then the footprint has more than doubled. At the same time, vertebrate wildlife populations have declined by more than half in just four decades. In 1970 it reached 1.0 Earths, in 2000 it was 1.2 Earths, in 2014 it was 1.5 Earths, and in 2017 it was 1.7 Earths.[5] In other words, by August 2, 2017 humanity had used up what nature can supply in that year. The rest of the year we were over budget, running an overdraft, negotiating hopeful loans (with whom?). Who would run a business like this? All perpetuated by capitalism, socialism, the World Bank (as if it owns the world) and the world's finance ministers.

In the mid-1970s (that's when the tide began to turn) Marie-Louise Von Franz wrote:

> Every utilitarian approach to the unconscious, or just wanting to make use of it, has destructive effects, just as, we are now beginning to realize, it has in outer nature. For if we only exploit our forests, animals, and the minerals in the earth, then we disturb the biological balance and either we or later generations have to pay a very big bill. Nature seems to want to keep its own balance and set its own purposes and have its

---

4. English Standard Version, Genesis 1:28.
5. http://data.footprintnetwork.org/

own biological whole and does not want to be exploited by one-sided utilitarian calculations."[6]

Biomass

We are but a very small part of the total sum of life and death—humans make up one ten-thousandth (0.01%) of the Earth's biomass. Plants make up 80%, bacteria come in a distant second at 13% and fungi third at 2%. But in the last 10,000 years, human activity has slashed plant biomass by half and reduced wild mammals by 85%. Farmed poultry today makes up 70% of all birds on the planet, with just 30% being wild. If you think that's bad—60% of all mammals on Earth are livestock, mostly cattle and pigs, 36% are humans and just 4% are wild animals.[7]

And feast on this: Body mass, or obesity, has doubled globally since 1980 without any significant change in genetic factors that contribute to obesity. In 2005, the global adult human biomass due to obesity was 3.5 million tonnes, the equivalent of 56 million people of average body mass. North America has 6% of the world population but 34% of biomass due to obesity. Asia has 61% of the world population but 13% of biomass due to obesity. One tonne of human biomass corresponds to approximately 12 adults in North America and 17 adults in Asia. If all countries had the BMI distribution of the USA, the increase in human biomass of 58 million tonnes would be equivalent in mass to an extra 935 million people.[8] As a Constitutional right, it seems, open carry doesn't only apply to guns. Could we think of excess, non-genetic weight as a planetary misdemeanour? Or how about 20% of McDonald's profits funding the treatment of obesity-related problems?

A recent paper in *Nature* said, "We find that Earth is exactly at the crossover point; in the year 2020 ($\pm$ 6), the anthropogenic mass [the mass produced by human activity], which has recently doubled roughly

---

6. Von Franz, *Individuation and Fairy Tales*, 29.

7. Bar-On, Phillips, & Milo (2018). The biomass distribution on Earth. *Proceedings of the National Academy of Sciences*, *115*(25), 6506–6511. https://doi.org/10.1073/pnas.1711842115

8. Walpole et al. (2012) The weight of nations: An estimation of adult human biomass. *BMC Public Health*, *12*(1), 439. https://doi.org/10.1186/1471-2458-12-439

every 20 years, will surpass all global living biomass. On average, for each person on the globe, anthropogenic mass equal to more than his or her bodyweight is produced every week".[9] Pappas, in the Scientific American, gave us a startling comparison:

> Roads, houses, shopping malls, fishing vessels, printer paper, coffee mugs, smartphones and all the other infrastructure of daily life now weigh in at approximately 1.1 trillion metric tons—equal to the combined dry weight of all plants, animals, fungi, bacteria, archaea and protists on the planet. The creation of this human-made mass has rapidly accelerated over the past 120 years: *Artificial objects have gone from just 3 percent of the world's biomass in 1900 to on par with it today.* [italics added] And the amount of new stuff being produced every week is equivalent to the average body weight of all 7.7 billion people.[10]

As we have seen, plants make up 80% of the total biomass of living matter. This vastly outweighs the bacteria which are about 15% of the total. The other groups, in descending order, are fungi, archaea (cellular organisms without a nucleus), protists (single-celled organisms with a nucleus), animals, and viruses, which together account for the remaining 5%. The biomass of humans is 0.01% of the total. Wait a moment—what does this say? One tenth of one percent of living matter produces artificial, dead-dead matter equivalent to 99.9% of all other living matter.

The Club of Rome

The Club of Rome was founded in the 1960s by a world-wide group of experts from a range of disciplines. Their goal was to understand the future state of world civilization. They commissioned the Massachusetts Institute of Technology to prepare a series of quantitative reports on

9. Elhacham et al. (2020). Global human-made mass exceeds all living biomass. *Nature*, *588*(7838), 442–444. https://doi.org/10.1038/s41586-020-3010-5
10. Pappas, *Human-Made Stuff Now Outweighs All Life on Earth*. Scientific American. https://www.scientificamerican.com/article/human-made-stuff-now-outweighs-all-life-on-earth

how the Earth might develop in terms of, for example, population, raw materials, and pollution. *Limits to Growth*, funded by the Volkswagen Foundation, was published in 1972. It described a computer simulation of exponential economic and population growth with limited resource supplies. Two of the scenarios saw "overshoot and collapse" of the global system by the mid- to latter part of the 21st century, while a third scenario resulted in a "stabilised world." Thus far its projections have proven largely accurate. In 1992 their 20-year review found that we had already overshot the Earth's carrying capacity. The 1992 Rio conference, and the Rio + 10 conference in Johannesburg conference were failures. The 2015 Paris Agreement on climate change was Trumped when the USA withdrew in 2017.

Dana Meadows, principal author of Limits to Growth, provided a 30-year update in 2004. In 2014 Graham Turner said, "Regrettably, the alignment of data trends with the LTG dynamics indicates that the early stages of collapse could occur within a decade, or might even be underway. This suggests, from a rational risk-based perspective, that we have squandered the past decades, and that preparing for a collapsing global system could be even more important than trying to avoid collapse."[11] Limits to Growth is a scientific and quantitative document and suffers from the limits of both those enterprises. It has left out the most important factors—the psyche of the Earth and the psyche of humans, both collective and individual.

---

11. Meadows et al. *Limits to Growth-The 30 Year Update*, 2004; Graham Turner and Lauren Rickards, eds. "Is Global Collapse Imminent?". www.sustainable.unimelb.edu.au (Research Paper No. 4), 2014. http://pinguet.free.fr/turner814.pdf

12

TWIN TOWERS

GETTING ABOVE THINGS

THE TOWER REPRESENTS the human desire to grow and rise above the earth, to look down upon, dominate and break away from nature, like space programs that strive to "loose the surly bonds of earth". The tower connects heaven and earth, materially and spiritually. Standing at the top of the tower—the man-made mountain—brings us up out of our daily round. We elevate ourselves above others and the land around us. We can see ourselves and others as objects. There! See—far below! We get some objectivity and take a different perspective on life.[1] We get above the muck and mire of betrayal and human suffering. We can see the whole circle of life around us.

Sublimatio

The tower is an image of the alchemical procedure of sublimatio (from the Latin sublimis, up to the line, to the limit, elevated, raised up). This is process of turning something solid or liquid into air or vapour, thus it rises up and becomes sublime. All images that associate with being high,

---

1. As The Who put it, "I know you've deceived me, now here's a surprise / I know that you have 'cause there's magic in my eyes / I can see for miles and miles and miles…"

elevation, and upward movement—ladders, stairs, elevators, climbing, towers, mountains, or flying, are symbols of sublimatio. Psychologically, this is one way of dealing with a concrete problem in life. We get above it, we see it as part of a larger pattern or landscape, and see its meaning. We are above the storm not in it. Forsaking his "fleshly nook" to witness "constellations and vast regions" from his tower, Milton wrote:

> Or let my lamp at midnight hour,
> Be seen in some high lonely Tower,
> Where I may oft out-watch the Bear,
> With thrice great Hermes, or unsphere
> The spirit of Plato to unfold
> What worlds, or what vast Regions hold
> Th' immortal mind that hath forsook
> Her mansion in this fleshly nook.

Religious revelation is often described as an ascent toward the divine. For example, Moses ascending Mount Sinai; the visions of Ezekiel; Muhammad ascending through the seven heavens; or the shaman climbing the ladder to the upper world. In psychological terms an ascension is an experience of the archetypal realm which releases us from the personal ego-bound attitude. The danger is that one floats off into this realm and abandons earthly concerns like the laundry and the budget. This is as dysfunctional as the dangers of the opposite alchemical process of coagulatio—living in the gutter of life. To paraphrase Keats, our soul is made in the vale between tower and gutter. Or as Flaubert wrote to Turgenev on 13 November 1872, "I have always tried to live in an ivory tower, but a sea of shit is beating against its walls".[2]

Monotheism wants to ascend—to be raptured up to God, to be transported to the paradise of the martyrs, but it always strengthens its opposite. Think witch burnings, or sexual abuse in the Catholic or fundamentalist churches. Its the hard-on under the clerical robes. Or notice that the Dalai Lama asked a young boy to "suck his tongue". Too much holiness invites its opposite. However, indigenous priests, clever

---

2. Ferber, *A Dictionary of Literary Symbols*, 231.

women, or medicine men make less pretence at goodness and tend to have a foot in both worlds, spiritual and secular.

The higher we get from the earthly entanglements the more we can see. So we get grand visions, emotional upliftings, great theories of everything, and complex "models" multiply. (Parts of this book are examples of sublimatio). The first picture of the Earth from space, or Darwin's Origin of Species are examples. In fact, the whole of human evolution could be seen as the gaining of objectivity, the getting of wisdom, and seeing our world from the outside. However, this is a point of view not the truth or a fact. It takes no account of who is deciding truth or fact. The sublimatio and the tower live in the realm of perfection, Platonic forms, and a Heaven where all is immortal, infinite and perfected. But the model is not the reality. We live in a body made of earth not air.

Before turning to the twin towers let's be reminded that money, finance and economics have been instruments of ever increasing sublimation over millennia. After all, growth and the getting of more is what economics is all about. Professions such as investment banking are more likely to inhabit the upper floors of skyscrapers. They are removed from "I'll give you two of these for one of those" in the basement.[3] From barter, to coinage, to paper money, to stock markets to... wait for it... floating rate bonds, zero interest bonds, deep discount bonds, auction-rated debentures, secured premium notes with detachable warrants, non-convertible debentures with detachable equity warrants, secured zero interest partly convertible debentures with detachable and separately tradeable warrants, differential shares, securitised paper, collateralised debt obligations, inverse float bonds, perpetual bonds, and municipal bonds... and yes, sub-prime mortgages. It's a house of cards waiting to collapse.

Towers of air

As two-leggeds made from the body of the Earth, we want to leave and ascend. Life is a vale of tears and we leave the tribulations behind us

---

3. Ferguson, *The Ascent of Money: A Financial History of the World.*

when we die and ascend to heaven. We are lifted away from the clodding
earth and closer to the vap'rous heavens, and the mystery of the sky. The
ivory tower is the place of intellectual pursuits or esoteric nerdiness at
the expense of everyday practicalities.But we lose connection with the
land beneath and are deprived of the direct experience of its blood and
breath. John Keats argued that, rather than a vale of tears, the world is
the vale of soul-making. He wrote:

> The common cognomen of this world among the misguided and
> superstitious is 'a vale of tears' from which we are to be redeemed by a
> certain arbitrary interposition of God and taken to Heaven—What a
> little circumscribe[d] straightened notion! Call the world if you Please
> "The vale of Soul-making" Then you will find out the use of the
> world... I say 'Soul making' Soul as distinguished from an Intelligence
> —There may be intelligence or sparks of the divinity in millions—but
> they are not Souls till they acquire identities, till each one is personally
> itself. Intelligences are atoms of perception–they know and they see
> and they are pure, in short they are God–how then are Souls to be
> made? How then are these sparks which are God to have identity given
> them–so as ever to possess a bliss peculiar to each ones individual exis-
> tence? How, but by the medium of a world like this?... Do you not see
> how necessary a World of Pains and troubles is to school an Intelligence
> and make it a soul? A Place where the heart must feel and suffer in a
> thousand diverse ways!... This appears to me a faint sketch of a system
> of Salvation which does not affront our reason and humanity—I am
> convinced that many difficulties which Christians labour under would
> vanish before it.[4]

As with all symbols, there two sides. In the Song of Solomon (7:4) the
"tower of ivory" is the admiring bridegroom's adoration of the neck of
his beloved. The "Maiden in the Tower" is a common theme in fairy
tales as in the tale of Rapunzel or Tennyson's "The Lady of Shalott."
She is the pure yet inaccessible maiden who is sequestered in the tower.
The phallic tower is a Christian symbol of the virgin's chastity. The

---

4. John Keats, Letter to George and Georgiana Keats, March 19, 1819.

tower is sheltering and protective of the purity of the feminine, so that she remains psychologically and spiritually virginal and one unto herself. The tower is the secluded retreat where rest, contemplation and creative work can emerge unhindered by the demands of daily life. Here she can give birth, parthenogenetically, kept apart from the phallic intrusions of goals, schedules and timelines.

We see the dark side of the archetype in the controlling father who wants to meet and approve his daughter's boyfriends. Or, more darkly, the young woman who gets killed by her father or older brother because she has kept the company of young men without being accompanied by a male relative. It is the confining phallic power of the masculine that separates it from the feminine earth, keeping it dry and airy and disowning the messiness of water and earth. The ivory tower of academia is the rarefied intellect untouched by the disturbances of life. Apocryphally, a Cambridge don was once heard to say, "Sex and relationships... they play havoc with good scholarship".

Towers are spoke of in many mythologies as being associated with both life and death. In Arthurian legend, the Holy Grail, which had miraculous healing powers and provided sustenance in infinite abundance, was kept in the castle of the Fisher King. In Greek mythology Hero and Leander lived on opposite sides of the narrows of the Dardanelles, now in modern-day Turkey. On the northern shore Hero, a priestess of Aphrodite, lived in a tower and each night she would light a lamp in the window of the tower to guide her lover, Leander, as he swam across to her from Abydos on the southern shore. He stayed with her until daybreak and then swam home again. But winter came, with its stormy weather, and still Hero lit the lamp and still Leander braved the seas. Then one night, during a violent storm, the lamp was blown out by the wind and Leander, losing his way, was drowned. Next morning Hero looked down and saw his body washed up on the shore. In her grief she flung herself from the tower, falling to her death beside her lover.

The hero or heroine's journey is beset with struggles and dangers before reaching the maiden in the tower. In fact the maiden in the tower may be unattainable—which is the whole point. The loss of the relationship, the memento, the opportunity, the death of what was desperately wanted, the true love, are all perhaps necessary losses so that a deeper life might emerge.

King Acrisius was disappointed by his lack of male heirs and asked the oracle of Delphi if this would change. The seeress told him that he would never have a son, but his daughter would, and that he would be killed by his daughter's son. At the time, Danaë, the daughter of Acrisius and Eurydice, was childless and, meaning to keep her so, King Acrisius shut her up in a bronze chamber to be constructed under the court of his palace. Other versions say she was imprisoned in a tall brass tower with a single richly adorned chamber, but with no doors or windows, just a sky-light as the source of light and air. For the rest of her life she was to be buried in this sky-tomb closed off from others. However, Zeus desired her and came to her as golden rain which streamed in through the roof of the chamber and down into her womb. Soon after, their child Perseus was born.

Unwilling to provoke the wrath of the gods or the Furies by killing his offspring and grandchild, Acrisius cast Danaë and Perseus into the sea in a wooden chest. But at the request of Zeus the sea was calmed by Poseidon and and the pair survived. They were washed ashore on the island of Seriphos where they were taken in by Dictys, the brother of King Polydectes, who raised Perseus to manhood. Polydectes was charmed by Danaë but she had no interest in him. Consequently, he agreed not to marry her but only if her son would bring him the head of the gorgon Medusa whose gaze turned men to stone. Using Athena's shield, Hermes' winged sandals and Hades' helmet of invisibility, Perseus was able to evade the Medusa's gaze and decapitate her.

Later, after Perseus brought back Medusa's head and started for Argos he learned of the prophecy and instead went to Larissa, where athletic games were being held. By chance, a now-aging Acrisius was there and Perseus accidentally struck him on the head with his javelin (or discus), so fulfilling the prophecy.

We hear a similar story in Irish myth. Balor was the one-eyed god of death and the most formidable of the Fomorii, the violent and monstrous sea gods who ruled Ireland before the arrival of the ancient and magical race of the Tuatha de Danann. So dreadful was his one eye that he destroyed whoever he looked upon and his eyelid had to be levered up by four servants. It was prophesied that he would be slain by his own grandson. To avoid this fate he locked his only daughter Ethlinn in a crystal tower on Tory Island. Nevertheless, she bore a son Lugh Lámhfada who fulfilled the prophecy by killing Balor in battle, taking out the giant's eye with a slingshot.[5]

One could now intone: "The moral of this story is..." but that would be preaching from the ivory tower. Archetypal myths, stories and dreams create an alchemical reaction between dream and dreamer that changes both. The psyche of the listener creates its own meaning according to the individual's developmental level of consciousness. These seeds lie dormant until conditions are ripe for them to emerge into consciousness later in life, not as a thought or a belief—which are the handmaidens of emotion—but as a reorientation of life's compass.

The Released Man

The Tower card in the European tarot usually depicts a tower being hit by lightning and two figures falling from either side of the tower. This card is usually interpreted as a violent upheaval that brings one down to earth, a reality check, a rude awakening, the world being turned upside-down, a life-changing event, the rug being pulled out from under you, or a bolt from the blue. It represents the collapse of old values and beliefs, the destruction of long-established situations, the puncturing of inflation, the discarding of what has petrified, or towering rage, ambition, pride and arrogance. What has been built brick by brick is destroyed in a flash and ego-driven hopes are shattered. Jung said, "Lightning signifies a sudden, unexpected, and overpowering change in psychic condition".

The shadow side of this card represents emotional disgrace, ruin, and downfall. Physically, it suggests misfortune, sudden unexpected adversity, or bankruptcy. Mentally, it represents a loss of meaning. Spiritually, an existential disorientation, and nothing worth living for. The light side of the card suggests the shattering of egocentric ambitions. Physically, it suggests a natural disaster that sweeps clean.

---

5. Ellis, *A Dictionary of Irish Mythology*, 39.

Mentally, is represents a disaster resulting in liberation, with the collapse of the old to make way for the new. Spiritually, it points to illumination, awakening, or the dissolution of a materialistic attitude. Edward Edinger's description fits:

> That's the way it happens in psychological experience. First one has the event, the crippling, agonizing event, and then in the process of trying to assimilate it, come to terms with it, one may discover its archetypal background—that there's a large enough context to it, a more than personal meaning. And even though that does not eliminate the pain of the experience, it makes the pain meaningful. To discover the archetypal background is indeed healing, I think chiefly because with that discovery ego is released from the identification with an archetypal experience. What is so intolerably burdensome is to carry personally a weight of meaning that is transpersonal. When one can get out from under that excessive weight by the process of disidentification, then there's a sense of release.[6]

In the Xultun tarot this card is called the Released Man and it also represents the ego's liberation from the trials of the preceding cards and the power of their archetypes. That is, if the ego is available for learning from the experience. As well as a collapse the Released Man can also be a revelation, an awakening and an epiphany. Moments of illumination rarely come plodding step by step. They may come all at once in a blinding flash but take years to understand them and live them. After living through the experience we might develop an emotional, lived understanding that is not cognitive but cellular, rising up from darkness of the body. This takes time, often years. The top-down revelation, an awakening and an epiphany, in the twinkling of an eye, with quick results, is usually preferred.

Spirit is not limited by space and time, it knows nothing of gradualness, incremental change, and the measured response. Like lightning, it is all or nothing. Spirit seeks union with matter without regard for human concerns, and does not make a distinction between a conscious

---

6. Edinger, *Ego and Self: The Old Testament Prophets*, 92.

human being and an unconscious one. For spirit the result is the same—the lightning bolt has touched matter—but for the human the result is vastly different depending on the degree of consciousness. For one who is unprepared it does feel like the collapse of their whole world. For one who is more conscious it feels like a release or a revelation.

The difference in interpretation, revelation or ruin, also depends on the perspective—spirit or ego. Ladders, steps or stairs are symbols of ego development and growth, moving to a higher state of consciousness, and the process of spiritualisation. But when an archetype falls into matter it undergoes a kenosis, an emptying, and a great narrowing. In dreams and visions this is often symbolised as a divine being falling to earth and in the card we see twins falling from the tower. For spirit this descent is a great constriction, humiliation and downfall; for the ego it is an awakening, an ascension and a profound liberation.

Collapse

In God's ambivalence, reaching for the heavens is punished by destruction, collapse and levelling. God says worship me but don't get big ideas or get too close. Perhaps the best known tower is the Tower of Babel. The Bible tells the story that after the Great Flood the whole earth was of one language and one speech. The people journeyed westward and found the land of Mesopotamia and settled there. They said let us build us a city and a tower, whose top may reach unto heaven; and let us make us a name, lest we be scattered abroad upon the face of the whole earth. And the Lord came down to see the city and the tower and said, "Behold, the people are one, and they have all one language, and now nothing will be restrained from them, which they have imagined to do. I shall confound their language, that they may not understand one another's speech and scatter them over the face of the earth". According to a Midrash the builders of the tower said, "God has no right to choose the upper world for Himself, and to leave the lower world to us; therefore we will build us a tower, with an idol on the top holding a sword, so that it may appear as if it intended to war with God".[7] When the people

---

7. Wikipedia, *Tower of Babel.*

attempted to build a ziggurat that reached heaven, God destroyed the tower and caused confusion (balbel in Hebrew) by rendering them incapable of understanding each others' language.[8]

As we have seen, stories and tower myths are about the separation of love, virginity, and pure thought from the storms of the material world. The tower is the refuge from the sordid world below or it can be the contemplative refuge of the sage or the poet. Or it can be the reaching upwards to attain the unattainable. But what concerns us here is the inevitable movement downwards that was already set in motion when the foundations of a tall tower are laid.

Tower myths come mainly from Europe and the Middle East, what used to be called the "Cradle of Civilisation". There are some exceptions such as the creation legend of Washo people of the Sierra Nevadas and Lake Tahoe. This myth tells of a great upheaval which caused the mountains to catch fire, the flames rising so high that the stars melted and fell to earth. This was followed by a flood, and some of the men who tried to escape the deluge by building a high tower were changed into stones. The Bambula of the Congo have a myth which says that men wanted to know more about the moon. They set a long pole in the ground, and a man climbed up it holding a second pole which he tied to the first. A third pole was added, and so on. When this tower had reached a great height, it collapsed, killing the people working on its construction, victims of their curiosity.[9]

Tower myths are less frequently mentioned in the mythologies of Asian cultures, and even less so in indigenous cultures in Africa or the Americas. The Western mind might view this as an inevitable consequence of their primitive level of development. An alternative view might be that the "undeveloped" cultures have not taken the wrong turn into the Middle East-European-Western cul-de-sac of inflation and giantism that began two or three millennia ago. They have kept their feet on the ground and walked on the earth.

Towers are symbolic of things that are virginal and untouched and need to be protected from the slings and arrows of life by being elevated

---

8. Shalit, "Inflation, Hubris and the Tower of Babel", 106-107.
9. Graves, 198.

upwards. Being imprisoned in and by the phallos means the feminine is supposedly protected from its intrusion but she has already been violated by her forced virginity. The towers of Wall Street would not exist if not for open cast mining in the Amazon.[10] Every CBD is a horizontal tower.

People build structures to reach upwards the moon, heaven, the perfection of the upper world, to touch the divine, to be god-like, to be adored, to give good phone, to get good ratings, and get squillions of dollars or votes. Nothing wrong with any of these but eventually it all ends in tears. What goes up must come down. Global extroverted culture was not ready for Covid-19 and threw a tanty. A meme during the lockdown said: "Introverts please check in on your extrovert friends... They are not okay. They have no idea how this works".

Northrop Frye (1912–1991) was an eminent Canadian literary critic who discerned the archetypal stories in, for example, the Bible and William Blake's writings. In the 1962 CBC (Canadian Broadcasting Corporation) Massey Lectures, titled The Educated Imagination, he said. "The particular myth that's been organising this talk... is the story of the Tower of Babel in the Bible. The civilisation we live in at present is a gigantic technological structure, a skyscraper almost high enough to reach the moon. It looks like a single world-wide effort, but it's really a deadlock of rivalries; it looks very impressive, except that is has no genuine human dignity. For all its wonderful machinery, we know it's really a crazy ramshackle building, and at any time it may crash around our ears".[11]

Let's go now from myth to material.

Towers of sand

In 2020 the world has about 1800 skyscrapers above 150 metres concentrated in nine cities. Sand is a non-renewable resource. Beach sand suit-

---

10. The Australian mining company BHP, the largest in the world, has offered US$26bn compensation for the Samarco disaster. In November 2015 a tailings dam collapsed leaving 19 dead and making it Brazil's biggest environmental disaster.
11. Cook, 107.

for making concrete is in high demand and there is even a black market for it. Desert sand is unsuitable for concrete. 50 billion tons of beach sand and fossil sand is used each year for construction. Towers are built of sand and steel and, to state the obvious, the sands of time are running out.

> My name is Ozymandias, King of Kings;
> Look on my Works, ye Mighty, and despair!
> Nothing beside remains. Round the decay
> Of that colossal Wreck, boundless and bare
> The lone and level sands stretch far away.
> —Percy Bysshe Shelley

So here come the figures… The construction sector is by far the largest emitter of greenhouse gases, accounting for 37% of global emissions. After air and water, sand is our most used natural resource. The world consumes 50 billion tons a year—enough to cover the area of the UK. That is twice the amount produced by every river in the world. A mile of a highway requires 15,000 tons of sand. Concrete is 75% sand and the sand used is marine sand found on beaches and at the bottom of rivers, lakes and oceans. Desert sand won't work as wind erosion makes the grains too round to make concrete.[12]

Cities are made of concrete. The number of people living in urban areas has more than quadrupled since 1950 to some 4.2 billion today—more than half the world's population. Another 2.5 billion will join them in cities by 2050. China (1.4 billion) and India (1.4 billion) and the USA (330 million) are the three most populous countries in the world. China now has 102 cities with a population of over a million. Europe has 38. China has the largest urban area in the world around

---

12. https://www.unep.org/resources/report/building-materials-and-climate-construct ing-new-future; Ludacer, Rob. 'The World Is Running out of Sand -- and There's a Black Market for It Now'. Business Insider Australia, https://www.businessinsider.com.au/ world-running-out-sand-resources-concrete-2018-6; Vince Beiser, 'Why the World Is Running out of Sand', https://www.bbc.com/future/article/20191108-why-the-world-is-running-out-of-sand; 'How the Scramble for Sand Is Destroying the Mekong, www.bbc. com/news/business-50629100; www.sandstories.org

Guangzhou where 45 to 60 million people live. Between 2011 and 2014, China used more concrete than the USA did in the entire 20th century. Again, in those three years, China built the equivalent of every highway and road bridge in the USA, and the Hoover Dam.

The best quality sand comes from riverbeds. It's the cheapest—take your boat into the middle of the river and suck it up from the bottom. The bed of the Mekong River has been lowered by several metres over a length of several hundred kilometres. Beach sand is disappearing. Up to 90% of the world's beaches have shrunk an average of 40 meters since 2008. Almost 70% of Southern California's beaches could be completely eroded by 2100.

Not only is sand used for building up it's also used for building out. Singapore imported 17 million tons for its 50-square mile land expansion. China is using tons of sand to build up the Spratly Islands as military bases in the South China Sea. The Palm Islands and The World were major island building projects in Dubai requiring 186 million cubic metres of sand. This so depleted the sea floor around the United Arab Emirates, a desert nation, that they had to import sand from Australia to construct the world's tallest building, the Burj Khalifa. Go figure!

Skyscrapers—the epitome of achievement, business and civilisation —rely at their roots on sand, that most shifting of elements, not rock, not clods of earth, not gravel, but sand that runs through the fingers and into the hourglass. Manhattan is sinking.[13] We will run out. Convince me that we won't. There is a black market already. There will be squabbles, fights, and business wars. No one asked the sand if it wanted to become concrete. No one said, "Thank you for your service".

Towers of old

Let's look at the highest towers in history beginning with the oldest.

---

13. In 2023 it was discovered that Manhattan was sinking under its own weight. "They found that the average subsidence rate across the city is 1-2mm/year, but in areas such as Queens and Brooklyn, it is significantly higher, up to about 4.5 mm a year. And globally, sea levels have risen 98.5 mm in the past 30 years (a mean of 3.3 mm/year)." New York City Is Sinking Under The Weight Of Its Own Buildings

The temple of Gobekli Tepe, in southeastern Turkey towards the Syrian border, is probably the oldest. Part of a temple complex, it is about 6 metres in height and dates from about 10,000 BCE. The tower of Jericho (about 8,000 BCE), in modern day Palestine, was 8.5 metres high and 9 metres at its base. The top of the tower was reached by twenty-two steps, a number that may hold meaning to those familiar with the tarot. About 4,000 years later the Anu Ziggurat (White Temple) was built in Uruk, a Sumerian city, in modern-day Iraq. It got up to 13 metres. In Egypt 1500 years later, and in quick succession around 2600 BCE, came the step pyramid of Djoser, and the pyramids of Meidum, Bent, and Dahshur, all of which were between 60 and 100 metres. Then came the Great Pyramid of Giza weighing in at about 6 million tonnes and 147 metres tall. It held the crown for thousands of years. It was only just surpassed in the 13th century by the spire of Old St Paul's Cathedral. In the Americas the highest Maya temples of the Classic period (200–900 CE) at Tonina (74 metres), Teotihuacan (71 metres) and Tikal (70 metres) were modest in comparison.

These were the visible towers, resplendent and impressive. What has been unnoticed is that well before the pyramids were built most cultures went, not upwards, but down into the body of the Earth or sideways along the face of the Earth. The majority of stone cairns, menhirs, dolmens, megaliths, barrows, and passage graves were rooted in, or went down into, the earth. The European megaliths of Stonehenge or Carnac are better known but megaliths are found world-wide. And to not forget the Inca roads, the Maya cenotes, the Nazca lines, and Angkor Wat, the largest temple site, in area, in the world. Ah but, you say, the Egyptians developed more advanced technology that enabled them to build higher. And I'd say, that's when our problem began.

Fast forward to 13th century Europe. St Paul's Cathedral was begun in 1087 CE and completed in 1314 with a spire that topped out at 149 metres. (Although there is debate about its exact height and the contemporaneous Lincoln Cathedral may have been 160 metres). The central spire of Lincoln Cathedral was destroyed in a storm in 1549 and Old St Paul's was gutted in the Great Fire of London in 1666. The rebuilding came soon after and it was officially declared complete in 1711. At 111 metres (365 feet) high, it was the tallest building in London from 1711 to 1963. Then came other European cathedrals in the 1500s and 1600s of similar height in France and Germany. These only exceeded the pyramid at Giza because it had eroded and was 10 metres lower. It was not until the Rouen (151 metres) or Cologne (157 metres) cathedrals of the late 1800s that the apex of religious buildings and monuments was reached.

Now the monuments, not to God but to human endeavour, took over and we find the Washington Monument (1884) at 169 metres and the Eiffel Tower (1889) at 330 metres. The latter remained the tallest until the modern era of "skyscrapers". In the early 1930s the competition was between the Chrysler building (1930, 319 metres), the Empire State building (1931, 381 metres), and the Bank of Manhattan Trust Building or 40 Wall Street (1930, 283 metres). In 1995 the latter was renamed the Trump Building.

The Empire State building (a strange name in a country so fervently republic and isolationist) was the tallest for 40 years until building tall got its second wind after World War II. The first World Trade Centre tower—which we shall come to later—was built in 1972 at 471 metres. This was followed by the Sears Tower (1974, 442 metres), the Petronas Towers in Kuala Lumpur (1998, 452 metres), the Taipei 101 in Taiwan (2004, 509 metres), and in 2007 the Burj Khalifa in Dubai which stands 830 metres tall.

In medieval times the tower as church spire was a pissing contest between religions. In modern times the tower as skyscraper is a pissing contest between cultures. Who has the biggest one, the longest one, the highest one?

Twin Towers

It is difficult to write about a tragedy such as 9/11. Three thousand people died in such a horrible way and the trauma and hurt, physical and emotional, is still fresh. We are too close. Another two or three generations would be respectful. But we may not have that time available to us.

The idea of establishing a World Trade Center in New York City was first proposed in 1943 but plans were put on hold in 1949. In the

1950s, to help stimulate urban renewal in Lower Manhattan, David Rockefeller suggested that the Port Authority build a World Trade Center there. On September 20, 1962 the Port Authority of New York announced Minoru Yamasaki as lead architect.[14] Ironically, Yamasaki was inspired by Islamic architecture, having previously designed Saudi Arabia's Dhahran International Airport with the Saudi Binladin Group. Yamasaki's plan incorporated twin towers. His original plan called for the towers to be 80 stories tall, but to meet the Port Authority's requirement for 10,000,000 square feet of office space, the buildings would each have to be 110 stories tall. Both planes hit the towers above the 80th floor.

The World Trade Centre complex housed more than 400 companies engaged in various commercial activities and, on a typical weekday, an estimated 50,000 people worked there. It was so large that it had its own zip code: 10048. The Twin Towers appeared in numerous TV shows and movies and became an icon of New York on par with the Empire State Building and the Statue of Liberty. Completed in 1973, it was an expression of the global and economic power of the USA.[15]

On September 11, 2001 the first plane struck the North Tower between floors 93 and 99 at 8:46 am. Seventeen minutes later at 9:03 am the second plane struck floors 77 to 85 of the South Tower. The intense fire caused by aviation fuel caused the structural steel in the towers to collapse. The south tower gave way first at 9:59 am, only 56 minutes after being hit. The north tower collapsed less than a half hour later, at 10:28 am.[16]

The number of 3,000 dead is small compared to other wars and disasters.[17] The USA has never been invaded or occupied. But the fact that there had been no recent attack on mainland USA (other than the

---

14. This was 39 years before 9/11. For the significance of the time period of 39 years see Owen, *The 27 Club* and *Jung and the Moon Cycles*.

15. See *The 27 Club* for the temporal relationship with 9/11 and the movie *The Towering Inferno*. The movie started filming in May 1974 and finished filming twenty-seven years later on September 11, 1974. The film's opening credits included a dedication: "To those who give their lives so that others might live, to the firefighters of the world, this picture is gratefully dedicated."

16. https://en.wikipedia.org/wiki/World_Trade_Center

17. Recent examples are: 1952 Great Smog of London, 12,000; 1969–1973 US bombing

1993 World Trade Centre bombing) since the war of 1812; its aim at the heart of American business; the deliberate and malevolent way it occurred; the fires and the jumping; the deaths of brave firefighters; and the heroism of Flight 93, are more than sufficient to give 9/11 eternal and memorial significance. But it is more than that and we would not do justice to its defining singularity, the depth and breadth of the event, if we did not consider it from all directions.

The tower is a way of symbolically connecting heaven and earth but like space programs that strive to "loose the surly bonds of earth" it also represents the inflated desire to break away from the earth and to dominate nature. In the past, the threat was from below—too much instinct, too much earth—so cultural norms, laws, religions and seemly behaviours were developed. But now the threat is from above, from too much spirit.

In the Tower card of many tarot decks we see twins falling from the tower or temple, twin bolts of lightning, flames coming from the tower, and the tower being struck by lightning about two-thirds of the way up. The similarity of these images with the tragedy of 9/11 is striking—the twin planes striking the twin towers, where the planes hit, the flames, the destruction of the towers, and people jumping headfirst from the towers. One of the photos of a "jumper" with legs crossed in a figure four is very similar to the Tower and Hanged Man cards.

Usually spirit seeks out the place where the veil between the worlds is thinnest, where spirit and matter are in closest proximity. In its desire to make human contact, spirit circles the edges of the herd, so to speak, looking for those who are furthest from the protection afforded by the collective at the centre of the crowd. It looks for the most marginal, the most vulnerable, the most receptive, the most defended, the most inflated or the most inflatable. If the worlds are out of balance, if the other world is not fed with our gifts of beauty, then a correction, or a nudge, or a sign will occur to suggest a change or a compensation. Here, we might think differently about indigenous cultures supposedly "appeasing" their gods. Psychologically, if our attitude is too concrete or

---

of Cambodia, 40,000–100,000; 1975 Failure of the Banqiao Dam, China, over 100,000; 1984 Bhopal chemical disaster, 8,000.

one-sided then we invite the unconscious to take drastic measures like sending down bolts of lightning or arranging collapse in our lives.

I wrote the following three paragraphs in late 2000 and early 2001.

The inflation of the Western psyche has grown unchecked in the last one thousand years and particularly in the last fifty years. It has difficulty accepting limitations and is suffering from a dissociative denial of the reality that the planet we live on is alive and accordingly may be ill and or dying. The inflation is fuelled by the uncritical acceptance of heroic attitudes such as, "In this land of opportunity and freedom anyone can become anything," and the economic fantasy of everlasting four percent annual growth.

The heroic world economy is unsustainable, in spite of the euphemism of "sustainable development." Were it not for the pathological breakdown in reality testing, even a single statistic would convince us of our destructiveness. For example: nearly eighty percent of the world's indigenous forests have been destroyed since 1970; the Grand Banks fishery off Newfoundland, the richest fishing ground in the world, was closed in 1992 and cod stocks continue to decline; between 1950 and 2000 more resources were consumed than in the whole history of the human race; and the Johnny-come-lately awareness of global climate change.

But the global heroic ego, for all its priapic, hyper-masculine competitiveness, has feeble self-esteem and is narcissistically vulnerable. Commercial self-esteem and "business confidence" is a such a delicate thing, swinging between grandiose, blustering, aggressive competition, on the one hand, and tantrums and tears on the other when its omnipotence is frustrated. A compensatory deflation of the Western psyche (or the American psyche as the quintessence of this inflated consciousness) that has severed itself from the natural world was a certainty. The puffed-up house of cards has no internal strength or scaffolding and a collapse was bound to happen.

A pancake dream

On Sunday September 9, 2001, two days before 9/11, I had a dream. But first some background.

I was studying at the Jung Institute in Zurich in the late 1980s. There I had a dream in which I laid out Jung's life on the Moon Cycles, an indigenous teaching based on the length of a human pregnancy and characterised by 9-month, 3-year and 27-year cycles. Every birth and death (in either matter or in spirit) sends out ripples in the fabric of time that follow a pattern: nine months (a pregnancy, from conception to birth), three years (four pregnancies which make up a Little Moon, a small circle of development) and 27 years (nine Little Moons make a Big Moon, a major circle of development). In the life of humans we are a child until age 27, an adolescent from 27 to 54, become an adult at age 54, and an elder at age 81.

Until I had the dream I never consciously thought of describing someone's life using this teaching. More than ten years later (no deadlines and fevered scribbling here), the dream led me to write a book called Jung and the Moon Cycles. It was published in 2002. In the writing of it, I discovered a number of unusual patterns in Jung's life that had not been recognised or written about before.

I began writing in 2000 and in the chapter on the Little Moon of the Big North Moon—the place of double Wisdom and Knowledge— when Jung was between 72 and 75 years of age, I dealt with his writing of the book he called Aion, a text that is closely related to the themes of this book. As I finished the section on Aion the events of 9/11 occurred. Now to the dream.

> I am in a place like the Jung Institute but not quite. I am there to look at something. I am somehow known for my work on Jung or I have some credibility because of what I have written on Jung. I am surprised at this. I am shown up to the attic by a young secretary who is a librarian or a member of the Jung family. I am led into a room where there are letters or papers or things that are shown only to certain people. She has some authority to make this decision. The small attic is no more than 4 or 5 paces across, the woodwork is only roughed in, and

the floor boards show. There are also 3 or 4 other researchers who are writing at desks. The young woman steps off the narrow stair, which I am still standing on, onto the attic floor and goes to open the door to the archive room that leads off the attic.

Suddenly the weight of all the people on the attic floor makes it start to collapse—first the rough wooden bannister, then the floorboards and then the walls. Then the whole house, which is 4 or 5 stories high including the attic, starts to collapse floor by floor. I run down the stairs and am ducking under collapsing floors and beams just keeping ahead of each floor as it collapses. I finally get to the ground floor and run out onto a city street with billowing clouds of dust behind me as the whole building pancakes.

I thought a lot about the personal aspects of the dream—the first place to look—but I won't amplify the dream other than to add my reactions as I wrote them down in the days after I had the dream. Initially, I thought it had to do with some de-idealisation of my attitude toward Jung and Jungian work. The young woman leads me to the inner sanctum but the ponderousness of the intellect, research and academic interest, perhaps the wrong attitude, not knowing how much is too much, makes the whole edifice collapse. It also reminded me of the 16 card in the tarot, the collapsing Tower hit by a bolt of lightning about two-thirds of the way up. The Xultun Tarot depicts two people falling out of the tower head first with legs crossed, in the shape of the number four, like the Hanged Man card.

When I had the dream I was in South Africa, six hours ahead of New York. I had the dream sometime Sunday morning, September 9. Two days later, on the following Tuesday morning New York time, the two towers of the World Trade Centre were hit by planes and collapsed. I saw it unfold on CNN on Tuesday afternoon—the towers collapsed floor by floor and the dust billowed out along the streets behind fleeing New Yorkers. This meant that my dream was about 48 hours ahead of 9/11. This horrific event had happened in the dream, in the other world, and that's how long it took to happen in the physical world.

Initially I thought that explosives had brought down the buildings as they collapsed like a demolition job. At the time I was running a workshop in rural South Africa and the only network we could get was CNN which said that the temperature had reached over 1500 degrees C, the structural steel had started to melt and the floors pancaked on each other, just as in my dream, followed by the great cloud of toxic smoke.

The texture of time

It was only the day after 9/11 that I got the feeling that the dream was not only personal but also about the tragedy in some way. In terms of the sequence in the dream, when the woman goes to get the hidden material it is then that the collapse begins. In the dream I felt that the material had been stored because it was interesting but its full significance had not been realised. I wrote at the time: "I had a feeling that has frustratingly evaporated as I write this that there was a connection between this apocalyptic tragedy and something that Jung did not disclose or that he left behind to be understood."

At the time I was finishing my book on the Moon Cycles and Jung's life. On Thursday afternoon, two days after 9/11, I decided to look at the Moon Cycles in relation to the events of 9/11. I found that they had occurred 40 years and 3 months after Jung's death on 6 June 1961. The Moon Cycles say that we travel around the Big Moon of Trust and Innocence from birth to age 27 and around the Big Moon of Death and Change from 27 to 54.[18] Halfway through this Big Moon, from age 39 to 42, is the Little Moon of double death and change—the apogee of our lives halfway between sunrise and sunset. Half way through this Little Moon at age 40½ is the time of triple death and change. So 9/11 occurred when Jung's death was in the place of triple Death and Change forty and a half years later. I only notice this relationship, this connection, this correspondence. I make no assumption about a link, neither do I dismiss it.

The unidirectional, Newtonian view is that time is only linear and causal, such that current events cause future things happen, and only when there is a demonstrable link of cause and effect. So according to

---

18. This rarely means physical death but rather the deaths (losses, separations, or ageing) that are part of life.

this view, any connection, of whatever nature, between Jung's death and 9/11 would remain unnoticed. But time is bi-directional, and multi-directional, without regard for our linear, unidirectional bias. Future dreamings cause current events to happen. Or to put it another way, things are dreamed of in the fifth dimensional world before they happen in the three dimensional world.

We see this is in degraded form in the encouragements we give to young people to Dream Big! and Follow your dream! However, the linear view of time holds to the shibboleth of objectivity, representative samples, repeated observations, and accurate measurement. Bi- or multi-directional time does not discard objectivity but also values subjectivity. It's not what you are considering but, as importantly, who is considering it. The observer is the observation. It's just good science, really.

So the Moon Cycle connections between the events of 1961 and 2001 showed up on my radar. They got my attention. They are the visible ripple in the fabric of time by the upwelling of an archetypal force thousands of years in the making. When an archetype is in your neighbourhood synchronicities happen, in knots and patterns. Time has a texture and its shape and form, albeit ever-changing, that can be seen and felt. The temporal nodes and tinctures discussed in this book relate primarily to what has happened in the past to bring us to the place we are in now.

Listening to what happens

It is a sign of how deeply unconscious the inflation is in Western culture that a deflation had to occur in such a tragic and deadly way as 9/11. The terrorists got the penis (the World Trade Centre) and the testicles (the Pentagon), but fortunately not the head or the heart (possibly the White House or Capitol Hill, but we may never know where Flight 93 was headed). And it had to be that drastic because we are not listening.

So what might this oracle, this "reaction of our environment" as Jung put it, tell us? The message is not too hard to hear. It was the *World Trade* Centre, the epitome of the business of business that collapsed to the ground. It was *two* towers that collapsed in the ground. Strangely, in the excellent collection of essays edited by Luigi Zoja,

Jungian Reflections on September 11, there is no mention of the symbolic significance of the event. It may literally be the collapse of world trade (which Covid-19 threatened), or the banking system, the world currency structure, an earthquake, or a tsunami. We don't know what the two collapses will be, how they will happen or how catastrophic they will be, the only thing that is predictable is their unpredictability. But happen it will, twice. One not too long after the other. And it may happen twice many times.

This book has been a piecemeal process over many years, thoughts never meaning to dress up as a book, and the river of events has always run by faster than I can write or would wish to write. So I find that a paragraph I have written gets overtaken rapidly by events as they come from the other world of possible futures descending through time into the material world. I was aware that matter would ask for its due at some point in some way. However, I couldn't have guessed Covid-19.[19]

Often we cannot see the specifics of an archetypal pattern until decades after the event, until we have some objectivity and are able to see it from the outside rather than being consumed by it and being unable to see its totality. Much of this chapter was written in 2000–2001, well before and just after 9/11. We never know at any particular point in time if the events I describe have happened, are happening, or are yet to happen. An archetype is a process has been repeated thousands of times before in human history. Or, to the contrary, a repeated event in the past creates an archetype. Each time the form is different but the pattern is the same.

Such an archetypal corrective, like a natural catastrophe, takes no prisoners. The planes, the plans, the terrorists, the victims, the extremists, the religions and the politics of 9/11 are all bit players in an ongoing archetypal drama about the compulsory downsizing of Western culture. From the ashes of the grief and tragedy, no consciousness of the meaning of 9/11 has arisen and it continues to be viewed simplistically as the actions of evil men against a good nation. Which it was—but that

---

19. As I edit the final draft of this book the CrowdStrike IT outage occurred on July 19, 2024 shutting down media websites, banks and airlines worldwide.

is not all it was. The process of collapse will continue in other ways and forms, mostly shocking and unexpected.

The USA had it coming. I recoil from saying that. But do not mistake it for a geopolitical statement, personal animosity, or an insensitive or disrespectful comment. The bruising and deflation of the American ego was the result of an inevitable historical process.[20] It is significant that it was the World Trade Centre that was hit—the ramrod straight, up-thrusting centre of commerce and business, in the city that never sleeps, in the "greatest country in the world". The WTC held many of the world's stockbroking firms and merchant bankers. Then came the Pentagon, but the White House or Capitol Hill were spared. It also came nine months into the term of a good ol', good versus evil president. George Bush said of 9/11 in a testamental sort of way, "This is about good and evil and good will prevail".

Fair enough, the ones who did this need to be dealt to, and most of them have been. But there has been little self-reflection and zero objectivity but this takes time, generations indeed. There is not much hope that the USA will ask why did this happen to me, at this time and in this way. Would this compensation have been avoided if Bush had decided not to grant oil leases in Alaska, or if Gore had become President? Now that sounds too much like divine retribution, or its ecological equivalent, but there you have it. There was no healthy narcissism and navel gazing, or curious, non-partisan, non-blaming, non-paranoid inquiry. In 2016 life had to raise bigger red flags and the USA got Donald Trump, replete with pathological narcissism. It's a 100% American product—Made in the USA.

---

20. As of mid-2024, with the resignation of Joe Biden, and the Republican nomination of Donald Trump, the inflation looks set to continue.

13

HISTORY

COLONISING-UP

THE HISTORICAL, economic, political and mercantile forces driving European exploration are well documented. But what about the psychological, psycho-historical or archetypal compulsions that drove this invasion of other lands and places that were considered free for the taking? It goes much further back than the birth of Christ —a favourite date in medieval Europe—but I will mention Jung's view of the forces operating over the first 1500 years of the Christian era leading up to the recent 500 years of destruction.

Jung began writing *Aion: Researches into the Phenomenology of the Self* around late 1947 and it was published in 1950. He said that "The model of the Self in Aion is based on Ezekiel's vision".[1] Jung was 72 and had recovered from a critical illness in 1944. He had experienced the six years of WWII, together with the emerging realisation of the scale of the Holocaust. In the Foreword he says that the book is about the change in the psychic situation over the Christian aeon, which coincides with the the Platonic month of the fishes, in other words, Pisces. Aion is about the archetypal significance of the Age of Pisces and the coming of the Age of Aquarius, and how the workings of archetypal processes during

---

1. Jung-Kirsch Letters, 173.

the Piscean era resulted in the Christ image (frequently associated with the fish) becoming one-sidedly spiritual and lacking in substance and instinct.

This self-created conflict between matter and spirit sharpened about halfway through the aeon. Around 1000 CE heretical sects like the Cathars (*katharoi*, the pure ones) arose and the split between matter and spirit became even wider. During the 13th and 14th centuries the Cathars believed that all visible matter, including the human body, was created by Rex Mundi (the King of the World and Satan) who was the God of the Old Testament. They believed that matter was therefore tainted with sin; Christ did not incarnate in physical form in a material body so they refused the Eucharist; and humans were actually angels who had been seduced by Satan before a war in heaven against the army of Michael. They were pescatarians and avoided eating anything that was a by-product of sexual reproduction. They were persecuted for their heresies by the Catholic Church, who held that there was only one God who created all things visible and invisible. The Cathars taught that to regain angelic status one had to renounce the material self completely. Until one was prepared to do so, they would be stuck in a cycle of reincarnation, and condemned to live on the corrupt Earth.[2]

From the point of view of the Earth this was all just silliness—one god, two gods, three gods, who cares? All things have free will so let's just leave them to it. Until now. The spiritual and cultural descendants of this two-legged foolishness have left a gash in the beauty web of matter that lives today in misogyny, pro-choice, second amendment, climate change, ecological coma, and a profound contempt for matter. All this set the stage for the final quarter beginning around 1500 CE. Edward Edinger captures what happened:

> An absolute psychological explosion in the collective psyche took place then, as though the Holy Ghost descended with a vengeance. We had the Reformation, the Renaissance, the age of exploration, the birth of science and art, and critical examination of all the sacred scriptures that up until then could not be touched, just as one had not, until then,

---

2. https://en.wikipedia.org/wiki/Catharism

dared examine the human body. In 1543, Vesalius, having robbed the gallows for corpses for dissection, brought out his first major work on human anatomy. Nothing was sacred anymore.[3]

In 1687 Sir Isaac Newton (1642–1726) published his *Philosophiæ Naturalis Principia Mathematica* usually abbreviated to Principia Mathematica, leaving out the natural philosophy. Before the advent of science, natural philosophy was the study of nature. Newton was an alchemist, a natural philosopher, as well as a devout Christian. John Maynard Keynes (1883–1946), the father of macroeconomics, said Newton was not the first of the age of reason but the last of the magicians. Based on the Bible, Newton calculated that the apocalypse would occur in 2016, 2034 or sometime before 2060. Perhaps he was not too far off.[4] Newton's scientific work formulated the immutable "laws" of physics and mathematics under which all natural phenomena, such as gravity or motion, operated. Concurrent with Newton's writing the colonisation of the Americas and subjugation of indigenous peoples to European "laws" was well under way.

With the coming of Christ a pendulum had swung violently to one side and was now swinging violently in the opposite direction. Jung summarises:

> A factor that no one has reckoned with, however, is the fatality inherent in the Christian disposition itself, which leads inevitably to a reversal of its spirit—not through the obscure workings of chance but in accordance with psychological law. The ideal of spirituality striving for the heights was doomed to clash with the materialistic earth-bound passion to conquer matter and master the world... but the spirit of medieval Christianity that underwent strange pagan transformations, exchanging the heavenly goal for an earthly one, and the vertical of the Gothic style for a horizontal perspective (voyages of discovery, exploration of the world and of nature)....

---

3. Edinger, *The Aion Lectures*, 79.
4. www.newtonprojectca.files.wordpress.com/2013/06/reply-to-tom-harpur-2-page-full-version.pdf; https://en.wikipedia.org/wiki/isaac_newton#occult

It is as if, with the coming of Christ, opposites that were latent till then had become manifest, or as if a pendulum had swung violently to one side and were now carrying out the complementary movement in the opposite direction. No tree, it is said, can grow to heaven unless its roots reach down to hell.... We hear of a reign of a "thousand years" and of a "coming of the Antichrist," just as if a partition of worlds and epochs had taken place between two royal brothers. The meeting with Satan was therefore more than mere chance; it was a link in the chain.[5]

So the birth of Christ, an indelible marker of time in Euro-Christian consciousness, was not the beginning of an epoch but simply an inevitable way-station in an archetypal movement upwards to spirit and away from the Earth. Inevitably, Jung put this in religious, and specifically Christian, terms as Satan or the Antichrist coming at the end of times or, its opposite, the second coming of Christ.

However, the Christian apocalypse is not quite a hostile takeover by Christ's dark brother, nor the Saviour's second coming lasting for eternity. The latter would inevitably lead to a disembodied existence for humankind for eternity—no flowers, no skin, no wind, no taste of lips and wine. But both may have kernels of truth within their husks. There will not be a Satanic apocalypse in spirit but rather in matter—the Earth may die. The destruction of matter and the Earth itself has been brought about by monotheism's abhorrence and disdain for woman and Earth.

Christianity, the religious virus carried by the Catholic Conquistadors and the Protestant Puritans exploding out of Europe, carried the seeds of its own demise which we are living though now— not through the Antichrist, or the end of time, or the Rapture, or Armageddon—but through the death of the very ground we walk upon. Sponsored and brought to you by civilisation and progress.

Exploding Europe

We have fled the Old World and the New World has been exploited.

---

5. CW 9, par. 78.

When the first European explorers sailed the south eastern seaboard of what is now the USA they could smell the scent of flowers miles offshore. They didn't wonder, they didn't ask permission of the people, the plants, or the animals, or the land itself. They took inventory.

The particular cul-de-sac that is Western consciousness originated in a very small part of the world——Europe. Bounded to the southeast by the Caucasus Mountains, the Black Sea and the Bosphorus, and to the east by Ural Mountains, the Ural River and the Caspian Sea, it is the world's second-smallest continent (only Australia is smaller) and covers only about 2.0% of the Earth's surface.

All cultures see themselves as the centre of the world. The ceremonial name of Lake Atitlan is Rumuxux Ruchiuleu in Tzutujil Maya, or the Belly Button of the Earth.[6] Many indigenous cultures did, and still do, refer to themselves simply as The People. Their lands were a mythic place where the natural and spiritual worlds touched, where the World Tree spans the heavens above and the depths below. It was a place where the connection with the ancestors—all humans related by bond or blood to the land, who lived in the other world—was unbroken. There was no need to travel, to invent wheels, chariots, roads, balloons, planes, or submarines that would carry humans over great distances vertically or horizontally—all markers of so-called "civilisation". The People didn't need to flee anywhere, they were already home.

Europe was subjected to severe religious strictures for over a thousand years after the death of Christ. The Christian desert hermits of the third century, the anchorites, and the stylites, gave rise to the traditions of Christian monasticism and the great, grey cathedrals and abbeys of Europe. This monastic enthusiasm increased greatly in the 11th and 12th centuries. The Church of Rome ruled. Until it didn't. But like all great archetypal changes this crumbling happened slowly.

Petrarch, the Italian scholar of the early 1300s, coined the notion of the "Dark Ages" which belonged to the thousand years between the fall of Rome and the Renaissance. The term became more popular during the 18th-century Age of Enlightenment. Europe, myopically disregarding the great advances of Arabic and Chinese science, saw its own

---

6. Prechtel, *The Disobedience of the Daughter of the Sun*, 92.

small patch reborn from the dark ages of intellectual stagnation and religious influence. Saint Augustine (354–430 CE) held that curiosity was one of the three most deadly sins, along with pride and lust. In the first millennium after the birth of Christ, this introversion and contraction was like a great inhalation before the psychological explosion of intellectual and physical discovery that began with the Renaissance. Literature, philosophy, art, music, politics, and science blossomed with a new freedom that began in Italy in the early 1400s and by the 1600s had spread to the rest of Europe. Parallel to this great release were the so-called "voyages of discovery".

Voyages of discovery

With such a history of religious constriction combined with the coming of the Renaissance, Europe desperately needed to flee to other places using what we would now call "technology". The Norse had briefly inhabited L'Anse Aux Meadows in Newfoundland around 1,000 CE and then settled the southern tip of Greenland over the succeeding centuries. They had contact with Native peoples (Thule and Beothuk) whom they called skraelings, meaning barbarian or foreigner.

Starting in 1419 the Portuguese, the great seafarers in their small caravels, set forth when Henry the Navigator explored Madeira, the Azores, and the coast of West Africa as far as Sierra Leone. In 1488 Bartolomeu Dias rounded the Cape of Good Hope. In 1498 Vasco da Gama reached India. In 1500, the Portuguese nobleman Pedro Cabral became the first European to come upon Brazil. From 1519–1521, Ferdinand Magellan circumnavigated the globe.

However, Spain was not be left out and in 1492 Christopher Columbus's three ships set sail hoping to reach India as an alternative route to the Silk Road for the prized silk and spices of the east. Columbus made landfall in what is now the Bahamas and called the indigenous people he met *indios,* which is Spanish for Indians. Indigenous peoples of America have been called this ever since.

We might wonder what if the Taino, Arawak, Inuit, Mohawk, Abenaki or Mi'kmaq had set out eastward across the Atlantic, hoping to find an alternative route to the distant land of China? And, on arriving at the furthest western reaches of, say, Portugal or Ireland, named the strange inhabitants they found there the "Chinese"? Would white Chinese-Europeans now be pressing for reparation and recompense for all the lands that were stolen by the Mohawk colonisers? You bet!

History levels and humiliates—in the sense of bringing us down to earth, taking a knee, drawing closer to the soil, the humus, beneath our feet. It's hard to stay puffed-up in the present when we are reminded of our past. So, in an age of "make America great again", let's not confuse the USA with the continent that stretches from from Baffin Island to Patagonia.

The continent of America, including North, Central and South America, is named after Amerigo Vespucci (1452–1512) the Italian explorer. Like Columbus, Vespucci travelled to the New World in 1499 and again in 1502 but, unlike Columbus, Vespucci wrote about it. His accounts of his travels were published in 1502 and 1504 and were widely read in Europe. Columbus thought he had reached Asia but Vespucci realised it was a new continent and was the first to call it the New World, or Novus Mundus, in his books. In 1507 a German cartographer, Martin Waldseemuller, drew up a map based on Ptolemy's projections and Vespucci's journals that showed this "new" continent, as a sliver of its eastern coastlines, that lay between the Atlantic and Pacific.

Of the thousand or so maps originally made only one survived. Rediscovered in Germany in 1901, it was grandly called the "Birth Certificate of America". The Waldseemuller map was purchased by the Library of Congress in 2003 for $10 million.[7] Keen we are on preserving physical things that are dug up or "discovered" like Egyptian pyramids, the ruins of Zimbabwe, or Maya temples. The Library of Congress paid $10 million for a 500 year-old map but paying the same $10 million for reparation to indigenous people for past thefts, or for the preservation of one of the thousands of endangered languages, would never be thought of. The spoken word takes second place to the written word.

The convention at that time was to put east at the top of a map. However, the Waldseemuller map placed north at the top of the map

---

7. Ramani, 'The Epic Story of the Map That Gave America Its Name'. http://www.bbc.com/travel/story/20180702-the-epic-story-of-the-map-that-gave-america-its-name.

thus putting Europe pretty much at centre of the map. This, together with naming of an entire, inhabited continent after a European man who only visited, demonstrates the European attitude and ambition of the time. It predicted how Europeans would plunder lands and resources, erase cultures, and kill millions. As Toby Lester summarises in his book, "It's a birth certificate for the world that came into being in 1492—and it's a death warrant for the one that was there before".[8]

All countries and continents were seen as feminine so Waldseemuller used the feminine Latinised name of Amerigo to name the new continent "America". Ironic? All the other continents—Asia, Africa, and Australia—also have names ending in *-a* indicating the feminine gender. But the name Europe derives from the Greek goddess Europa who has particularly masculine connections. Her name comes from the Greek, *eurus*, meaning broad or wide, and *ops* meaning face or countenance. Broad was an epithet for the earth in early Indo-European religions. So we might think of Europe as referring to something like the face of the broad earth.

The daughter of a Phoenician king, Zeus had fallen in love with Europa, so turned himself into a white bull and carried her off to Crete on his back. She bore three sons to him. Her seduction, abduction, ravishment or rape (all much the same in Greek mythology) was painted as "The Rape of Europa" by Rembrandt, Titian and Goya.[9]

The psychological and masculine lineage of Europe is revealed by the myth. Zeus gave her five gifts, all with masculine qualities. The masculine wants to act on the world so it can change what is. The feminine wants to absorb the world so it can understand what is. It is the instinctual nature of the feminine to receive the projections of those around her and mould herself to them. Not as an act of inferiority and submission but as a way of getting inside things, feeling them, relating, joining, and knowing them in a different way from the masculine. The

---

8. Lester, *The Fourth Part of the World: An Astonishing Epic of Global Discovery, Imperial Ambition, and the Birth of America.*

9. Although we weren't there at the time, we might equally say that Europa seduced the all-powerful Zeus by taking advantage of his all-vulnerable weakness for women. To concretise and modernise this particular story as one of a "power imbalance" is to detract from, and diminish, the power of women.

light side of Europa or Pasiphae is receiving knowledge and illumination through enveloping, consuming, and joining with the masculine power of the bull. What comes of this union is the quality that monotheism refers to as wisdom or Sophia.

This masculine archetype of expansion, knowledge and illumination appeared in matter centuries later (oh dear, those archetypes, they do take their time) as the voyages of exploration and the later period of the Enlightenment, but also as colony and empire—all originating from Europe.

Colonising-up

At the same time, profound secular and spiritual upheavals and protests were happening in medieval Europe. In Germany, Martin Luther (1483–1546) protested the spiritual power of the Pope. According to one account, Luther nailed his "Ninety-five Theses" to the door of All Saints' Church in Wittenberg on 31 October 1517. He proposed that faith alone, not "indulgences", brought salvation and that the Bible, not the Pope, was the only source of divine knowledge from God. In England, Henry VIII (1491–1547) protested the secular power of the Pope. He threw a hissy because Pope Paul III would not annul his marriage to Catherine of Aragon, his first wife (of six), so he set up his own Church of England, and dissolved all the monasteries, priories, and convents in England in the late 1530s. It has been estimated that, in England at the time, one adult man in fifty was a member of a religious order. The result of these protestations was Protestantism in its various forms (Anglican, Calvinist, Lutheran and Huguenot) which rapidly spread throughout England, Scotland and northern Europe. It ended the absolute power of the Catholic Church of Rome that had lasted almost 1500 years.

Meanwhile, back across the Atlantic, the flurry of colonisation gathered pace. In 1493 John Cabot had laid claim to Newfoundland for Henry VII of England. In 1494 Portugal and Spain signed the Treaty of Tordesillas which divided the world outside of Europe between them along a north-south meridian 1,560 kms west of the Cape Verde islands. This was the basis for the division of South America between

Portuguese Brazil and the other Spanish-speaking countries. It was later ignored by the British, Dutch and French. In 1510 Vasco Núñez de Balboa founded the first permanent settlement in the Americas in present-day Panama and in 1513 he crossed the Isthmus of Panama and became the first European to see the Pacific Ocean from the shores of America.

Inland, between 1519 and 1532, Cortes slaughtered the Aztecs in Central America, and Pizzaro did likewise to the Incas, in South America. For France, the voyages of Jacques Cartier between 1534 and 1542 laid claim to the country of Canada (an Iroquois name for a nearby settlement) and the lucrative fur trade by canoe of *les voyageurs*. In 1605 Samuel de Champlain founded Port Royal at present-day Annapolis Royal, Nova Scotia and later Quebec City in 1608. New France was the area colonised by the French in North America during a period extending from the exploration of the Saint Lawrence River, by Jacques Cartier in 1534, to the cession of New France to Spain and to Great Britain in 1763. At its peak in 1712 (prior to the Treaties of Utrecht by which the French, Spanish and British re-arranged the map of North America) the territory of New France extended from Newfoundland to the Rocky Mountains and from the Hudson Bay to the Gulf of Mexico.

In the first half of the 1600s, almost every country in Europe had been involved in the Thirty Years' War (1618–1648). An estimated five to seven million died out of a total European population of about 70 million. Initially a Protestant–Catholic conflict, by 1648 Spanish power had collapsed which left the colonial possessions of the Portuguese and Spanish empires up for grabs. By then the Dutch had the largest mercantile fleet in Europe—larger than all the other European seafaring nations put together—and they annexed most of Portugal's territory in the East Indies giving them control over the enormously profitable spice trade. In 1652 Jan van Riebeeck established Kaapstad (Cape Town) as a supply station.

In 1607 the first permanent British settlement in North America was built at Jamestown, Virginia. In the first half of the 17th country a multitude of colonies were established in what is now eastern Canada, the eastern USA and the Caribbean by Great Britain, Sweden

(Delaware), and the Netherlands. What is now New York was briefly New Amsterdam until 1667 when it was ceded to the British and renamed after the Duke of York, later to become King James II.

More than decimation

If a Roman legion mutinied, supposedly one in every ten (thus decimation) legionaries were killed. During the 1600s First Nations peoples were more than decimated. A case in point—Manhattan. Often described as the cultural, financial, media, and entertainment capital of the world with Times Square being the "crossroads of the world" on New Year's eve. (Grandiosity abounds). In 1524, the Florentine explorer Giovanni da Verrazzano sailed as far as the mouth of the Hudson River. In 1609 Henry Hudson, an Englishman, sailing for the Dutch West India Company, sailed up the eponymous river as far as Albany hoping to find a northwest passage to India. (In 1610 he explored what came to be known as Hudson Bay, the northern passage for the fur trade). In the Dutch National Archives in The Hague, Netherlands, is a letter dated November 5, 1626 written by the Dutch merchant Pieter Schagen. He wrote, "They have purchased the Island of Manhattes from the savages for the value of 60 guilders".

At the time of first European contact there were about 10,000 Native peoples living on Long Island. The Shinnecock and the Montauk with the Canarsee and Lenape straddling either side of Manhattan. The Manahatin, Lenape, and Munsee Indians were all indigenous to lower Manhattan according to their respective histories. The word Manhattan originates from the Lenape description manna-hata, which means "island of hills".

In another 1626 account, Peter Minuit—appointed director-general of New Netherland by the Dutch West India Company—purchased Manhattan from the Lenape, or Delaware Indians, for $24 worth of trade goods, sometimes described as "trinkets". This likely referred to wampum. Made from quahog shells and strung into belts, this was used ceremonially by tribes along the eastern seaboard for storytelling, exchange, and recording treaties and historical events. This story is often quoted with a unspoken subtext of what a good deal it was and how the white man bought something for nothing from the savages—the most expensive real estate in the world bought for twenty-four bucks. Suckers!

However, Europeans had a strange belief that land could be owned —the result of a couple of thousand years of social mutation. The population of Europe in the early 1600s was about 70 million, about 12 percent of the world population. European culture with its attendant social and economic structures was in a global minority. The sale of land was transacted through written title in perpetuity. Once title was established, landowners built fences, walls and other barriers to bar trespassing by others. But for Native peoples at the time, it was proper for gifts to be exchanged for safe passage through their lands or for temporary occupation by visitors.[10]

A few hundred Dutch settlers then farmed the lower end of Manhattan until the British conquered New Amsterdam in 1664 and renamed it New York. "By 1741, it was estimated that only 400 natives remained on Long Island. By the time of the American Revolution in 1775, Indians were a rare sight on the island, having been driven away from their beloved 'Paumanok' (Land of Tribute)".[11]

In 1713, the Treaty of Utrecht was signed. Spain gave British slave traders the contract known as the Asiento de Negros (the "agreement of blacks". This was a monopoly contract between the Spanish Crown and various merchants for the right to provide 144,000 enslaved Africans a year to colonies in Spanish South America. Around six million Africans were taken as enslaved people to the Americas, at least one third of them on British ships. It has been estimated that overall about 12 million Africans were captured to be taken to the Americas as slaves.Of that 12 million over 55 per cent were taken to Brazil and Spanish South America. About 35 per cent were taken to the West Indies. Notably, fewer than 5 per cent were sold in North America.[12]

Now the European countries began to fight over the spoils of the

---

10. 'America's First Urban Myth?', http://blog.nmai.si.edu/main/2011/08/americas-first-urban-myth.html
11. 'Long Island Indian Tribes-Richmond Hill Historical Society', http://www.richmond hillhistory.org/indians.html.
12. https://www.bbc.co.uk/bitesize/guides/zqv7hyc/revision/2

world. Britain, France, Portugal, Spain, the Netherlands, Sweden, Scotland, Denmark and Norway all had a go and by the 1700s the colonisation of the Americas was well established. The late 1700s and early 1800s saw the same in India, Africa and Oceania.

But not only was there a geographical explosion out of Europe that claimed land it did not own but also a similar philosophical, economic and political expansion that claimed ideas it did not own. (Although the narratives of discovery and invention would pretend otherwise). Both were signs of malignant inflation and hubris. European colonisation, in its urgency to escape the colon of Europe, was way too far up itself. In the feverish escape from religious oppression it, in turn, became the oppressor.

The mid-1800s was prime time for colonisation. For example, after signing The Treaty of Waitangi in 1840 Britain sent 18,000 soldiers to fight the New Zealand Wars (1845-1872). After the New Zealand Settlements Act of 1863 the iwi where I live had 80% of their land confiscated (raupatu) by the 1890s.[13]

By the end of the 19th century extroverted European colonisation had spread around the globe and the scramble for colonies was almost over. The league table had Britain well in the lead. Canada, Australia, South Africa, India, and New Zealand were the bigger ones with dozens of other colonies, protectorates, dependencies, overseas territories and so on over the centuries.[14] Spain was a fading second (Central and South America, and the Philippines). France, a disgruntled third with North and Saharan Africa, French Indo-China, Quebec (for a time) and scattered islands such as Mauritius, Réunion, Martinique, St. Pierre et Miquelon, and French Polynesia. These were followed by the colonial also-rans—Portugal (Brazil, Mozambique, Goa, Macao), the Netherlands (South Africa, Dutch East Indies, Dutch Antilles), Germany (South West Africa), Belgium (Belgian Congo), Denmark (Greenland), and Italy (Abyssinia and Somalia).

---

13. https://www.boprc.govt.nz/media/295675/Ngai-Te-Ahi-Hapu-Management-Plan-Final-23-07-2013.pdf
14. www.britishempire.co.uk/timeline/colonies.html; www.worldatlas.com/articles/former-british-colonies.html

The USA, however, colonised itself. No different than the Europeans crossing the Atlantic, the USA colonised by spread westward across the woodlands, the prairies, and the mountains, bringing with it George Washington's "civilising" process for Native Americans to prepare them for "citizenship". Washington concluded the Treaty of New York in 1790 with the Creeks [which] "established a policy and process of assimilation called "civilization" aiming to attach tribes to permanent land settlements. Under the policy tribal members would be given 'useful domestic animals and implements of husbandry" to encourage them to become "herdsman and cultivators" instead of "remaining in a state as hunters".[15]

England

Medieval Europe was not a great place to live. Fifteenth century England was feudal with a rigid social order of peasants, knights, nobles, and the king or queen. Peasants farmed common arable land or land owned by the king or nobleman and paid tithes in produce and services.

Beginning in the 13th century land began to be "enclosed" or fenced in and the ownership of the common land transferred to a new "owner". Once enclosed, use of the land became restricted to the owner. It ceased to be common land for communal use and was often converted from arable to pasture for sheep and the growing wool industry.[16] Under Henry VIII the enclosures gathered pace. By the 17th century half of all open land was enclosed and 50–70 percent of the English population were landless labourers, compared with 10–20 percent in the 16th century. Enclosure was driven by population growth and inflation. In 1500 England's population was about 2.5 million and rose to about 5.5 million in 1650.

The enclosures resulted in the destruction of whole villages and the loss of land meant that peasants had to seek work and be paid a "wage".

---

15. www.mountvernon.org/library/digitalhistory/digital-encyclopedia/article/native-american-policy
16. Olson-Raymer, 'The Europeans - Why They Left'. n.d. http://users.humboldt.edu/ogayle/hist110/expl.html.

By the 1700s the enclosures had created a landless working class that provided the labour required in the new industries developing in the north of England. These labourers—men and their families—became economic migrants who had to uproot and move long distances to search for work in urban areas. Mortality was high. On average, women had 7-8 pregnancies during their lifetime. A third of all children died before reaching age five, and half died before age 10. Less than half the population reached adulthood. Once a child reached the age of 10, they could expect to live into their early 30s, and for those who survived to 25, their life expectancy was into the late 40s.

Before 1450, over 90% of Europe's population lived in small rural communities. Within a century, there was not enough land to meet the needs of all the people due to the population growth and the enclosures, and the cities became even more overcrowded and dangerous. In the late 1600s the population of London was about half a million. The Russian, Peter the Great (1672–1725), described the city in 1698:

> The narrow streets were piled with garbage and filth which could be dropped freely from any overhanging window. Even the main avenues were dark and airless because greedy builders, anxious to gain more space, had projected upper stories out over the street... For women, the age of consent was twelve [it remained so in England until 1885]. Public floggings were a popular sight, and executions drew vast crowds.... The most ghastly execution was the penalty for treason: hanging, drawing and quartering. The condemned man was strung up until he was almost dead from strangulation, then cut down, disemboweled while still alive, beheaded, and his trunk was then chopped into quarters.[17]

What was to become the global economy began to rev up at this time. The world's first stock exchange was created in 1602 in Amsterdam by the Dutch East India Company. From the late 1400s to the 1700s Western Europe experienced a major cycle of inflation (that's the economic kind not the psychological kind) referred to as the "price revo-

---

17. Massie, *Peter the Great: His Life and World*, 212-13.

with prices on rising sixfold over 150 years. This was driven in part by the influx of gold and silver from the Americas. In comparison, from 1290 until 1500 Sweden had 0% inflation.

The 1700s were a time of great upheavals in politics, philosophy, art and science. The century was called the Age of Enlightenment or the Age of Reason. It promoted science, freedom of thought, rationalism, intellect, social reform and humanism. It opposed superstition, the divine right of kings, and the bondage of ecclesiastical dogma. Originating about 1650 to 1700, The Enlightenment was sparked by philosophers such as Baruch Spinoza (1632–1677), John Locke (1632–1704), Voltaire (1694–1778), and Immanuel Kant (1724–1804). In 1687 Sir Isaac Newton published *Principia Mathematica* with his discoveries of the Laws of Motion, gravity and calculus. According to Kant, the Enlightenment was "Mankind's final coming of age, the emancipation of the human consciousness from an immature state of ignorance and error,"and the dictum of the age was "Dare to know".[18]

Nasty, brutish and short

At the end of the English Civil War that lasted from 1642–1651, Thomas Hobbes (1588–1679) wrote *Leviathan or The Matter, Forme and Power of a Common-Wealth Ecclesiasticall and Civill*. The frontispiece is of a giant crowned man holding a sword and a crozier. His body is composed of the faces and bodies of people looking up at his face. He towers over a pastoral landscape and a quotation from Job is above his head reads, "There is no power on earth to be compared to him". The title is taken from the Leviathan (a dragon, serpent or sea monster) of the Book of Job. God illustrates his majestic power by showing Job that only he can overcome the fearsome Leviathan.

Hobbes argued that civil war and the brute situation of a state of nature, the anarchy of "the war of all against all", could only be avoided by strong, undivided government and rule by an absolute monarch. It remains one of the founding documents of Western political philosophy. The state of nature is a term in political theory referring to the state

---

18. Porter, *The Enlightenment: Britain and the Creation of the Modern World*.

of uncivilised societies before governments. Hobbes is perhaps best known for his description of the life of the savage in the state of nature. He wrote:

> In such condition there is no place for industry, because the fruit thereof is uncertain, and consequently no culture of the earth, no navigation nor the use of commodities that may be imported by sea, no commodious building, no instruments of moving and removing such things as require much force, no knowledge of the face of the earth, no account of time, no arts, no letters, no society, and which is worst of all, continual fear and danger of violent death, and the life of man, solitary, poor, nasty, brutish, and short.[19]

These words were written by someone who had never travelled further than Paris. Commodities, trade, commodious building, mechanical instruments, clocks, and the arts and letters of Thomas Hobbes are all good and civilised. Just as when a new medication is introduced it is subject to extended trials and the costs and benefits are weighed carefully before approval. This did not happen with the benefits of the Enlightenment which were considered to be wholly good. Those who do not have such Hobbesian things are bad, inferior and savage and can be quelled.... the redskins, the natives, the beaners, the savages, the Mexican, the Negro, the kaffirs, and so on.

But it was English urban life that was brutish and short. The savages were doing fine, thank you. (Ask any Australian aborigine whose culture had been doing just that for more than 50,000 years). Over the next century England exported its racial superiority across the Atlantic where it puffed up even further into the American notion of "exceptionalism".

Independence?

Politically, out of the theocracies and aristocracies of the Middle Ages emerged Oliver Cromwell's Puritan Revolution in England in 1649, the

---

19. Hobbes, *Leviathan*, XIII. 9.

American Revolution in 1776, and the French Revolution in 1789. The phrase "life, liberty and the pursuit of happiness" of the Declaration of Independence was likely adapted from the English philosopher John Locke's writings. Locke, along with Bishop Berkeley (1685–1753) and David Hume (1711–1776), was one of the original British empiricists in the tradition of Francis Bacon and William of Ockham. He believed that the mind was a blank slate or tabula rasa at birth and that knowledge is determined only by experience derived from sensory perception. This was mostly aimed at the churches' monopoly on truth via doctrine, dogma and revelation. But, fatally, it limited perception to only the physical world and what was "sensible" by smell, touch, sight, hearing and taste. Doctrinal proof was replaced by empirical proof.

Western culture is heir to the empirical tradition which wove its way into the American Revolution and the Declaration of Independence. Although many Americans, I imagine, would hissy-fit at any suggestion that their country was anything less than a brand new creation of freedom and democracy. In fact, like monotheism, it re-enacted the archetypal theme of violent separation from its origins. If you don't think that Europe and its ideas are deeply embedded under the skin of the U.S. of A. just look at the architecture of the Capitol—all Ionic columns, Parthenon facades, and a dome like St Paul's Cathedral in London. Thomas Jefferson wanted the Capitol to resemble the Roman Pantheon, ironically the Temple of All Gods (not just one). And what about all the Old World names—Athens, Georgia, New York, Paris, Birmingham, Washing-town, and Memphis?

In 1776 Adam Smith, the Scottish philosopher and economist, wrote *The Wealth of Nations* in which he argued that private competition free from regulation produces and distributes wealth better than government regulation. Smith believed that individuals and businesses seeking their own interests regulated the economy most efficiently "as if by an invisible hand."

Thomas Paine, the English author and pamphleteer, who one was one of the signatories of the Declaration of Independence, wrote *The Age of Reason* in 1793 in which he advocated deism, reason and free-thinking, and argued against institutionalised religion. Deists held that religious knowledge (called natural religion) is either inherent in each person or accessible through the exercise of reason. Deism advocated a rationalist religion and criticised the supernatural, miracles and revelation, and the specific teachings of any church. They emphasised reason and opposed fanaticism and intolerance. Deistic views were also held by Benjamin Franklin, Thomas Jefferson, and George Washington.

The march of science

In 1798 Thomas Malthus published *An Essay on the Principle of Population*. His work was the first to apply statistics to population and it was the forerunner of modern demographics and epidemiology. His work also became a cornerstone of the later eugenics movement. He reasoned that the capacity of the earth's resources could never increase quickly enough to sustain the needs of a human population that was undergoing unchecked growth. This is the world today—too many people, not enough food, or water, or air, or space.

Carl Linnaeus (1707–1778) was a Swedish botanist and zoologist. Linnaeus published *Systema Naturae* in 1735. The 1700s and 1800s was time of observation and classification in the natural sciences, in the tradition of the parish parson who became an expert on a particular species or the Victorian illustrator of flowers. Linnaeus was the father of modern taxonomy (the classification of plants and animals into groups from biggest to smallest: Domain, Kingdom, Phylum, Class, Order, Family, Genus, and Species) and binomial nomenclature (the naming of species where the first part of the name is the genus to which the species belongs and the second part is the species within the genus. For example: the Linnaean name for humans is Homo (genus) and sapiens (species). As a result, all known life on this planet has been given a Latin name. He was famous in his time and Goethe said of him: "With the exception of Shakespeare and Spinoza, I know no one among the no longer living who has influenced me more strongly."[20]

In 1642 Abel Tasman, the Dutch explorer, had briefly visited what is now known as Tasmania and the western shoreline of New Zealand but continental Australia remained unexplored. At the time it was

---

20. https://en.wikipedia.org/wiki/Carl_Linnaeus

believed that there had to be a great land mass, Terra Australis, the "Great Southern Continent," stretched across the South Pacific to balance the land masses of Asia and Europe. Without it, the scientists of the time believed, it would not be possible for the earth to rotate properly on its axis. As late as 1770, the central and south Pacific was virtually unknown to Europeans. Between 1768 and 1779 Captain James Cook explored and mapped the North and South Pacific.

One of the burning scientific issues of the time was the problem of how to measure accurately the distance of the earth from the sun. Such a measurement, it was believed, would contribute greatly towards a much better understanding of the universe and how it operated. In 1716, the astronomer Edmond Halley (he of Halley's Comet) suggested that an accurate calculation could be obtained by taking simultaneous measurements of the transit of Venus from widely spaced geographical locations. There had been a transit of Venus in 1761 but the observations made were not precise enough to yield an accurate calculation. The next transit of Venus was calculated to occur on June 3, 1769 and the Royal Society of London, eager to extend Britain's role in scientific endeavour, proposed a journey to the South Pacific to measure the second transit of Venus from Tahiti. Captain James Cook was chosen to lead the expedition, the first of three that Cook made, and the Endeavour began its voyage on August 25, 1768.

Cook duly observed the Venus transit and then opened his sealed orders from the Admiralty. He was directed to proceed westward and search for the Great Southern Continent. He circumnavigated New Zealand and mapped its coastline. Then in April 1770 he reached the southeast coast of what we now know as Australia. He declared it *terra nullius* (land belonging to no-one or empty land) and called it New South Wales.

By the mid-1700s Britain's "Bloody Code," where execution was the punishment for hundreds of relatively petty crimes, mostly against property, was coming to an end. Transportation to the North American colonies had become the preferred alternative. But in the 1780s, after the American War of Independence, the British government was forced to look elsewhere. On 20 January 1788, eleven ships with 775 convicts aboard arrived at Botany Bay. (Now on 26 January each year Australia

Day commemorates the arrival of the grandly-named "First Fleet." Aboriginal peoples call it "Invasion Day"). Over the next two hundred years Aboriginal peoples were hunted for sport and their culture was decimated. The first covenant that had lasted for over 40,000 years was broken. It remains to be seen if there will ever be a second covenant.

In the mid-1700s the Industrial Revolution gathered steam, so to speak. Jethro Tull had invented the seed drill in 1701. Abraham Darby first used coke, replacing charcoal, to fuel his blast furnaces for cast iron at Coalbrookdale in 1709. The year 1761 is considered the beginning of the Industrial Revolution when a ship canal was opened to Manchester, its birthplace. In 1764 in the village of Stanhill, Lancashire, James Hargreaves invented the spinning jenny. In 1776 James Watt, of Glasgow, built the first steam engine. In 1779 the world's first iron bridge made from the now-cheaper cast iron was built across the Severn Gorge at the village of Ironbridge, Shropshire. Thomas Telford (1757–1834) built roads, bridges and canals across England and John McAdam (1756–1836) invented tarmacadam, or tarmac, to bind and smooth the surface of the gravel or soil roads. Now machines replaced hands, and steam replaced muscle. The industrial revolution and its cities were born.

The spirit of the times saw progress, expansion and economic and political reform. But William Blake (1757–1827) the English poet, painter, and visionary saw "dark, satanic mills." Blake penned the words, "And did those feet in ancient time," in the preface to his epic poem Milton.[21] It was revived by Robert Bridges, the Poet Laureate, in 1916 for patriotic ends to "brace the spirit of the nation [to] accept with cheerfulness all the sacrifices necessary." It was sorely needed because in the first day of the Battle of the Somme, on July 1, 1916, the British Army suffered its bloodiest day with 19,000 dead.

As a result of the Industrial Revolution, over the two centuries after 1800 the world's average per capita income increased over tenfold, and the world's population increased over sixfold. Economist Robert

---

21. Blake's poem was later set to music and renamed "Jerusalem". It is also known as the opening music by Vangelis in the film "Chariots of Fire".

Lucas[22] said, "For the first time in history, the living standards of the masses of ordinary people have begun to undergo sustained growth... Nothing remotely like this economic behaviour has happened before."[23] But basic double-entry accounting seems to be missing. For every credit there must be a debit. Who or what has paid the price for all this growth?

Whatever in creation is despised, cast out, ignored, dishonoured, repressed, or split-off, will find its way home somehow, somewhere, sometime. All things are part of the gathering-together circle. They return, not in their original form, but in degenerate or distorted form. Europe had fled its dark roots, became over-spiritualised and un-earthed. As compensation, the gods and goddesses, the archetypal forces that had been denied, reappeared in the form of debased matter. Jung said, "The gods have become diseases." The gods also became machines.

In the end, The Enlightenment (capital T, capital E) was a local remedy, sorely needed to rescue a small over-Christianised, over-crowded, area of the planet from itself. As enlightening as the 1700s may have been for those in Europe, for indigenous peoples world-wide, it was the beginning of a 300-year holocaust.

---

22. The winner of the 1995 Nobel Prize in Economics who developed the hypothesis of rational expectations.
23. https://en.wikipedia.org/wiki/Industrial_Revolution

14

——————

WATCHING AMERICA SELF-HARM
IMPRISONED BY FREEDOM

People demand freedom of speech to make up for freedom of thought, which they avoid. —Søren Kierkegaard

DEAREST READER, in this chapter I am observantly critical of the USA but please note that I have no entrenched animus toward the country—there are many things I like and admire.

The USA is the secular good King. It carries the image of what is best in each of us—the light side of the Self. They are a nation that attempts to represent what is best in the human race; our aspirations; our desire to see justice done; to balance fairness and kindness with firmness and resolve; and for each human being to be considered as an equal without regard to class, race, abilities, origins, religion or gender. This human experiment has never before been conducted on such a scale with such diversity. The land and the history have given immigrants a fresh start, a clean slate. Such an epochal adventure is bound to fail, and fail nobly, and rise from that failure to start again. But stumbling steps are a reflection of the immensity of the task not the lack of nobility in the effort. The USA deserves our wholehearted support, warts and all. Why? Because its failure tips the scales, measurably, toward cruelty and heartlessness; toward despots and dictators both political and religious; and emboldens the tyrannical King, the dark side of the Self.

So I offer my heartfelt thanks to the USA for staying the course, for drafting the Constitution, for its bright-eyed creative spirit, for its irrepressible confidence in life, for sending its young men and women to distant shores to die in the fight against a darker future, and for welcoming to their shores those seeking a brighter future.

But all that is not my business here. I will bang on about the USA because it is the poster child for grandiosity. It's the leading light, the index case, the demonstration project, for the thinking, making, and doing of how to destroy our planet.[1]

I will also say that it's not the fault of the USA. They are just the poor buggers at the pointy end of ten thousand years of growth, inflation, and bad planetary housekeeping. But that's also irrelevant—they have pushed themselves forward for the job and at some point life asks each of us to take (or decline) responsibility for what we are not responsible for. Or the planet has to live with our neglect.

China suppresses dissidents—but we rarely know their fate. Russian dissidents fall out of windows, get poisoned, or their planes explode. In contrast, in the USA, an ex-president, who has interfered with an election and encouraged an insurrection, has to turn up at court to face criminal charges and get his mugshot taken. So if I had to choose between the three I'd much rather live in the USA. Even though it considers itself the best and greatest country in the world—though other democracies work just as well—there is always room for change. I will make some suggestions to the Republic for self-improvement.

Horror vacui

When the psyche has no limits, like a gas in a vacuum, it expands and inflates to occupy the space given to it. Nature is supposed to abhor a vacuum. It's the molecular equivalent of the doctrine of *terris nullius* in

---

1. I wrote most of the sections that follow in late 2021 and early 2022. Sadly, as of January 2024 it looks like the USA may be in for another episode of self-harm if Trump becomes President.

Australia which was considered by the British to be "desert and unin-habited". If it's empty, own it, populate it and use it. It's a relic of the *horror vacui* (nature abhors a vacuum) of Aristotelian physics. Following Plato, Aristotle said that, by definition, a void is nothing and nothing cannot be said to exist and, being featureless, it could not be encountered by the senses. Actually, nature will allow such nothingness. It is called spirit or the unconscious, undetectable by the five senses but well-known to our sixth sense. It is what we encounter as a reality but which the senses cannot perceive because it does not have length, breadth, height, weight, or duration. But it has its own recognisable patterns or laws which differ from those of matter.

The adolescent American psyche struggles with boundaries and limitations. One of the laws of the psyche is that all things have a natural size, shape and purpose. It is their gift and their nature. If you try to become something else other than who you are then life will give you problems. It was Oscar Wilde who reputedly said, "Be yourself, everyone else is taken".[2] In 1925, on a visit to the USA in an interview with the New York Times, Jung commented on the American illusion that anyone could become anything she or he wished.[3]

But both the psyche and the Earth have limits. For an individual, you are fortunate if you encounter your limits otherwise you remain a a perpetual pre-schooler or, if you are unlucky, a perpetual adolescent. With the Earth, the so-called Anthropocene is the first time we have had to encounter planetary limits. The oppositional kicking, screaming and tantrumming against being told "No, you can't do that" has already begun.

The idea of everything and everyone having their right size is anti-thetical to the American dream where anyone can become any thing if they try hard enough, pray hard enough, or work hard enough. Understandable given the religious and social oppression the colonisers and immigrants had experienced in Europe. But their views have never been revised. Expansionism and business growth have been socially

---

2. Not clearly attributable to Oscar Wilde. https://quoteinvestigator.com/2014/01/20/be-yourself

3. *C.G. Jung Speaking: Interviews and Encounters*, 397.

constructed solutions that have worked reasonably well—that is, they have not encountered any significant restraints—for the last 500 years. But soon or later they don't work in the psyche or the Earth, they being one and the same—one internal, the other external.

We see this biological limitation with evolutionary and environmental pressures that regulate the size of animal populations or the body mass of a species. In the psyche, when our natural size is exceeded or subceeded then, like a pendulum swinging to its furthest reach, the opposite force will come into play. Jung called this the self-regulation of the psyche. What goes up must come down, the tide comes in and the tide goes out, the breath inhales and the breath exhales. There are no straight lines in nature. All things move in circles as Black Elk (1862–1950) told John G Neihardt:

> Everything the Power of the World does is done in a circle. The sky is round, and I have heard that the earth is round like a ball and so are all the stars. The wind, in its greatest power, whirls. Birds make their nests in circles, for theirs is the same religion as ours. The sun comes forth and goes down again in a circle. The moon does the same, and both are round. Even the seasons form a great circle in their changing.... The life of man is a circle from childhood to childhood, and so it is in everything where power moves. Our tepees were round like the nests of birds, and were always set in a circle, the nation's hoop, a nest of many nests, where the Great Spirit meant for us to hatch our children.[4]

Vacuums of the mind

The geography of colonisation affected the psyche of the colonisers. Wide-open spaces produce vacuums of the mind into which rush all kinds of unhinged ideas about freedom—particularly for European colonists in the 1600s and 1700s. This is most noticeable in the history and traditions of the USA where the colonisers spread westward. We don't hear a similar story about the eastward colonisation of Russia.

---

4. Black Elk, and John G Neihardt. *Black Elk Speaks: being the life story of a holy man of the Oglala Sioux.* 1988.

Mongolia and Siberia, with China on the other side, were much less appealing to European habitation.

The inflation that came with European exploration released an appetite, long buried under 1500 years of religious and political constriction, a greed that wanted the whole thing, nothing less. The USA was geographically exceptional. Here I am not referring to the self-created doctrine of exceptionalism. It was exceptional in that no other continent afforded such ease of expansion. There was unlimited land ripe for the taking with only "Red Indians" to oppose them. This is still alive and streaming on Prime video. The ten episodes of the TV movie *1883* "follow the Dutton family on a journey west through the Great Plains toward the last bastion of untamed America".

This geography affected the collective psyches of all those immigrants who came to the continent. But they were strangers to the land, they had to survive, and hard work and expansion in God's name impelled them westward. Their nostalgia trailed behind them in British place names like New England, Manchester, Norfolk, Glasgow, Dunleith, or Aberdeen. The land was forgiving in its geography and bountiful in its gifts. Not too hot, not too cold. The colonisation of Canada was different. Wagon trains don't travel well in muskeg or permafrost. Canoes do but the rivers run mostly north-south draining into Hudson Bay or the Great Lakes. As *les voyageurs* and *courier du bois* knew, the portages were long, and the mosquitos were worse. The French were there first anyway. Samuel de Champlain established the first settlement of Port Royal in modern-day Nova Scotia in 1604. The Mayflower did not land at Cape Cod until 1620.

The further white immigrants lived from a major centre (because that's where big government is), the more rural of mind and politics they were. The further west they went, the more conservative and redneck they became, and the more First Nations were marginalised. Convince me there is no correlation. In the USA there's Texas through Colorado and the western states up to Montana. Over the border there's the provinces of Alberta and, to a lesser extent, Saskatchewan. Similarly in Australia, there are the states of Western Australia, Queensland, and Tasmania. In the USA, when the settlers got over the Rockies they seemed to come to their senses, downsize a bit, and swing back to the centre, like the Pacific states of British Columbia through Washington and Oregon down to California.

The colonisation of Australia produced a similar wild west, anti-authoritarian, counter-dependent, hyper-independent cast of mind but it was generally less truculent and much less religiose than the USA. I give you ockers, bogans, sheilas, sandpaper, and the beloved larrikin. Australia is about the same size and width as the contiguous states of the USA. Yes, that's right. The first European sighting of Australia was of Cape York by the Dutch in 1606. James Cook named the east coast New South Wales and claimed it for Britain. A penal colony was established at Sydney Cove, Port Jackson on January 26, 1788. The date is now Australia's national day. Hmm! The first settlers were mostly British continuing into the post-WWII years with the "ten pound Poms".

For Europeans there was not much between Sydney and Perth except uninhabited desert. Exploring the outback was much less appealing than crossing the Mississippi. Though the immensity of the continent did not prevent them from shooting Aboriginal people for sport. Historically, being of similar ancestry and similar cultural psyche, Australia has had a trans-pacific affiliation with the USA but there has also been a strong but ambivalent tie to the "old country" of Britain. Again, I give you cricket and The Ashes.

The largest land masses on Earth all lie in the northern hemisphere so we might consider Asia's history for comparison with North America.[5] The Mongol empire under Khagan dynasty (Genghis Khan 1162–1227 to Kublai Khan 1215–1294) stretched from the Pacific to Eastern Europe by the end of the 1300s, and was the largest land-based empire in history. Although the Mongol culture was a nomadic, horse culture the sheer breadth of the Mongol Empire (7000 kms from Poland to the Pacific compared to 5000 kms from Europe to North America) meant that it would fragment eventually. Later, the Ming dynasty (1368–1644) was Confucian and inward-looking and China was considered to be the centre of the known world. Nevertheless, the great treasure fleets under Admiral Zheng-He sailed out from 1405 to 1433 to

---

5.   In 2023 over 50% of the world's population lives within the circle of India, Southeast Asia and China.

South East Asia, India, East Africa, Arabia, and perhaps much further.[6] The fleets had dozens of ships four or five times the size of Columbus' Santa Maria with livestock, men, and women on board. They were sent out to control the maritime trade routes and exact tribute from the distant countries rather than to colonise. After the mid-1400s maritime exploration declined and China returned to relative isolation until the Catholic and Protestant missionaries established themselves in the 18th and 19th centuries. All in all, the social and political forces involved in Chinese expansion were quite different from those driving the exodus from Europe across the Atlantic.

Ungrounded

We know that individuals are more vulnerable to developing a narcissistic and grandiose personality when early attachment is unsound, and they don't have a "secure base." The preschooler who is a bossy "little emperor" comes to experience the limits of his or her powers within a loving but firm parental relationship. So it was with exploration and colonisation. The settlers, the refugees, and the migrants were not indigenous. They fled from a distant land. Consequently, the psyche was not "grounded" in a "good-enough" relationship with the earth underneath its feet. They didn't know their place. When we are separated from matter and the sacredness of spirit within matter, and spirit is consigned to live in a distant heaven reserved for the faithful few with an omnipotent God, then human grandiosity and narcissism will increase without limit. "It's all mine. I can do what I want with it. I can bend it to my will. God said so". After all, the Old Testament God had commanded humankind to have dominion over all.

Although inevitably saturated with the zeitgeist of his time (as we are with ours), Jung, always relevant to today because he spoke from outside his time, put it this way:

> The foreign land assimilates its conqueror. But unlike the Latin
> conquerors of Central and South America, the North Americans

---

6. Menzies, *1421: The Year China Discovered the World*.

preserved their European standards with the most rigid puritanism.... Thus, in the American, there is a discrepancy between conscious and unconscious that is not found in the European, a tension between an extremely high conscious level of culture and an unconscious primitivity. This tension forms a psychic potential which endows the American with an indomitable spirit of enterprise and an enviable enthusiasm which we in Europe do not know.... Our contact with the unconscious chains us to the earth and makes it hard for us to move, and this is certainly no advantage when it comes to progressiveness.... *Plurimi pertransibunt*—but he who is rooted in the soil endures. Alienation from the unconscious and from its historical conditions spells rootlessness. That is the danger that lies in wait for the conqueror of foreign lands, and for every individual who, through one-sided allegiance to any kind of -ism, loses touch with the dark, maternal, earthy ground of his being.[7]

The gift of defeat

The defining of self-esteem, self-identity, and the freedom to be oneself is accomplished on the outside through opposition to an external "enemy" (natural or human). James Hillman points out that "For all the utopian nobility of the Declaration of Independence, the text actually presents a long list of grievances against the enemy of them all, the king".[8] Of the 1331 words in the Declaration 60% of them complain (the twenty-seven grievances) about what George III has done or not done. The 27th grievance reads: "[The King of Great Britain] has endeavoured to bring on the inhabitants of our frontiers, the merciless Indian Savages whose known rule of warfare, is an undistinguished destruction of all ages, sexes, and conditions". So George III was the essential foil needed to bring about independence.

The enemy throws into relief our strengths and weaknesses.

---

7. CW 10, Mind and Earth, par. 103. This chapter bears further reading as Jung writes about the relationship between place and race or culture with particular reference to the American psyche.
8. Hillman, *A Terrible Love of War*, 25.

Individually, the same happens with physical hardship that might be considered "character building". It separates the "men from the boys", it's Marine boot camp, hard work and sports, or the Duke of Edinburgh awards. It allows or compels one to find one's limits, resilience and strength that is as yet undeveloped. This is necessary. But sooner or later we encounter a physical, psychological or spiritual limit, a boundary, somebody bigger, something more powerful, something we can't do, an enemy we cannot overcomes, where we can go no further despite our heroic efforts. This is the gift of defeat. For the modest, overly humble, self-effacing, diffident or retiring person (it's hard to find antonyms equivalent to grandiose) it is the gift of success. Both success and defeat may be resisted in equal measure depending on the person's introverted or extroverted nature.

The American psyche was geographically blessed and born from opposition to George III, but it has not yet matured to a place where it can function without an enemy. That said, it is ahead of other cultures that are immersed in autocratic regimes. The USA provides robust opposition and and through that an unreliable stability. But the psychological law says that, unless a mediating third intervenes, at some point the enemy without will become the enemy within and the group, government, regime or society will inevitably begin to fight with itself. Post-Obama, and since Trump, the second civil war has begun.[9]

Veneration and the missing King

Worship and adoration, to be in awe of something greater than oneself, either secular or spiritual, to be struck by wonder, is a cellular need, like thirst, hunger, sex or meaning. All cultures have had kings (mostly) who were worshipped as the divine representatives and intermediaries between the powers above and the secular world. The young king was virile and sprayed his fertile seed over the Earth and it became plentiful. We see this in the meaning of husbandry—one who is the spouse, the husband, of the Earth. Ploughing and tilling has been found as early as 3500 BCE. The first ploughing in spring was a sacred event. The moist

---

9. Written in late 2016 and early 2017 at the beginning of the Trump presidency.

brown soil was then penetrated by the ard, the hoe, the mattock, or the ploughshare, guided by human hand. Through the eyes of the Earth herself, the brown soil, made moist by spring rains, lay waiting to receive the hardness of the mattock, opening itself to new seed, new life and fruitfulness.

But the king inevitably became weak and frail as his powers waned and the crops failed. Then he was ritually killed.[10] Ploughing turns over the uppermost soil bringing up nutrients to the compacted surface while burying weeds and the remains of last year's crop. This is what happens in the death of the ruling ego. The old worn-out attitude that is past its prime and has outlived its usefulness or developmental stage must be killed before new life can emerge from the ground of the psyche.

The secular power of the British monarchy has been on a downward slide since the Magna Carta of 1215. But those who bray for its abolition are short of an understanding of what it means for those who see in the monarch those noble qualities that they aspire to or admire, albeit from afar. In psychological terms the person-in-the-street projects onto the monarch the qualities of the Self. They bring out the best in us. We are all on our best behaviour when we meet the Queen. How else to account for a vestigial monarchy that costs millions in upkeep? If dismantled and deprived of an object onto which to project the contents of its psyche, the collective would just seek another object to worship, admire, love, or hate and fight with.

This is what has happened in the USA. The need to worship, respect, and adore are needs of the heart and of the soul. So what if there is no king to fight or praise? Love of country, patriotism and the Second Amendment stepped into fill the gap, all inflamed by and mixed up with the Judeo-Christian God's need to be worshipped. The separation of church and state has come full circle, turned on itself, and now almost everyone has a "faith". The Constitution has become the object of worship and is accorded the same reverence, emotion, holiness, sanctity, touchiness, and freedom from criticism (aka free speech) that it was framed to protect. In most of the world lèse-majesté—to do no wrong

---

10. Frazer, *The Golden Bough*, Chapter 24.

to majesty, in other words you cannot criticise the king as, for example, in Thailand—is no longer illegal but it remains alive and well as an unwritten law in the USA. But compared to Stonehenge, the Magna Carta, Notre Dame Cathedral, or the Winter Palace, it's the oldest thing they've got.

The USA calls itself the leader of the free world (but I don't recall any democratic election for this post) and prides itself on freedom. This as it should be, on one level. On another level it's all wrong. The shadow of freedom is hidden beneath faith and the Constitution. True freedom is sacrificed to both. Fleeing from persecution in Europe the necessity of outer religious freedoms for the Pilgrims have turned into their opposite. External laws, whether they be secular or spiritual, are ready-made, off-the-shelf, rules of conduct for those who lack inner authority. The less inner authority we have the more vulnerable we are to collective viruses like the polls, the ratings, the reviews, the conspiracy theories, and the extremists—whether socialist or capitalist. And the more the "rule of law" is needed.

In his Farewell Address of 1796 George Washington wished that the Constitution be "sacredly maintained" following James Madison's wish that "veneration rather than critique" become the collective attitude to the Constitution, for "only veneration would generate the stability requisite to maintaining even the wisest and freest governments". But Thomas Jefferson's later warning has gone unheeded. In 1816 he wrote that "Some men look at constitutions with sanctimonious reverence and deem them like the Ark of the Covenant, too sacred to be touched.... institutions must advance also, and keep pace with the times. We might as well require a man to wear still the coat which fitted him when a boy".[11] So much for the originalists.

A tension of opposites

In 1887 Lord Acton wrote "Power tends to corrupt, and absolute power corrupts absolutely." The absolute monarchy of Louis XIV (1638–

---

11. Levinson, "Pledging Faith in the Civil Religion; Or, Would You Sign the Constitution?", 29.

1715) the Sun King, who reputedly pronounced *L'état, c'est moi* (I am the state) was the pinnacle of absolutism of the European monarchs in the 1600s and 1700s. They were unrestrained by the churches, governments, or elites, and their power was claimed to be received from God. All things contain their opposite and the Bourbon excesses led eventually to the French Revolution of 1789 just as the Russian Empire and the Tsars were overthrown by the Russian Revolution in 1917.

This same archetypal tide brought about the US Constitution in the year of 1789. The ebb and flow between the need for individual authority (because sometimes bureaucracy is thick as a brick) and the need for collective authority (because sometimes people are thick as a brick) is an archetypal tension. Both are forms of government by the people for the people and this conflict of opposites will continue. All we can do is to resist the swings to the extremes. That is, until a mediating third intervenes. In indigenous cultures this was the Earth, the physical environment through which spirit moved. A "medicine sign", a synchronicity, the alignment of the heavenly bodies, might indicate the path to walk. The destruction of this secular and spiritual self-regulating being, the precursor of and identical with Jung's Self, is the subject of this book.

The immigrants and settlers were diaspor'd from their own lands fleeing religious persecution in Europe. Each culture has its own DNA (I mean that literally but more of that another time) and the persecuted became persecutors. They were not indigenes and the long black veil trailing behind them was hardness of heart, hardness of belief, and hardness of drink. The land was to be occupied and owned, and rights were "God-given". The influx was overwhelmingly Christian beginning with the Pilgrims in 1620 followed by the Puritans, themselves wanting to purify Protestantism. They valued prudence, soberness, diligence, education, independence and responsibility. They banned the Papists (even John F Kennedy, a Catholic, was mildly suspect in the 1960s) and hung the Quakers. The more the settlers pushed west the harder they became. The idealisation of "America", and the denial of its history, continues to the present day. The tensions, conflicts and contradictions within the American psyche are so riven and fractured that after eight years of the best of America (Obama) we then had four years of the worst of America (Trump).

Self-colonisation

Alexis de Tocqueville (1805–1859), a French diplomat, visited America in 1831 and wrote *Democracy in America* (in two volumes, 1835 and 1840). We should recall that in the early 1700s France was the leading world and diplomatic power with colonies world-wide. New France covered much of eastern and central Canada and central USA from northern Labrador to Louisiana until it was ceeeded to Britain by the Treaty of Paris in 1763. The Treaty of Versailles gave all former British lands in New France below the Great Lakes to the United States. In 1803 Napoleon sold the lands in the Mississippi basin from New Orleans to the Canadian border to the United States in the Louisiana Purchase.

The art of French diplomacy has left us with words such as communique, détente, coup d'etat, and tête-à-tête. Benjamin Franklin and Thomas Jefferson imported much of the Enlightenment ideals from their time in Paris in the 1780s. "Jefferson found himself impressed by the decorum of the international diplomatic corps he encountered [in Paris] and their ability, no matter the controversy at hand, to maintain civil discourse.... I would wish [my] countrymen to adopt just so much of European politeness...[12] De Tocqueville's book became popular in both Europe and the USA well into the twentieth century as a statement and prediction of the American success story.[13] I quote at length, with italics added, to give the reader a sense of the tone and form of the developing American psyche.[14]

> The chief circumstance which has favoured the establishment and the maintenance of a democratic republic in the United States is the nature

---

12. https://www.monticello.org/site/research-and-collections/minister-france
13. https://hbr.org/2001/01/tocqueville-revisited-the-meaning-of-american-prosperity
14. Tocqueville, Chapter XVII: Principal Causes Maintaining The Democratic Republic – Part I.

of the territory which the American inhabit. Their ancestors gave them the love of equality and of freedom, but God himself gave them the means of remaining equal and free, by *placing them upon a boundless continent, which is open to their exertions....* In the United States not only is legislation democratic, but nature herself favours the cause of the people.

In what part of human tradition can be found anything at all similar to that which is occurring under our eyes in North America? The celebrated communities of antiquity were *all founded in the midst of hostile nations, which they were obliged to subjugate before they could flourish in their place.* Even the moderns have found, in some parts of South America, vast regions inhabited by a people of *inferior civilization,* but which occupied and cultivated the soil. *To found their new states it was necessary to extirpate or to subdue a numerous population,* until civilization has been made to blush for their success. *But North America was only inhabited by wandering tribes, who took no thought of the natural riches of the soil, and that vast country was still, properly speaking, an empty continent, a desert land awaiting its inhabitants....*

That continent still presents, as it did in the primeval time, rivers which rise from never-failing sources, green and moist solitudes, and fields which the ploughshare of the husbandman has never turned. In this state [as if it had been kept in reserve by the Deity] it is offered to man, not in the barbarous and isolated condition of the early ages, but to a being who is already in possession of the most potent secrets of the natural world, who is united to his fellow-men, and instructed by the experience of fifty centuries. *At this very time thirteen millions of civilized Europeans are peaceably spreading over those fertile plains,* with whose resources and whose extent they are not yet themselves accurately acquainted. *Three or four thousand soldiers drive the wandering races of the aborigines before them;* these are followed by the pioneers, who pierce the woods, scare off the beasts of prey, explore the courses of the inland streams, *and make ready the triumphal procession of civilization across the waste.*

In 1801, President Jefferson described settlers' intentions for expansion: "However our present interests may restrain us within our own limits, it is impossible not to look forward to distant times, when our rapid multiplication will expand itself beyond those limits and cover the whole northern, if not the southern continent, with a people speaking the same language, governed in similar form by similar laws."[15]

The pre-Columbian population of the Americas is notoriously difficult to judge (estimates range from 10 to 100 million) but for North America a median figure might be 50 million. This had remained steady until the 1500s. The 150 years after Columbus's arrival brought a toll on human life (80-90% loss of population) that is comparable to all of the world's losses in World War II.[16]

On 20 May 1862, US President Abraham Lincoln signed the Homestead Act into law—the greatest land giveaway in American history. The government gave away 270 million acres of "public land" out west—10% of the USA—to people who built a home, lived on it and farmed it for five years.

In 1894 the U.S. Census Bureau warned against accepting Indian "legends" as facts. "Investigation shows," the bureau said, "that the aboriginal population within the present United States at the beginning of the Columbian period could not have exceeded much over 500,000."[17]

Ironically, and tragically, the Constitution of the USA and its democracy is based in part on the Iroquois (Haudenosaunee) confederacy which was formed in the 1400s and perhaps as early as the mid-1100s. Around the time of the 1987 bicentennial of the U.S. Constitution the U.S. Senate passed a resolution acknowledging that "the confederation of the original 13 colonies into one republic was influenced by the political system developed by the Iroquois Confederacy, as were many of the democratic principles which were incorporated into the Constitution itself."

---

15. Dunbar-Ortiz, 'Yes, Native Americans Were the Victims of Genocide | History News Network', 2016 accessed 12 July 2022, http://historynewsnetwork.org/article/162804.
16. See Dunbar-Ortiz, *An Indigenous Peoples' History of the United States* and Stannard, *American Holocaust: The Conquest of the New World*.
17. Lewis Lord, 'How many people were here before Columbus?' https://web.archive.org/web/20080305224956/http://www.usna.edu/Users/history/kolp/HH345/PRE1492.htm

War is normal

Western consciousness took a wrong turn a while back and doesn't know it's lost. Over the last 10,000 years the human race has had a profound effect on matter or, as we think of it today, the environment. The word environment (French, *environ* meaning encircled by) was first used in its modern sense in the mid-1950s by the then fledgling science of ecology. But this neutered, bloodless term continues to bind us in a straitjacket of distance and objectivity, where our consciousness of the mess we are in stretches to sorting our rubbish into plastic and paper, and braying about environmental action.

It calls forth the adolescent psychology of Greenpeace and the Rainbow Warrior to ride into battle and protect the vulnerable.[18] It helps the English pretend that there is still such a thing as "the country-side" or that there are parts of the USA that are still a "wilderness." The word belies the long, tragic history of the evisceration of blood and life from the body of matter.

George Santayana was right—those who do not know history are doomed to repeat it. But that is only half the story. George Bernard Shaw was equally right when he said that what we learn from history is that we learn nothing from history.

Before the modern era this precious history was held within the stories, myths and legends of the People. Not only were people connected to their turangawaewae (home ground, a Maori word literally meaning "a standing place for the feet") and the lineage of the land where they stood—the creek where great-grandfather fell and broke his leg; the hill that is the belly-button of the world; the cave four long-songs ride away where the earth-snake lives; the bend in the mighty river past the mountain where the taniwha lives—but also to its lineage in spirit. The names of the ancestors and the ancestors of the ancestors—human, animal, insect, plant, and mineral—were known to all. The songs and the prayers kept the material and spiritual world in good rela-tion, for if those two lovers and adversaries, spirit and matter, were ever allowed to stop singing their holy song, if they were forgotten, if their

---

18. Paul Watson, formerly of Greenpeace, is still getting himself arrested.

praise-names were not sung, if their holy fight ever stopped, if peace ever broke out, then the world would end.[19]

But let us not confuse modern notions of peace and harmony with being in right relationship with our siblings on this planet. We extend these courtesies and charities to other humans but not to the natural world. Peace, justice, harmony, and cooperation are human constructs that we have fashioned for ourselves in the one-sided conduct of human affairs.[20] As James Hillman said, war is normal. Our longed-for peace and harmony, in spite of 10,000 years of evidence to the contrary, is not the peaceable garden of the tofu-eaters, where everything has the same nature, the lion lies down with the lamb, and everyone loves everyone else. For sure, this only brings about its opposite which we are living now. Harmony and balance is where all things live according to their own nature, spiritual and instinctual, where all things walk with the beauty and terror of their own nature.

Silliness

Every culture, nation, organisation, group, or family has a collective shadow. Its form depends on the prevailing forces in collective consciousness and the history of the culture. All cultures have their slaveries, quirks, follies, and cruelty, as well their shining magnificence and brilliant achievements. But all light must cast a shadow. The dominant cultural value or trait, the cultural persona, is a defence against, and a compensation for, the feared opposite trait which is often unacknowledged, denied or unconscious. I say trait, a term often used with regard to personality disorders, because each culture has a personality and an associated personality disorder. A sort of cultural DSM.

For example, Jewish humour and devotion to life (l'chaim) compensates the traumatic history of persecution and death. The idealisation of the hero, the difficulty accepting limitations, and the fantasy of four percent annual growth, are the shadow of the magnificence of the Declaration of Independence. The fear of dependency and domination

---

19. With acknowledgements to Martin Prechtel.
20. The vicious nature of the gods. http://www.pantheon.org/articles/n/niobe.html

is the shadow of the American idealisation of freedom. The English gave the world sports and "fair play" as compensation for its colonial shadow and class elitism. Jung told Laurens van der Post that one of the most striking qualities of the English spirit is their love of sport and genius for inventing games.[21] The Mafia and sibling hostility (e.g. the barbed banter between the Cuomo brothers, one a Mayor of New York and the other a CNN host) are the shadow of the close-knit Italian family. Lest these characterisations seem stereotypical, we should remember that stereotypes exist only because an archetype, an ingrained pattern across humankind, such as the hostile brothers, stands behind them.

Let's name some of these quirks and sillinesses that belong to the USA. Just at random and just for fun.

The self-styled greatest country in the world is incapable of sustaining more than two political parties. All we get is Democrats and Republicans. I deal with the inherent problems of this arrangement in "Divided we stand. United we fall". In the world of business ("America's business is business" said President Calvin Coolidge in 1925) this arrangement would be considered a duopoly and anti-competitive. So much for voter choice in the election free market.

Said parties have their colours all backwards (red for Republicans and blue for Democrats). Silly me, here I thought that red was for socialism as in pinkos and the "red tide of communism" and blue was a button-down, blue-blood, conservative colour.

It was called the "the most significant overhaul of the nation's gun laws in decades" by the New York Times—but it was really just tinkering with the ambulances strewn at the bottom of the cliff. The June 2022 gun "control" legislation was titled the Bipartisan Safer Communities Act. Nothing about guns. Everything about the miracle of bipartisan agreement.

It's always a shooter never a gun-man, gun-woman, or gun-person. Does the NRA not want the g-word mentioned?

While I'm at it, the USA is all for banning abortion and saving life from the moment of conception. But it quickly abandons the "every life is precious" prayerful sermonising after the child is born. The sanctity

---

21. Laurens van der Post, *Jung and the Story of Our Time*, 46.

of the Second Amendment seems to be way more important than the scores of school children who have been shot and killed in mass shootings.

In Prague, on 21 December 2023, fourteen people were killed by a gunman. The Czech Prime Minister announced a national day of mourning for December 23. A national day of mourning? In the USA there would be 365 days of mourning, or more, if the idea occurred to anyone. For more read "It's the gun, stupid!"

The Star Spangled Banner (beautiful but hard to sing, apparently) is about a naval battle against the British in 1814 and the tune is based on a British drinking song. Many national anthems are exhortations to death and war but the USA is one of the few (or only) one that is about an actual battle.

The USA is unable to look after its own. It is still quibbling over health care which is left in the hands of insurance companies, and it is nowhere near anything like Canada's Medicare or Britain's NHS. Its health care is the most expensive in the world and it spends twice as much as other OECD countries.[22] And during Covid, the richest country in the world ran out of baby formula.

The US poverty rate (the percentage of the population living on less than USD4 a day) is 1.7% which is at least twice as much as other developed countries (Germany 0%, France 0.3%, Australia 0.7%, Canada 0.7%).[23] In some places like the Mississippi Delta and much of Appalachia life expectancy is lower than in Bangladesh and Vietnam.

Linguistically, the USA is the breeding ground of kute kontortions of the English language like Krispy Kreme donuts which looks like a grade one spelling mistake trying to look faux-French with a bit of crème. For a more prosaic comparison, check out Canada's Tim Hortons (sic) named after Tim Horton (1930-1974) an NHL hockey player who founded the coffee and donuts chain.

---

22. AFL-CIO, The U.S. Health Care System: An International Perspective, https://dpeafl cio.org/programs-publications/issue-fact-sheets/the-u-s-health-care-system-an-international-perspective

23. Angus Deaton, "The U.S. Can No Longer Hide From Its Deep Poverty Problem." *The New York Times*, January 25, 2018, sec. Opinion. https://www.nytimes.com/2018/01/24/opinion/poverty-united-states.html

The USA cleaves to the "old country" (remember the Kennedys and Camelot) and still measures things in colonial pounds, gallons and miles. Miles per gallon as a measure of fuel consumption is still used in the USA, the UK (but the UK gallon is larger), and Canada (alongside L/100kms). Most of the world uses litres/100 kms.

It is fascinated with the British monarchy but lives in paranoid fear that George III will return or some ruler/federal government/world conspiracy is plotting, deep state, to take away their "God-given rights". Now it has its own, home-grown wanna-be absolute monarch aka Donald Trump.

In the absence of titles like Sir or Lord, the male line is kept alive by monarchical patronyms such as John D Rockefeller III, for example, like George III but nowhere near Louis XIV. Or an initial as a first name to replace the Duke or Earl—like R. Anthony Brunheimer.

It is one of only four countries in the world that use the month-day-year date convention. The others are the Federated States of Micronesia and Palau (both island nations in the Pacific) and Belize (formerly British Honduras). Everyone else uses day-month-year.

The American parochial ignorance of geography is legendary. Trump wanted to buy Greenland but it's not clear if he knew where it was. Visitors to Toronto from the US have asked "Can I get to Vancouver by subway? How long is the drive to the Arctic Circle? American visitors to Sydney have asked if they can get to Uluru in a day. Perhaps forgetting that Australia is about the same size as the USA and the drive to Uluru takes about 4 days. And then there is the common usage of giving the country name after a well-known capital city as in London, England (just to avoid any possible confusion with say London, Arkansas), or as in Paris, France (not to be confused, *mon dieu*, with Paris, Texas).

The back windows of pickups are still draped with the Confederate flag. In the 1970s after a minor diplomatic stoush between the USA and France, a bumper sticker could be seen that read: "Ban French Fries". Mostly on aforesaid pickups.

The American sporting psyche has a short attention span. It can maybe stretch to a long afternoon of baseball but a five day Test match? No way! In so-called "track and field" it can pay attention for the 10 seconds of a 100 metre sprint or 45 seconds for the 400 metres. But above that Americans are notably absent. Per capita the USA has had several outstanding middle- or long distance runners but there has never been any depth at the club level, of which there are but a few. Sport is mostly organised around universities and participation ends after college.

The scarcity of attention span is best seen in American football. Called such although the ball is hardly ever kicked with a foot and ironically the game where the ball is kicked is called soccer not football. Defensive tackles hardly ever touch the ball in a game. It's a 60 minute game of four 15 minute quarters. But the average NFL game takes 3 hours and a bit to complete with the shortest being 2.5 hours and the longest 4 hours. The ball is in play for an average of 18 minutes.[24] In most other sports (football 90 minutes, rugby 80 minutes, ice hockey, field hockey and lacrosse all 60 minutes) the action goes full-on for the regulation time. In American football a play lasts an average of a really exhausting four seconds and each play is meticulously scripted by the book. No room for the unexpected or improvisation here. So much for sport as unscripted drama. After all these intellectual and physical demands the boys in the heavy armour must have a forty-second break so everyone can recover, have time for the TV commercials, and have a committee meeting in the middle of the field. They should try rugby.

Then there's the grandiose "World Series" of baseball. World? It's only played seriously by a handful of countries. Compare that to football (soccer) which is the world's most popular sport and is played in almost every country in the world. Cricket is the second most popular game. Neither ever got off the ground in the States. But then there's no need for heavy armour, coaches, colleges, and sponsors. With cricket—sticks for wickets, a tennis ball, and a piece of wood. With football—two coats for goal posts and a tin can.

Since writing this I ran across a similar—and better—list. It seems that the original was penned way back in 2000 but John Cleese's version is the most recent. Enjoy!

---

24. https://www.mirror.co.uk/sport/other-sports/american-sports/how-long-super-bowl-lasts-13626956

It's the gun, stupid!

In the name of freedom and independence the USA sentimentally clings to the Second Amendment. It might have been a good idea in 1791 but 200-odd years later armed Americans mostly need to defend themselves against, er, other armed Americans. The NRA says that the best protection against a bad buy with a gun is a good guy with a gun. On May 24, 2022 in Ulvade, Texas, nineteen good guys with guns waited for an hour in the hallway of a school before tackling the one bad guy with a gun. Nineteen children and two teachers died. Mass shootings continue with the support of the Second Amendment and little protection from good guys with guns. No need for terrorists, the USA homekills. Not doing something about guns is a uniquely American form of DSH (Deliberate Self Harm).

Here's some figures. According to data compiled by the University of Sydney's GunPolicy.org, the UK's annual rate of gun deaths per 100,000 people was 0.2 in 2015 versus the United States' rate of 12.09. In 2017, the site estimates, the UK had 5 guns for every 100 people. The US had 120 guns per 100 people, twice that of the next-highest scoring country, Yemen.

In 2021, the US had the highest number of gun deaths ever and 2023 was its deadliest year for mass shootings. Despite having less than 5 per cent of the global population, the US possesses nearly half of the world's civilian-owned guns.[25]

Compare this now. On March 15, 2019 in Christchurch, New Zealand, 51 people were massacred at prayer in two mosques. On his way to a third mosque the perpetrator was arrested—without being shot and killed—by two unarmed police officers. Gun laws were changed within a month.

After the Dunblane, Scotland massacre of 16 five and six year-old children and a teacher on March 13, 1996, Lord Douglas Cullen led the

---

25. "America Fell for Guns Recently, and for Reasons You Will Not Guess | Aeon Essays."
    Megan Kang. "America Fell for Guns Recently, and for Reasons You Will Not Guess | Aeon Essays, 09 April 2024." https://aeon.co/essays/america-fell-for-guns-recently-and-for-reasons-you-will-not-guess

inquiry. By the end of 1997 virtually all handguns were banned in the UK. Since then there has been only one mass shooting, in 2010. Of background checks, he said:

> Despite the fact that there is room for improvement in the certification system I conclude that there are significant limitations in what can be done to exclude those who are unsuitable to have firearms and ammunition. There is no certain means of ruling out the onset of a mental illness of a type which gives rise to danger; or of identifying those whose personalities harbour dangerous propensities. On this ground alone it is insufficient protection for the public merely to tackle the individual rather than the gun.[26]

Six weeks after Dunblane, on April 28, 1996, 35 people were killed at Port Arthur, Tasmania (site of a former convict prison from the 1830s). In 1987 a frustrated Barry Unsworth, then premier of New South Wales, had stormed out of a national gun summit in which Tasmania had resisted changes proposed after two mass shootings in Melbourne that year, declaring: "It will take a massacre in Tasmania before we get gun reform in Australia". Within 12 days of the Port Arthur killings the federal and state governments passed the National Firearms Agreement which included a ban on all semi-automatic rifles and all semi-automatic and pump-action shotguns, and a system of licensing and ownership controls, and a mandatory buy-back scheme.[27]

So it's really not that hard, guys, particularly for a country that prides itself on yes-can-do and anything-is-possible. But repealing the Second Amendment and changing the gun laws is not going to happen for a few generations or so, if ever. The mass shootings and hand-wringing will go on, and get worse. But it would be like—actually the same as—banning the Bible (although the Torah and the Q'uran would

---

26. Cullen, *The Public Inquiry into the Shootings at Dunblane Primary School on 13 March 1996*. 1.11.
27. Calla Wahlquist, "It Took One Massacre: How Australia Embraced Gun Control after Port Arthur." *The Guardian*, March 14, 2016, https://www.theguardian.com/world/2016/mar/15/it-took-one-massacre-how-australia-made-gun-control-happen-after-port-arthur.

be easier). Nevertheless, after Ulvade the fateful words were finally spoken. In an interview with MSNBC Michael Moore said, "It's time to repeal the Second Amendment" and Biden said that the Second Amendment is not absolute.[28]

Cultures and cults hold sacrosanct their beliefs, books, dogma, gods and spirits. All are rooted in the honouring, veneration, or feeding of the other world. Fish on Fridays, Protestant good works, Catholic Mass, or Quaker silence. But not guns. Guns and their use are not anchored in a deeply held spiritual reality. They are a stick with one end. Being subject to the vagaries of humans, tethered by neither earth nor heaven, they are a free radical. They are born of the Second Amendment ("A well regulated Militia, being necessary to the security of a free State, the right of the people to keep and bear Arms, shall not be infringed"). James Madison compared the federal government of the United States to the European kingdoms. He argued that state militias "would be able to repel the danger" of a federal army, "It may well be doubted, whether a militia thus circumstanced could ever be conquered by such a proportion of regular troops". The fear of the federal government and deep state conspiracies still rules the US psyche.

Paranoia, characteristic of the omnipotence born of emigration and occupation, is bred deep in the American psyche.[29] For all the paranoia about deep state, creeping socialism, and threats to national security, the USA is a country that has never been physically occupied or invaded—at least not since the Mayflower landed. To state the obvious, the USA, as it was to later become, was the original invader. It was born from invasion by post-Columbus Europeans who have occupied indigenous lands for 500 years.[30]

The USA declared war on Britain in War of 1812. It was thought of as the second war of independence. Although disputed by historians, one of the causes was the American wish to annex Canada. However,

---

28. Kathryn Watson, "Biden Says 'the Second Amendment Is Not Absolute' after Texas Elementary School Shooting - CBS News," May 26, 2022. https://www.cbsnews.com/news/texas-school-shooting-biden-second-amendment-is-not-absolute/
29. David Bell, *Paranoia*; James Hillman, *On Paranoia (Eranos Lectures Series, 8)*.
30. Only 10 countries in the world have never been colonised by Europeans. www.worldatlas.com/articles/10-countries-who-were-never-colonized-by-europeans.html.

the USA has invaded dozens of countries since the War of Independence.[31] As late as the 1920s and 1930s elaborate plans were drawn up for a war on the British Empire, including the pre-emptive invasion of Canada.[32] And in two World Wars it was late to the party (1917 in WWI and 1941 in WWII) and only after it had been directly attacked at Pearl Harbor. Metal and muscle were needed.

America elected itself

(What follows was written from 2015 to the beginning of the Trump presidency in 2016).

> There are two Americas. One is the America of Lincoln and Adlai Stevenson; the other is the America of Teddy Roosevelt and the modern superpatriots. One is generous and humane, the other narrowly egotistical; one is self-critical, the other self-righteous; one is sensible, the other romantic; one is good-humored, the other solemn; one is inquiring, the other pontificating; one is moderate, the other filled with passionate intensity; one is judicious and the other arrogant in the use of great power. —William Fulbright, *The Arrogance of Power*.

From the end of WWII to the 1990s much of international politics was consumed with nuclear war and the standoff between the Soviet Union and the USA. After the collapse of the Soviet Union the stable chaos, however dysfunctional and dangerous, was tipped. There was a period of relief underpinned by denial. Communism had finally been conquered. The American way (including Amway) is the better way of life! But now the USA had no bridle on its grandiosity as the leader of democracy and the free world. The obvious question being: Who elected you? Even the news anchors on CNN (usually centrist and Democrat—as left as you can get in the USA anyway) often say "America, the greatest country in the world." This rendered Donald

---

31. Grossman, "From Wounded Knee to Syria: A Century of U.S. Military Interventions", https://sites.evergreen.edu/zoltan/interventions/
32. https://en.wikipedia.org/wiki/War_Plan_Red

Trump or similar as an inevitability. Just as it colonised itself (while maintaining a self-image of never having been a colonial power) it has narcissistically elected itself. The USA got the President it deserved.

Screeds have been written about Donald Trump, I shall add little to the noise here. In 1981, Donald Trump revealed his view on life when he told People magazine, "Man is the most vicious of all animals, and life is a series of battles ending in victory or defeat. You can't just let people make a sucker of you." This is the primal existence, the "war of all against all" which philosopher Thomas Hobbes (1588–1679) imagined was the natural state of humanity without civilised laws and regulations which create "social contracts." Hobbes believed that social contracts would soothe the savage beast. The Age of Enlightenment, which began after he died, saw the creation of laws and customs that solidified social contracts and expanded individual rights. "America is the greatest manifestation of the Enlightenment ideal, a nation committed to peace and equality for people of every sort."[33]

No-one seems to be wondering how half of this "greatest manifestation of the Enlightenment" voted for Donald Trump. Everything turns into its opposite over time and the great 500-year experiment that was the USA is now self-harming and will inevitably eat itself from the inside like story of Erysichthon.

America is bipolar by nature, by history, by geography, and by will. It loves a fight, wants more by way of manic growth and expansion, goes into a depression (the 1920s), inflates again to stop the scourge of communism in SE Asia, has big ideas, and thinks it's the boss of everyone as leader of the free world. Some might say that this diminishes the meaning of "real" bipolar disorder. I'd say expand the diagnostic criteria. Every culture has its own face, its own personality disorder. Perhaps a parallel DSM for cultures? Would that be racism?

American democracy is rigidly partisan. Bipartisan means two sides. After the massacre of children at Uvalde, Texas in May 2022, a feeble change of gun legislation was heralded as a bipartisan achievement. It was called the "Bipartisan Safer Communities Act". The bipartisan pat

---

33. https://www.cnn.com/2019/08/10/opinions/trumps-influence-is-spreading-like-a-virus-dantonio/index.html

on the back comes first, congratulations boys, but nothing about guns. The USA cannot manage, for all its greatness, the simple task of having more than two political parties. There must be a winner or a loser—Democrat or Republican. Just like nature they say, dog eat dog, winner takes all. No-name Independents are mythical beasts and of little account. In other countries they have a fairly robust role to play—NZ First in New Zealand, or the Liberal Democrats in the UK, for example.

The opposites are so far apart without much hope of mediation or finding a third way that the USA—subject to history, aka archetypal law, aka that's how such things have always rolled—will eventually tear itself apart. The internal forces and contradictions are such that a third rupture, a breakdown, is inevitable. One is a happening, two is a coincidence, and three is a pattern. The first rupture was the Declaration of Independence from Great Britain, the second was the Civil War (1861–1865), and the third will be the ever-widening split between radical left and radical right. This will be sharpened by conflict around the sanctity of the Second Amendment before it is made irrelevant by the destruction of the planet. Guns won't protect you against climate change, heat domes, and Texas becoming unliveable.

Trump is not *the* problem. He is, of course, *a* problem and needs to be dealt with and dealt to. The 74 million people who voted for him are the problem. Every age and every nation gets the leaders it deserves. Eight years of the best of the USA with Obama, now four years (we hope that's all) of the worst. Poor Trump, and poor USA, are the issue of a 500- and 5,000-year-old problem. But let's not cry any tears for either. They have free will, as they are wont to say.

In a 1986 paper Stephen Mitchell described the development of the narcissistic character. I should remind the reader that although he locates the origins of narcissism in infancy and childhood, it is an archetypal pattern—to which the title of his paper alludes—that can occur to an individual at any age or stage, and to any entity—psychological, group or cultural.

> Kernberg portrays the narcissistically-prone infant as so frustrated and hateful as to be unable to tolerate hope, the possibility of anyone offering him anything pleasurable or sustaining. So little is forthcom-

ing, the child concludes, and with such ill-will toward him, it is better to expect nothing, to want nothing, to spoil and devalue everything that might be offered. So, a "grandiose self" is established—complete, perfect, and self-sustaining. This position serves as both an expression of and a defense against the explosive oral aggression, and the only secure resolution in a world experienced as treacherous and sinister. The maintenance of the grandiose self becomes the central psychodynamic motive, resulting in a contemptuous character style and a disdainful manner of relating to others.[34]

Three recent books cover the ground here, so you and I don't have to. I mention these books as descriptions of what is occurring synchronistically on the Earth at the beginning of the 21st century. The archetypal tsunami of human narcissism is coming in. The orange road-kill is in your face. Civilisational narcissism has finally emerged to display itself openly rising from the depths of centuries of hidden admiration for it. To what end? For the purpose of its humiliation and down-sizing, I would suggest. At the same time in history we have a greedy global economy, evangelistic bully religions, a contemptuous paranoid president, and a dying planet. A perfect storm.

Trump is the epitome of individual narcissism and *pars pro toto* the narcissism of globalised civilisation. In October 2017 twenty-seven psychiatrists and psychologists published *The Dangerous Case of Donald Trump: 27 Psychiatrists and Mental Health Experts Assess a President*.[35] In March 2019 the second edition came out with contributions from thirty-seven psychiatrists and psychologists.[36] They are mostly, if not all, American and cover the bases brilliantly.

Some chapter titles, to give you a taste: "Unbridled And Extreme Present Hedonism: How The Leader of the Free World Has Proven Time and Again He Is Unfit For Duty". "Trump's Daddy Issues: A

---

34. Stephen Mitchell, "The Wings of Icarus—Illusion and the Problem of Narcissism", *Contemporary Psychoanalysis*, 107-132.
35. Bandy Lee et al., *The Dangerous Case of Donald Trump: 27 Psychiatrists and Mental Health Experts Assess a President*.
36. Bandy Lee et al., *The Dangerous Case of Donald Trump: 37 Psychiatrists and Mental Health Experts Assess a President*.

Toxic Mix for America". "Donald J. Trump, Alleged Incapacitated Person: Mental Incapacity, The Electoral College, and the Twenty-Fifth Amendment".

The book is very good regarding Trump's pathological narcissism although he avers himself to be a "very stable genius" and that he "aced" the MoCA. The Montreal Cognitive Assessment was created by Ziad Nasreddine, a Montreal neurologist in the late 1990s. It is a one page screening test, and that only, for cognitive impairment that has largely replaced the MMSE (Mini Mental Status Examination) on which it was based. It was administered to Trump by his personal physician Ronny Jackson. For someone who is not cognitively impaired it is relatively easy to "ace".

Trump is a textbook case of a Narcissistic Personality Disorder. All this being said, it does not need ten years of university to recognise a bullshitter. Neither should medical ethics regarding direct examination of a patient stifle stating the obvious when a clear and present danger indicates an ethical duty to warn.[37] People with problems like depression or anxiety are mostly a problem for themselves. Those with personality disorders are a problem for others. Half of America loves him, the other half is fascinated by him.

The third book is somewhat similar to the first.[38] Written by Jungian analysts, some chapter titles will give you a flavour: "The Trump Complex, the John Wayne Archetype and States of National Possession". "Trump and the American Selfie: Archetypal Defenses of the Group Spirit" ("Donald Trump is currently carrying around a selfie stick with the longest reach in the world. And, for a long time, America has also been carrying around a selfie stick with the longest reach in the

---

37. Bandy Lee is a forensic psychiatrist and primary author of the books cited. In March 2017, the American Psychiatric Association released a statement reaffirming the Goldwater rule that restricts comments related to the mental health of public figures without their consent or evaluation. In May 2020 she was terminated from Yale University because of "your repeated violations of the APA's Goldwater Rule and your inappropriate transfer of the duty to warn from the treatment setting to national politics." https://en.wikipedia.org/wiki/Bandy_X._Lee

38. Leonard Cruz and Steven Buser, *A Clear and Present Danger: Narcissism in the Era of Donald Trump*.

world."). Thomas Singer comments on the wound to the American group Self.

> The third and final component of this intertwined triad of forces in the group psyche is Trump's implicit promise of providing a cure for the wound at the level of the group Self. This is where his narcissism is most prominent and most dangerous. The unconscious equation can be stated as follows: "I am the Greatness to which America may once again aspire. By identifying with how great I am, you can rekindle your wounded American dream and make yourself and America great again." Or even more bluntly: "I have achieved the American dream; I am the American dream; I am the incarnation of the Self that the country aspires to". This, of course, is a massive inflation.... Trump's book *The Art of the Deal* characterizes his magnetic appeal: 'I play to people's fantasies. People may not always think big themselves, but they can still get very excited by those who do. That's why a little hyperbole never hurts. People want to believe that something is the biggest and the greatest and the most spectacular. I call it truthful hyperbole'.[39]

The Self or group spirit of America is built on more than three hundred years of progress, success, achievement, resourcefulness, and ingenuity, accompanied by almost endless opportunity and good fortune. We love and believe in our heroic potential; our freedom and independence; our worship of height and speed, youth, newness, technology; our optimism and eternal innocence. We have enjoyed the profound resilience of the American spirit, which has shown itself repeatedly through very difficult historical trials, including our Civil War, World War I, the Great Depression, World War II, the Vietnam War, the 9/11 attacks, the Iraq War, the financial collapse in 2008, and other major crises, including the one we may be in now. As a country, we have been blessed in our capacity to transcend loss, failure, and the threat of defeat in the face of crisis time and again, and this has contributed to a positive vision of ourselves that has been fundamentally solid at the core for a long time. Of course, that Self-image is

---

39. Trump grew up attending Norman Vincent Peale's church. Peale was the author of *The Power of Positive Thinking*, 1952.

subject to inflation, arrogance, and a morphing into *hubris*, in which we believe in our own exceptionalism and are blind to our causing grave injury to peoples at home and abroad.

There is an added section in the 2017 edition called "Humanity's Perpetuation and Survival" but the five chapters really do not go any further than Trump and the USA. The closest is the chapter entitled "The Age of Thanatos: Environmental Consequences of the Trump Presidency" which comments:

> Everyone is vulnerable to the ravages of climate change, but as conditions worsen and the cumulative toll rises, it is children who will be hurt the most. Already many "climate aware" young people are saying they will not have children because of the carbon footprint of adding another person to the planet but also because of the chaos they anticipate. Some admit to hoping for a pandemic, to reduce the "offending species," and to having conversations about "rational suicide." Fury is growing toward a government that is turning a blind eye to their futures.

The third of the books is Justin Frank's *Trump on the Couch*. It is an brilliant psychoanalytic study of Trump.[40] Frank is a Kleinian psychoanalyst and former clinical professor of psychiatry at George Washington University Medical Center. His study is more in-depth, psychological and trenchant than The Dangerous Case but he does not address planetary issues. However, he gives an excellent accounting of the contribution of Trump's childhood relationships—his distant mother, his authoritarian father, his alcoholic older brother, and his childhood cruelty and aggression. His understanding of Trump is conclusive, what you'd expect from his history, and it's not fake news.

But I come to footnote Trump not to praise him. He has the rigidity, weakness, and lack of adaptation associated with serious pathology. To wit, he is incapable of the following: having a beer, losing, being humiliated, being restricted, understanding emotional truth, not being

---

40. Frank, *Trump on the Couch: Inside the Mind of the President*.

transactional, having the strength to be weak, being schooled, and so on. He cannot tolerate reality.

Trump is the USA writ large—just listen to the tone of Thomas Singer's extolling of American virtues above. MAGA. Just as Trump's denouement, his comeuppance will come to pass, so will that of the USA.

All of the above could be said about China or Russia, and rightly so. The psychology of dictators is similar. But I am more familiar with the USA and it allows itself to be known. Think they are different? Just listen to Trump's proposals in a speech in July 2022 on his return to Washington after losing the election.

> He again called for the death penalty for drug dealers, but added praise for the "quick trials" that authoritarian countries like China use to combat the narcotics trade. He suggested construction of government-run tent compounds outside of urban areas to rehabilitate homeless people so that American cities could again be "clean, safe and beautiful". He also called for the presidential authority to deploy National Guard soldiers to fight crime in cities without a local governor's permission—harkening back to the clashes between the president and Democratic governors over whether to use US military forces during the sometimes violent Black Lives Matters protests in 2020.[41]

Planetary resentment

When the unconscious was re-discovered on the inside as an (almost) never-before-seen-thing, Freud and those who came after became captured by this and privileged inside over outside. They ascribed over-much importance to the dynamics of inner world, significant as they are. This led to the work of Melanie Klein and her recognition of unconscious phantasy and later, the Controversial Discussions (the schools of Melanie Klein vs. Anna Freud) in the 1940s. Out of this came the middle or Independent school including, for example, Donald Winnicott with his "good-enough" mother; John Bowlby with the

---

41. https://www.bbc.com/news/world-us-canada-62314119

importance of attachment; and later object relations theorists (such as Harry Guntrip, Ronald Fairbairn, Heinz Kohut, Otto Kernberg, and Stephen Mitchell), who brought some balance between inner and outer.

Projection (Latin; *pro*, before; *iactus*, throw) is throwing something out in front of oneself. It is a inner mental image, feeling, or representation that is seen as an external objective reality. Inner and outer get confused, what is me and what is the other get mixed up, and then there are "boundary issues". This complex is not conscious, otherwise it would be recognised by the ego and there would be no need for it be projected.

But if you throw something in front of you, you eventually trip over it. You meet it outside as fate—in your lover, spouse, boss, or addiction. It's the complex's way of getting your attention. Projection is preceded by denial, that is, one denies that one has such and such feeling or this or that attitude, but insists that someone else does. "I don't love (or hate) X, but Y does". Often it is reversed. "I don't love (or hate) X, but X loves (hates) me".

Narcissism and paranoia go hand in hand. Where there is one there is always the other. Trump is a good example. He is intensely needy. He desperately needs to be adored and applauded, to win, and to have the biggest dick in the room. Look at how he sits when he's not behind a table—red tie long and well-hung, hands steepled downward at crotch level, and we know what his self-declared big hands mean, don't we, nudge, nudge, wink, wink. And he's leaning forward so we don't see how fat he is. Then have a look at his signature—all tall standing-up things and skyscrapers. He is still trying to be good enough for, and better than, Daddy. Just read his family history. His need for worship is the same as that of Yahweh's. But more of that later..

The more traumatic, the more charged, the more conflicted, the more fraught the complex is, the more it will split because it is too painful or too denied by consciousness. One part becomes the conscious persona, the self identity—Trump the deal maker, the one who can bull-shit his way into or out of anything, who never apologises, who fakes it until he makes it, and who psychotically thinks that he can make whatever he thinks a reality. The other part sinks into the unconscious, and is projected onto and into others. What he does not want in himself he sees in others—deep state operatives, losers, contempt for weakness, shouty CAPITALS, and it's all Fake News. It's pretty much Psychology 101.

Trump is terrified of humiliation and failure (though that anxiety is buried deep) and of being seen as a "loser". He will thrash about in the corner like a rat in a trap and wriggle on the hook but is unlikely to suicide. He will probably go to his grave harbouring deep and lasting grievance and resentment, blaming everyone else, and without having learned anything about Donald Trump.

He is the narcissistic issue of, and is a symbol of, what has happened over centuries particularly, for geographic and historical reasons, in North America. He is a puppet in an archetypal drama. The Earth has been used for production and progress, and stripped of its mana. Like Trump, introspection is not our global culture's strong point, so we will go to our planetary grave full of grievance, resentment, and blame.

The prison of freedom

The flood of immigrants to North America was on a scale never seen before in the history of the human race in such a brief span of centuries. The Greek myths of Narcissus and Icarus are human-scale maps of the outcome of hubris and only take us so far in understanding the limitations of our so-called freedoms.

The colonisers confused their freedoms. They thought freedom was absolute and unlimited and could be sought only in the fight against oppression, against the deprivation of their "God-given rights", and against the tyranny they fled from. They believed the laws of nature could be overcome by progress and cleverness, and the laws of spirit could be side-stepped and ignored by obedience to an ambivalent God who was split between New Testament love and Old Testament revenge.

The psyche has limitations to its freedom as does nature and the civilisations born from it. What happens when such limitations are ignored? Well, here we are. The ultimate limitation is the destruction of the Earth, the very ground we stand on, the end game of our religious contempt for the holiness of matter. A story yet to written but who might remain to experience it?

The freedom of rugged individualism has a shadow. When the guard is let down and when the persona begins to crumble, the hard man turns into his opposite—the maudlin, sentimental, country music, tears and beers kind of man. Yes, the cowboy usually has a mother complex. He's a cow-boy. What does that look like? He becomes sentimentally soft and gooey when he thinks about his country, about the flag, and about patriotism.

For all the individualism of Western culture it is in thrall to its very own version of socialism. It is the hive, the pack, the herd, the group, the team, the subculture, the race, the congregation, the party, or the belief. Not that this is much different than other countries but everything is bigger in Texas. The seeming individuality of the hero is under the control and protection of the collective. Faith, the anthem, the hand on heart, are all unquestioned. This is the archetypal current that brought "civilisation" to the shores of Turtle Island.

The desire to be free of monarchy, church and big government was efficiently combined in the Constitution. But Americans are handcuffed by freedom. They are oppressed by the Constitution and the notion of freedom just as much their European forebears 300 years ago were oppressed by absolute monarchs. The inner world of most of 330 million individuals is still in cultural, national and political chains.

The Constitution is both King and Church—worshipped and feared in equal measure. Looks better, and in many ways is better if you run the secular ruler over it, but the psychological relationship with belief-worship-reverence hasn't changed. The Constitution was written as a document for the benefit of white, immigrant Europeans. Nothing in there about the 100 million First Nations peoples already there, nothing about the wolverines, the Jimmy blue crabs, and the wide, wide plains and prairies.

The more we strive for external freedoms the more internally imprisoned we become. Nor should it be any other way. The struggle to free others from outer oppression and dictatorship is an essential and unrelenting moral and human task. Moral? Nah, too principled and philosophical—it is something we feel, a cellular instinct, to be kind, to push against unfairness, to want to help another, to rise up against oppression. It is the right thing to do. Anyone who has spent time with 7 or 8 year-old kids will know that the rules of the group are keenly attuned to fairness and fair play.

But the task of freeing ourselves from our inner chains gets lost in the pressing need to right the wrongs of the world. For those whose fate it is to do so (here I think of Nelson Mandela or Desmond Tutu) the rest of us may be thankful for their lives. But internally we are enslaved by our beliefs and our culture. The freedom so trumpeted in Western culture is in bondage to its history and lineage.

All cultures are communal, sharing the common wealth. But our Judeo-Christian-Islamic lineage, our non-indigenous lineage, has bifurcated in the last several hundred years. Socialism and capitalism. Communism and democracy. A parallel but identical development has been the passionate intensity, the fevered debate, between faith and science, reason and religion, with travelling gospel shows like Richard Dawkins' "The Celebration of Science and Reason–The World Tour".[42]

The idea of the chosen people indicates an act of choosing, an exercise of free will. As Jung demonstrates in *Answer to Job,* it was through the very human stance of Job that God/Yahweh came to develop the faculty of free will, reflection and choice and become liberated from his (did you want that capitalised?) instinctual and amoral unpredictability.

Animals live under the heavy rule of instinct but humans have been given the blessing and curse of free will and the freedom to choose. But freedom to choose what? Individual freedom from what? Freedom from the rule of the mob? Freedom from the rule of the genitals? Humans have always feared and loved each other in equal measure. We like mob love, "I love humanity. I love people. Let's have a cuddle in our narcissistic notion that we are always kind and unconditionally loving toward each other." Not that these things are bad, it's just they cannot bear the weight of too much reality. We don't like mob hate. The swarming, the riot, the crowd, gang rape, torn limb from limb, social

---

42. Ironically, the 2011 hardcover edition of Richard Hawkins' *The Magic of Reality: How We Know What's Really True,* has a remarkably similar cover to Carlos Castaneda's *The Power of Silence*. Have a look.

disorder, and January 6. We hire governments to solve the problem and then complain they do it wrong—too much force, too little force.

But here's the rub: We like individual freedom but we want protection from it.

BIBLIOGRAPHY

CW refers to C. G. Jung, *The Collected Works* (1953–1979). Herbert Read, Michael Fordham and Gerhard Adler (eds.) Princeton: Princeton University Press.

MDR refers to C. G. Jung, *Memories, Dreams, Reflections.* New York: Vintage Books, 1989.

I have quoted Jung extensively, or paraphrased where I have reached the limits of fair use, to remain close to the spirit of his words and not intervene between Jung and the reader.

Some parts of this book are adapted from Owen, *Jung and the Moon Cycles, The Maya Book of Life,* and *The 27 Club.*

———

AFL-CIO. "The U.S. Health Care System: An International Perspective," August 15, 2016. https://www.dpeaflcio.org/factsheets/the-us-health-care-system-an-international-perspective.

Bar-On, Yinon M., Rob Phillips, and Ron Milo. "The Biomass Distribution on Earth." *Proceedings of the National Academy of Sciences* 115, no. 25 (June 19, 2018): 6506–11. https://doi.org/10.1073/pnas.1711842115.

Baring, Anne. "Cinderella: An Interpretation". In Murray Stein and Lionel Corbett, eds. *Psyche's Stories: Modern Jungian Interpretations of Fairy Tales*: Volume 1, 49-62, 2017.

Bayley, Harold. *The Lost Language of Symbolism: An Inquiry into the Origin of Certain Letters, Words, Names, Fairy-Tales, Folklore, and Mythologies.* New York: Dover, 2006.

Beinart, Peter. *The Icarus Syndrome: A History of American Hubris.* New York: Harper Perennial, 2011.

Beiser, Vince. "Why the World Is Running out of Sand." Accessed May 7, 2020. https://www.bbc.com/future/article/20191108-why-the-world-is-running-out-of-sand.

Bell, David. *Paranoia (Ideas in Psychoanalysis).* Icon Books, 2003.

Brailsford, Barry. *Song of Waitaha: Histories of a Nation.* First Edition. Wharariki Publishing Company, 2006.

Bulfinch, Thomas. *Bulfinch's Mythology: The Age of the Fable / The Age of Chivalry / Legends of Charlemagne.* 1st edition. The Modern Library, 1950.

Campbell, Joseph. *The Way of the Animal Powers.* Edited by Robert Walter. First Edition. New York: San Francisco: Alfred Van Der Marck Editions, 1983.

Castaneda, Carlos. *Tales of Power.* New York: Pocket Books, 1974.

Castaneda, Carlos. *The Power of Silence: Further Lessons of Don Juan.* Simon & Schuster, 1987.

Cook, David. *Northrop Frye: A Vision of the New World.* New World Perspectives. New York: St. Martin's Press, 1985.

Cruz, Leonard, and Steven Buser. *A Clear and Present Danger: Narcissism in the Era of Donald Trump*. Chiron, 2016.

Cullen, Lord. *The Public Inquiry into the Shootings at Dunblane Primary School on 13 March 1996*. https://assets.publishing.service.gov.uk/media/5a7cba0fe5274a2f304ef b63/3386.pdf

Davidson, Nick. "How Much Wetland Has the World Lost? Long-Term and Recent Trends in Global Wetland Area." *Marine and Freshwater Research* 65, no. 10 (2014): 934. https://doi.org/10.1071/MF14173.

Deaton, Angus. "Opinion | The U.S. Can No Longer Hide From Its Deep Poverty Problem." *The New York Times*, January 25, 2018. https://www.nytimes.com/2018/ 01/24/opinion/poverty-united-states.html.

Deloria, Vine Jr. *C.G. Jung and the Sioux Traditions: Dreams, Visions, Nature and the Primitive*. Edited by Philip J. Deloria and Jerome S. Bernstein. Spring Journal, 2009.

Diamond, Jared. *Collapse: How Societies Choose to Fail or Succeed: Revised Edition*. Penguin Books, 2011.

Dunbar-Ortiz, Roxanne. "Yes, Native Americans Were the Victims of Genocide." History News Network, December 5, 2016. https://www.historynewsnetwork.org/article/yes-native-americans-were-the-victims-of-genocide.

Dunbar-Ortiz, Roxanne. *An Indigenous Peoples' History of the United States*. ReVisioning American History. Boston: Beacon Press, 2014.

Edinger, Edward. *Ego and Archetype: Individuation and the Religious Function of the Psyche*. New York: Putnam, 1972.

Edinger, Edward. *Goethe's Faust: Notes for a Jungian Commentary*. Inner City Books, 1990.

Edinger, Edward and Deborah A. Wesley. *The Aion Lectures: Exploring the Self in C.G. Jung's Aion*. Inner City Books, 1996.

Edinger, Edward. *Archetype of the Apocalypse: A Jungian Study of the Book of Revelation*. Chicago: Open Court, 1999.

Edinger, Edward. *Ego and Self: The Old Testament Prophets*. Toronto: Inner City Books, 2000.

Edinger, Edward. *The Eternal Drama: The Inner Meaning of Greek Mythology*. Shambhala Publications, 2013.

Edmonson, Munro. *The Book of the Year: Middle American Calendrical Systems*. Salt Lake City: University of Utah Press, 1988.

Elhacham, Emily, et al. "Global Human-Made Mass Exceeds All Living Biomass." *Nature* 588, no. 7838 (December 2020): 442–44. https://doi.org/10.1038/s41586-020-3010-5.

Elk, Nicholas Black, and John Neihardt, *Black Elk Speaks: Being the Life Story of a Holy Man of the Oglala Sioux*. Lincoln, NB: University of Nebraska Press, 1932.

Ellis, Peter Berresford. *Dictionary of Irish Mythology*. Santa Barbara, CA: Abc-Clio Inc, 1989.

Ferber, Michael. *A Dictionary of Literary Symbols*. Cambridge: Cambridge University Press, 2007.

Ferguson, Niall. *The Ascent of Money: A Financial History of the World*. New York: Penguin Press, 2008.

Frank, Justin A. *Trump on the Couch: Inside the Mind of the President*. New York: Avery, 2018.

Frazer, James George. *The Golden Bough; a Study in Comparative Religion*. New York London, Macmillan, 1894. http://archive.org/details/goldenboughstudy01fraz.

Graves, Robert. *The Greek Myths: Complete Edition*. London; New York: Penguin Books, 1993.

Grossman, Zoltán. "From Wounded Knee to Syria: A Century of U.S. Military Interventions." Accessed September 16, 2019. https://sites.evergreen.edu/zoltan/interventions/.

Hannah, Barbara. *Jung, His Life and Work*. New York: Putnam, 1976.

Hillman, James. *And Huge is Ugly*, Tenth Annual E. F. Schumacher Memorial Lecture, Bristol, England, 1988.

Hillman, James. *On Paranoia (Eranos Lectures Series, 8)*. Spring Pubns, 1988.

Hillman, James. *A Terrible Love of War*. Penguin Books, 2005.

Hobbes, Thomas. *Leviathan: Or the Matter, Forme, and Power of a Commonwealth Ecclesiasticall and Civill*, 1651.

Hughes, Sylvia, *New Scientist*, 29 September 1990, www.newscientist.com/article/mg12717361.200-antelope-activate-the-acacias-alarm-system

Hunt, Stephen (ed.) *Christian Millenarianism*. C. Hurst, 2001.

Jeffrey, David L. *A Dictionary of Biblical Tradition in English Literature*. Wm. B. Eerdmans Publishing, 1992.

Jenkins, John Major. *Maya Cosmogenesis 2012: The True Meaning of the Maya Calendar End-date*. Santa Fe, NM: Bear & Co.. 1998.

Johnson, Samuel. *The Dictionary of the English Language*, 1755.

Jung, Carl Gustav (1953–1979) *The Collected Works*. Herbert Read, Michael Fordham and Gerhard Adler, eds. Princeton: Princeton University Press.

Jung, C. G. *Man and His Symbols*. London: Aldus. 1964.

Jung, C. G. *Letters, Vol. 1, 1906–1950*. Gerhard Adler and Aniela Jaffe (eds.) Princeton: Princeton University Press, 1973.

Jung, C. G. *Letters, Vol. 2, 1951–1961*. Gerhard Adler and Aniela Jaffe (eds.) Princeton: Princeton University Press. 1973.

Jung, C. G. *Word and Image, Bollingen Series XCVII, Vol. 2*. Edited by Aniela Jaffé. First Edition. Princeton, N.J.: Princeton University Press, 1983.

Jung, C. G. *C. G. Jung Speaking: Interviews and Encounters*. Princeton: Princeton University Press, 1987.

Jung, C. G. *Memories, Dreams, Reflections*. New York: Vintage Books, 1989.

Jung, C. G, and William McGuire. *Analytical Psychology: Notes of the Seminar given in 1925*. Princeton, N.J.: Princeton University Press, 1991.

Jung, C. G. and Ann Conrad Lammers. *The Jung-Kirsch Letters: The Correspondence of C.G. Jung and James Kirsch*. London: Routledge, 2016.

Kingsolver, Barbara (1998) *The Poisonwood Bible*. London: Faber & Faber.

Kline, Anthony. www.poetryintranslation.com/PITBR/Latin/Metamorph8.php

LaHaye, Tim and Jerry Jenkins (1995) *Left Behind: A Novel of the Earth's Last Days*. Wheaton, IL: Tyndale House.

Lawrence, D. H. *Apocalypse*. First Edition. Martin Secker, 1932.

Lawrence, Natalie. "Are plants conscious? Radical new experiments suggest they could be", 24 August 2022, www.newscientist.com/article/mg25534012-800-the-radical-new-experiments-that-hint-at-plant-consciousness

Layard, John. *Celtic Quest: Sexuality and Soul in Individuation*. Edited by Anne S. Bosch. Revised edition. Dallas, Tex: Spring Pubns, 1985.

Lee, Bandy X., Robert Jay Lifton, Gail Sheehy, William J. Doherty, Noam Chomsky, Judith Lewis Herman, Philip Zimbardo, et al. *The Dangerous Case of Donald Trump: 27 Psychiatrists and Mental Health Experts Assess a President*. New York: Thomas Dunne Books, 2017.

Lee, Bandy X., Jeffrey Sachs, Robert Jay Lifton, Gail Sheehy, William J. Doherty, Noam Chomsky, Judith Lewis Herman M.D, et al. *The Dangerous Case of Donald Trump: 37 Psychiatrists and Mental Health Experts Assess a President - Updated and Expanded with New Essays*. Updated, Expanded ed. edition. New York: Thomas Dunne Books, 2019.

Lester, Toby. *The Fourth Part of the World: An Astonishing Epic of Global Discovery, Imperial Ambition, and the Birth of America*. New York: Free Press, 2010.

Levinson, Sanford. *Pledging Faith in the Civil Religion; or, Would You Sign the Constitution?*, 29, William & Mary Law Review, 113 (1987).

Lopez-Pedraza, Rafael. *Cultural Anxiety*. Daimon Verlag, 1990.

Lord, Lewis. "U.S. News 08/18/97: How Many People Were Here before Columbus? Pick a Number," March 5, 2008. https://web.archive.org/web/20080305224956/ http://www.usna.edu/Users/history/kolp/HH345/PRE1492.htm.

Ludacer, Rob. "The World Is Running out of Sand -- and There's a Black Market for It Now." Business Insider Australia, June 12, 2018. https://www.businessinsider.com. au/world-running-out-sand-resources-concrete-2018-6.

Lyons, Oren and John Mohawk, eds. *Exiled in the Land of the Free: Democracy, Indian Nations, and the U.S. Constitution*. Santa Fe, NM: Clear Light Press, 1992.

Massie, Robert K. *Peter the Great: His Life and World*. New York: Modern Library, 2012.

McGuire, William, and R. F. C. Hull, eds. *C. G. Jung Speaking: Interviews and Encounters*. Bollingen Series 97. Princeton University Press, 1977.

Meadows, Donella H., Jørgen Randers, and Dennis L. Meadows. *The Limits to Growth: The 30-Year Update*. Reprint. London: Earthscan, 2009.

Menzies, Gavin. *1421: The Year China Discovered America*. Harper Perennial, 2008.

Mitchell, Stephen A. "The Wings of Icarus: Illusion and the Problem of Narcissism." *Contemporary Psychoanalysis* 22, no. 1 (January 1, 1986): 107–32. https://doi.org/10. 1080/00107530.1986.10746118.

Mutwa, Credo Vusa'Mazulu. *Song of the Stars: The Lore of a Zulu Shaman*. Barrytown, 2000.

New Zealand Department of Conservation, "New Zealand's Wetlands at Risk: 2 February 2018." www.doc.govt.nz/news/2018/new-zealands-wetlands-at-risk

Noll, Richard. *The Jung Cult: Origins of a Charismatic Movement*. Reprint edition. New York: Touchstone, 1997.

Olson-Raymer, Gayle. "The Europeans - Why They Left." n.d. http://users.humboldt. edu/ogayle/hist110/expl.html.

Ostrowski-Sachs, Margaret. *From Conversations with C. G. Jung*. 2nd edition. C. G. Jung Institute, 1977.

Ovid. *Metamorphoses*. Translated by Brookes More. Boston, Cornhill Publishing, 1922.

Ovid. *The Metamorphoses of Ovid*. Translated by Mary M. Innes. Harmondsworth, 1955.

Ovid. *Metamorphoses*. www.theoi.com/Text/OvidMetamorphoses8.html

Owen, Michael. *Jung and the Native American Moon Cycles: Rhythms of Influence*. York Beach, ME: Nicolas-Hays, 2002.

Owen, Michael. *The Maya Book of Life: Understanding the Xultun Tarot*. Kahurangi Press, 2011.

Owen, Michael. *The 27 Club: Why Age 27 Is Important*. Kahurangi Press, 2012.

Pappas, Stephanie. "Human-Made Stuff Now Outweighs All Life on Earth." Scientific American. Accessed September 14, 2021. https://www.scientificamerican.com/article/human-made-stuff-now-outweighs-all-life-on-earth/.

Perera, Sylvia Brinton. *The Irish Bull God: Image of Multiform and Integrated Masculinity*. Toronto: Inner City Books, 2004.

Porter, Roy. *Enlightenment: Britain and the Creation of the Modern World*. Penguin, 2001.

Post, Laurens Van Der. *Jung and the Story of Our Time*. Vintage, 1978.

Prechtel, Martín. *The Disobedience of the Daughter of the Sun: Ecstasy and Time*. Yellow Moon Press, 2001.

Ramani, Madhvi. "The Epic Story of the Map That Gave America Its Name." Accessed August 22, 2018. http://www.bbc.com/travel/story/20180702-the-epic-story-of-the-map-that-gave-america-its-name.

Sabini, Meredith (2002) *The Earth has a Soul: The Nature Writings of C.G. Jung*. Berkeley, CA: North Atlantic Books.

Sand Wars. Documentary. La Compagnie des Taxis-Brousse, Rappi Productions, 2013. Sand Wars (2013) - IMDb

SandStories.org - Finding solutions to the global sand crisis

Santillana, Giorgio and Hertha von Dechend. *Hamlet's Mill: An Essay Investigating the Origins of Human Knowledge and its Transmission through Myth*. Cambridge, MA: Harvard, 1969.

Shalit, Erel. *The Complex: Path of Transformation from Archetype to Ego*. Studies in Jungian Psychology by Jungian Analysts 98. Toronto: Inner City Books, 2002.

Stannard, David E. *American Holocaust: The Conquest of the New World*. New York: Oxford University Press, 1993.

Timmins, Beth. "How the Scramble for Sand Is Destroying the Mekong - BBC News." Accessed May 5, 2020. https://www.bbc.com/news/business-50629100.

Tocqueville, Alexis de. *Democracy in America*. Translated by Harvey C. Mansfield and Delba Winthrop. 1st edition. Chicago, Ill.: University of Chicago Press, 2002.

Turner, Graham, and Lauren Rickards. "Is Global Collapse Imminent?". www.sustainable.unimelb.edu.au (Research Paper No. 4), 2014. http://pinguet.free.fr/turner814.pdf

von Franz, Marie-Louise. 'The unknown visitor in fairy tales and dreams'. In *Archetypal Dimensions of the Psyche*. Boston: Shambhala, 1997.

von Franz, Marie-Louise. *An Introduction to the Interpretation of Fairytales*. Dallas, TX: Spring. 1970.

von Franz, Marie-Louise. *The Golden Ass of Apuleius: The Liberation of the Feminine in Man*, Spring, 1970.

von Franz, Marie-Louise. *C. G. Jung: His Myth in Our Time*. London: Hodder & Stoughton, 1975.

von Franz, Marie-Louise. *On Divination and Synchronicity: The Psychology of Meaningful Chance*. Toronto: Inner City, 1980.

von Franz, Marie-Louise. *Psyche and Matter*. Shambhala, 2001.

Wahlquist, Calla. "It Took One Massacre: How Australia Embraced Gun Control after Port Arthur." www.theguardian.com/world/2016/mar/15/it-took-one-massacre-how-australia-made-gun-control-happen-after-port-arthur.

Waitaha, Ngati Kowhai o. *Song of Waitaha: The Histories of a Nation (2nd ed.)* Christchurch: Wharariki Press, 2003

Walpole, Sarah et al. "The Weight of Nations: An Estimation of Adult Human Biomass." *BMC Public Health* 12, no. 1 (December 2012): 439. https://doi.org/10.1186/1471-2458-12-439.

Wickes, Frances. *The Inner World of Choice*. Englewood Cliffs, NJ: Prentice-Hall, 1963.

Williams, Terry Tempest. "Living in a woman's body: like Earth, we are changing quickly through the violence of climate collapse". www.theguardian.com/lifeandstyle/2022/feb/15/living-in-a-womans-body-like-earth-we-are-changing-quickly-through-the-violence-of-climate-collapse

Wolff, Robert. *Original Wisdom: Stories of an Ancient Way of Knowing*. Inner Traditions, 2001.

Zoja, Luigi. *Growth and Guilt: Psychology and the Limits of Development*. 1st ed. Routledge, 1995.

Zoja, Luigi, ed. *Jungian Reflections on September 11: A Global Nightmare*. Einsiedeln: Daimon-Verlag, 2002.

INDEX

Buddha, 41, 46, 62, 183–184
bulls, 63, 65, 69–70, 85–86
bullshitter, 269

C

calendars, 137, 139, 141
Calvinist, 36, 228
Calydonian boar hunt, 59, 61, 82, 85, 90, 114
Canada, 1, 41, 206, 229, 232, 245, 253, 259–
    260, 265
capitalism, 43, 62, 192, 251, 276
Castaneda, Carlos, 14, 103, 276
catastrophe, 25, 135, 147–148, 182, 190, 218
Catholic, 99, 122, 135, 146, 152, 170, 197, 221,
    223, 228, 247, 253, 264
CBT 169–170
cellular, 194, 203, 250, 276
Centaurs, 71, 86–87, 105, 130
ceremonies, 32, 39, 108, 141, 145–147, 168,
    171
childhood, 76, 169, 244, 267, 272
chimeras, 71, 105, 123
choice, 38, 56, 76, 91, 145, 165, 175, 185, 258,
    276
Christ, 33–34, 39, 47, 54, 139–140, 166, 168,
    170–171, 176, 220–225
Christchurch, 262
Christian, 28, 41–42, 46–47, 54, 59, 61, 65,
    82–83, 99–100, 105, 123, 139, 148–149,
    155, 161–168, 170–174, 183, 192, 199, 220,
    222–224, 253
Christianity, 37, 69, 100, 140, 147, 149, 169,
    183, 222–223
Churchill, 46, 180
Cinderella, 37
cities, 8, 42, 124, 147, 155, 180, 186, 190, 206–
    207, 234, 240, 272
civilisation, 4–5, 11, 17, 20, 28, 34, 38, 59, 130,
    138, 145-149, 178, 190, 205–208, 223–224,
    268, 275
civilised, 19–20, 22–23, 38, 69, 116, 169, 185,
    236, 266
cognitive, 169, 173, 184–185, 203, 269
collapse, 17–18, 25, 29, 36, 100, 138, 147, 195,
    198, 202–206, 211, 213–219, 229, 265, 271

colonisation, 3, 10, 21, 24, 28, 42, 68, 71, 100,
    123, 149, 160, 184, 220, 222, 226–233, 239,
    244–247, 253, 256, 258, 260, 265–266, 274
compensation (psychological), 29, 53, 57, 60–
    61, 75, 108, 114, 122, 153, 161, 175, 186,
    206, 212–213, 219, 241, 258
complex, 3, 8, 10, 33–35, 43, 75–77, 189, 198,
    209, 211, 270, 273–275
consciousness, 3–5, 7, 20–23, 25, 28–29, 35,
    46–62, 65, 70, 91, 116, 133–134, 143–146,
    149, 153, 156, 164, 172–176, 178, 202, 204,
    213, 218, 223–224, 235, 256, 258, 274
Constitution (USA), 1–2, 7–8, 152–153, 171,
    193, 251–252, 256, 275
covenant, 240, 252
crack-between-the-worlds, 51, 109
Creation, 3, 16, 28, 46, 50, 52, 110, 120, 139,
    149, 165, 171–172, 175, 194, 205, 235, 237,
    241, 266
cricket, 246, 262
culture, 2–5, 7–11, 17–19, 22, 24–25, 28–29,
    34–35, 37–42, 46, 56–57, 69–72, 77, 80,
    84–85, 88, 91–92, 97, 101, 103, 106–108,
    116, 119, 125–129, 137–141, 147, 149, 152,
    155, 160, 162, 165–171, 174–176, 183–184,
    186, 188, 190–191, 205–206, 209–210, 212,
    217–218, 221, 224, 227, 230–231, 236–237,
    240, 246–252, 257–258, 264, 267–268,
    275–276
cycles, 33–34, 48, 52–53, 55, 66, 100, 120,
    137–138, 141–143, 152, 179, 181, 211, 214,
    216–217, 221, 234

D

Daedalus, 59–60, 63, 65, 72–81, 94–95
Dagda, 68
Dawkins, Richard, 276
death, 9–11, 24, 30, 37, 43, 47–48, 50–52, 61,
    63, 72, 78–81, 89–93, 97, 112, 114, 121,
    125–130, 134, 137, 139, 143, 155, 158,
    160–161, 165–168, 173, 178, 180–182, 193,
    200–201, 214–217, 223–224, 227, 236, 250,
    258–259, 272
death-that-gives-death, 59
death-that-gives-life, 59, 125
decimation, 3, 230, 240

Jung, C G, 8, 13, 18–24, 33–41, 51, 55, 58, 98–
    104, 115, 138, 147–148, 152–157, 162–164,
    166–182, 190, 202, 211, 214–217, 220–223,
    241, 243–244, 248, 258, 276
Jungian, 18, 37, 60, 102–103, 106, 215, 218,
    270

K
kairos, 50, 137, 164–166
kaitiaki, 15, 166
Kernberg, Otto, 268, 273
Kierkegaard, Soren, 152, 242
king, 35, 46, 59, 63–74, 79–89, 94, 101–102,
    200–201, 207, 221, 227, 230, 233, 249–252,
    275
Klein, Melanie, 26, 74, 77, 271, 273
kronos, 164–165

L
labyrinth, 60, 65–66, 72–73
Lakota, 146, 176
land, 1–4, 7, 11, 15, 22–31, 53, 56, 59, 68–69,
    80–86, 96, 98, 104–107, 114, 123, 147,
    156–161, 174–178, 196, 199, 204, 208, 213,
    224–225, 231–234, 239, 245–248, 253–257
language, 2, 6–7, 9, 37, 57, 161, 190, 204–205,
    255, 260
Layard, John, 88
Lee, Bandy, 268–269
Letakots-Lesa, Chief, 38
Leviathan, 235–236
lightning, 10, 80, 86, 109, 116, 202–204, 212–
    213, 215
lime tree, 105
linden tree, 104, 113–114
Lopez-Pedraz, Raphael, 34, 183
love, 9–10, 12, 16, 27, 30, 34–35, 45, 56, 60–
    66, 92–98, 103–108, 112, 116, 130–135,
    143–146, 155, 158, 161–162, 165, 177,
    184–185, 201, 205, 227, 249, 251, 254, 258,
    270–277
lover, 13, 35, 68, 78, 84, 94, 102–103, 127,
    200, 273

M
magic, 13, 21, 51, 65, 67, 129, 196, 201, 276

male, 26, 43, 61, 67, 86, 88, 94, 98, 171, 185,
    200–201, 260
maori, 2–3, 9, 16, 23, 35, 41, 63, 127, 147, 176,
    257
marriage, 37, 61, 68, 94, 115, 184, 228
masculine, 37, 60–75, 83, 85–86, 89, 91, 95,
    115, 129–130, 149, 200, 227–228
Matariki, 16, 147
matriotism, 90
melancholy, 11, 108
Meleager, 86–95
memory, 6, 30, 49, 54, 91, 102, 110, 115, 119–
    120, 173
Mephistopheles, 155–163
Mercurius, 22, 108, 115–118, 156
mercy, 61, 145–146
Metamorphoses, 49–59, 73, 86, 93–98, 103–
    104, 129, 133, 137, 151
Milton, John, 50, 197, 240
Minotaur, 54, 59–60, 65–66, 69–71, 86, 94, 96,
    105
miracles, 61, 109, 238
Mississippi, 153, 246, 253, 260
mitakuye oyasin, 176
Mithraism, 69, 168
Mohawk, 1, 225–226
money, 29, 126, 150, 156, 158, 198, 277
monotheism, 3, 7, 37, 51, 61, 68, 85, 145–148,
    153, 163, 175, 184, 197, 223, 228, 237, 277
mother, 2–3, 5, 13–14, 26, 35, 53, 67, 74–78,
    88, 92, 95, 97, 100, 119, 139, 144, 149, 169,
    172, 174, 192, 272–273, 275
movement, 12–13, 20, 37, 42, 47, 52, 55–56,
    66, 123, 140, 144–145, 153, 169, 197, 205,
    223, 238
murder, 44, 71, 74, 77, 79, 99, 121, 146, 155–
    156, 179
mythology, 34–37, 41, 47, 54, 56, 67–68, 71–
    73, 76, 82, 99, 104–105, 113, 118–119, 133,
    137–140, 178, 185, 200–205, 227, 257, 274

N
narcissism, 16, 42, 47, 77, 91, 132–135, 219,
    248, 267–270, 273–274, 277
Native, 2, 17, 21, 37, 225, 230–236, 255

R

race, 4, 8, 15, 17, 45, 71, 236, 255, 267
Ragnarok, 112, 147
rapture, 40, 146–149, 197, 223
rational, 10, 25, 36, 40, 47, 60, 108, 133, 171,
    178, 184–185, 195, 235, 238, 241, 271
raupatu, 232
Reformation, 152, 221, 235, 240, 263
religion, 4, 7–11, 34–42, 46, 51, 68, 100, 106,
    108, 131, 138–139, 147–152, 164, 169, 171,
    181, 184, 197, 210, 212, 218, 223–228, 232,
    237–238, 244–246, 251–252, 268, 275–276
reparation, 27, 99–100, 163, 226
Republican, 219, 258–259, 267
responsibility, 5, 27, 157, 183–184, 242, 253
Revelation, Book of, 32, 40, 62, 147–149, 161,
    181, 184, 197, 203–204, 237
revenge, 29, 78, 85, 92, 130–131, 133, 275
revolution, 46, 140, 231, 236–237, 240–241,
    252
rights, 44, 155–156, 253, 260, 266, 274
right-wing, 40, 43

S

sacred, 3, 5–6, 10, 15, 37, 44, 48, 63, 68–72,
    105, 113, 118–123, 130, 142, 144, 147,
    165–166, 171, 221–222, 250, 252
Saint, 46, 99, 122–123, 148, 170, 225, 229
sandpaper, 246
Satan, 170, 221, 223, 240
savages, 3, 11, 20, 230–231, 236, 249
scepticism, 8, 103–104, 181
science, 5, 8–9, 42, 51, 106, 118, 171, 173, 182,
    185, 217, 221–225, 235, 238, 256, 276–277
Second Amendment, 171, 186, 221, 251, 259–
    267
second covenant, 240
secular, 46, 80, 138, 141, 147, 198, 228, 250–
    252, 275
self-harm, 242
Senoi, 11
Sensation (function), 13, 168
sentimental, 21, 43, 77, 84, 91, 108, 158, 262,
    275

separation, 20, 22, 64, 79, 120, 148, 152–153,
    165, 172, 205, 237, 251
seven, 2, 16, 54, 66, 99, 126, 128, 135, 147,
    189, 197, 229
sex 13, 66, 75, 79, 83, 86, 90, 200, 250
sexual, 35, 53, 67, 72, 74–75, 90, 129, 170,
    197, 221
Shakespeare, 9, 50, 90, 152, 238
shaman, 91, 171, 197
shouty, 8, 181, 274
silliness, 221, 257
Sirius, 16
sisters, 16, 30, 38, 46, 48, 61, 71–75, 80, 93, 95,
    135, 159, 183–187
snake, 45, 69, 72, 79, 109, 123, 125, 167, 176
socialism, 40, 192, 251, 259, 264, 275–276
Somme, Battle of the, 240
soul, 12, 14, 30, 33–37, 43, 46, 63, 74, 88, 99,
    106, 120, 122, 146, 153–156, 160, 176, 197,
    199, 251
South America, 3, 226, 228–229, 231–232,
    248, 254
specism, 45–47
spirit, 3, 6, 10–16, 22–24, 35–39, 44, 50–51,
    61–65, 83, 85, 92, 95–97, 99–111, 115–138,
    145–147, 154, 167, 170–172, 176–181, 197,
    203–204, 212, 214, 221–223, 240–248, 252,
    257–258, 270–271, 275
spirits, 11, 85, 110, 120, 133, 158, 264
spiritual, 3–5, 11, 24–25, 36, 46–47, 62–63, 79,
    83, 85, 91, 143–144, 149–150, 160, 165,
    168, 176–177, 196, 198, 200–203, 221, 224,
    228, 249–252, 257, 264
stars, 15–16, 37–38, 46, 56, 61, 65, 80, 120,
    138, 140, 144, 160, 172, 187, 205, 244
Styx, 54, 80, 92, 134
sublimatio, 196–198
suicide, 24, 271, 274
superbia, 116, 134–135, 187
superstition, 22, 104, 118, 153, 235
sustainable, 1, 17, 25, 195, 213
swamp, 53, 57, 106, 115, 160–161
synchronicity, 23, 97, 146, 166–167, 217, 252,
    268

ACKNOWLEDGEMENTS

I write mostly by myself without the benefit of critics, readers or editors. Unwise but it's what I seem to do. Thus all bad prose, tangled ideas, missing attributions, inconsistent style, and the like are mine alone. However, I say thirteen thankyous to my friends and colleagues Barbara Rockel, Sheila Cowburn, Di Koch, Alastair McLachlan, Kerry Sandison, Tania Jenkins, and Mike Holding for their invaluable comments and support.

This is not a scholarly review although I may reference sources as appropriate. Over the years I have absorbed the writings and wisdom of others by osmosis and reconstituted them from the valuable residue they have left. Many years later the original sources have been lost in the distant past—all metaphorically mixed and interbred such that their parentage and pedigree is murky and mongrel. Only now do they dance nicely with what I am writing. To those sources acknowledged and unacknowledged I offer my gratitude for what you have left.

Some of the material has been presented at various workshops over the years and more recently *Terra Mortis: The Pathology of Hope and the Death of the Earth* at the New Zealand Association of Psychotherapists Conference: Te Ipu Taiao, The Climate Crucible, March 2020; and *Our Ailments and the Earth* to the Vancouver Jung Society, March 2022.

I acknowledge that I live on the ancestral lands of Ngai Te Ahi hapu and the iwi of Ngati Ranginui and Ngai Te Rangi who are the kaitiaki of this whenua on which I stand.

Over the years Indigenous, Native and First Nations voices, worldwide, have become stronger. I offer my thanks and respect to all those who have restored their lands, languages and traditions. Here I shall offer acknowledgement of two such voices. I am grateful for their words and hope that this book may follow in the places their feet have walked.

Chief Seattle (Si'ahl in Duwamish, c. 1786–1866) was a Suquamish and Duwamish chief. The city of Seattle was named after him. His well-known letter was purportedly sent to President Pierce in 1855. It is often quoted but is of doubtful authenticity and does not appear on the Suquamish website. However, his similar 1854 oration is available there.

Vine Deloria, Jr (1933–2005), Yankton and Standing Rock Sioux, was Professor Emeritus of History, Law and Religious Studies at the University of Colorado. He was named by TIME magazine as one of the greatest religious thinkers of the twentieth century. He was the author of many books since the 1970s including *God Is Red: A Native View of Religion*; *Red Earth, White Lies: Native Americans and the Myth of Scientific Fact*; *Custer Died for Your Sins: An Indian Manifesto*; and *The World We Used to Live In: Remembering the Powers of the Medicine Men*. Drawn to Jung's writings in later life, he left a partially finished manuscript that was completed by his son Philip J Deloria, titled *C.G. Jung and the Sioux Traditions: Dreams, Visions, Nature and the Primitive (2009)*.

ABOUT THE AUTHOR

Michael Owen BSc, MA is a clinical psychologist in private practice in Aotearoa/New Zealand. He is a Member of the NZ Psychological Society, and former Member of the NZ Association of Psychotherapists.

He has been a psychotherapist and clinical psychologist for over forty years. After a first degree in zoology he led residential and wilderness therapy programs in Canada for high-needs children and adolescents, followed by post-graduate studies at the University of Toronto. He was Professor and Program Coordinator, Child and Youth Care, Humber College, Toronto.

Along the way he has trained in psychoanalytic psychotherapy, family therapy, and EMDR; and with Stanislav Grof, Michael Harner, Jon Kabat-Zinn, Virginia Satir, Carl Whitaker, and Thomas Verny amongst others.

Latterly, he was Senior Clinical Psychologist in Adult, and Child and Adolescent, Mental Health Services at Tauranga Hospital, New Zealand. He has studied at the C G Jung Institute, Zurich and has led wilderness retreats in Canada, New Zealand, South Africa and Botswana. Over many years he has worked with indigenous healers, medicine people, and elders in Canada, USA, Mexico and South Africa.

And no, he is not on Twitter, Instagram, Facebook or whatever. Never has been. Maybe sometime. Occasionally on Substack.

TERRA MORTIS: SERIES CONTENTS

PART I: A FEW ROUGH BEASTS

What's This All About: A Preface | Indigenous | A Few Rough Beasts | Oracles Ancient: Ovid and the Maya | Bulls and Purple Hair | The Lover Survives | The Heart of Heaven | Oracles Modern: Faust, Titanic and 9/11 | Jung and the Aeon | Titanic | Growth | Twin Towers | History | Watching America Self-Harm

———

Part II will be available in early 2025 from Kahurangi Press, Amazon and other booksellers in paperback and eBooks.

PART II: ALL THE ROUGH BEASTS

Disorder | Lovelock's machine | Ailments | Nature heals, nature kills | Bipolar | Psychopathy | Pre-Traumatic Stress Disorder | Soul and spirit | Narcissism | Panic | Attachment and Separation | The beauty and pathology of hope | Positive psychology | Melancholy | Despair | Abandoning hope | Suffering | Crucifixion

Matter | Earth and Self | Clues to a coma | Cutting | Space travel and Monty Python | Skin and bones | Inflamed | Element dreaming | Losing the memory of trees | Talking to the trees | Body | Fire-from-within | Fire-on-the-earth | What's dying? | Infants | Functions, floods and fire | Blood on the water | Bulimia terraforman | Ecological Laws

Science | Unclench | Priestess | Divination | Knowledge | Precision and proof | The rise of reason

Money | Mood | Moneta | Prosperity | Negative GDP

Monotheism | Faith and belief | Answer to Job | Revelation | Apocalypse soon

Remedies and Solutions, eh? | Grief | Diagnosis | Eco-shock | Gathering | Dreaming | All the Rough Beasts | Dire and unethical necessities

FROM KAHURANGI PRESS

Paperbacks from Kahurangi Press, Amazon and booksellers.

eBooks from Kindle and Apple

By **Michael Owen**

The 27 Club: Why Age 27 Is Important, Kahurangi Press, 2018.

The Maya Book of Life: Understanding the Xultun Tarot, Kahurangi Press, 2013.

Jung and the Native American Moon Cycles, Nicolas-Hays, 2002. Paperback, available from Amazon.

By **Peter Balin**

Xultun Tarot (Classic Edition), Kahurangi Press, 2011. Available from Amazon.

Visit xultun.com for the story of the creation of this unique deck in 1976—the first indigenous tarot.

Please note: This is not the unauthorised edition by Lotus Press, with muddy colours and smaller playing card size, which is listed on Amazon as a "newer edition".